100 Film Noirs

100 FILM NOIRS

BFI SCREEN GUIDES

Jim Hillier & Alastair Phillips

A BFI book published by Palgrave Macmillan

First published in 2009 by
PALGRAVE MACMILLAN

on behalf of the

BRITISH FILM INSTITUTE
21 Stephen Street, London W1T 1LN
www.bfi.org.uk

There's more to discover about film and television through the BFI. Our world-renowned archive, cinemas, festivals, films, publications and learning resources are here to inspire you.

Palgrave Macmillan in the UK is an imprint of Macmillan Publishers Limited, registered in England, company number 785998, of Houndmills, Basingstoke, Hampshire RG21 6XS. Palgrave Macmillan in the US is a division of St Martin's Press LLC, 175 Fifth Avenue, New York, NY 10010. Palgrave Macmillan is the global academic imprint of the above companies and has companies and representatives throughout the world. Palgrave® and Macmillan® are registered trademarks in the United States, the United Kingdom, Europe and other countries.

Series cover design: Paul Wright
Cover image: *The Killers* (Robert Siodmak, 1946, © Universal Pictures Company)
Series design: Ketchup/couch
Set by Cambrian Typesetters, Camberley, Surrey
Printed in China

This book is printed on paper suitable for recycling and made from fully managed and sustained forest sources. Logging, pulping and manufacturing processes are expected to conform to the environmental regulations of the country of origin.

British Library Cataloguing-in-Publication Data
A catalogue record for this book is available from the British Library

ISBN 978-1-84457-216-8 (pbk)
ISBN 978-1-84457-215-1 (hbk)

Contents

Acknowledgments

Our thanks go to Rebecca Barden for initially commissioning this book and for her customary tact, insight and patience. We are also grateful, in different ways, for the support and advice of the following: Alex Ballinger, Stella Bruzzi, Alison Butler, Sophia Contento, Audun Engelstad, Anders Futtrup, Alex Jacoby, Wujung Ju, Mark Kurzemnieks, Belinda Latchford, Fiona Morey, James Naremore, V. F. Perkins, Andrew Spicer, Sarah Thomas and Ginette Vincendeau. Finally, many of the ideas in this volume were developed during our classes in the Department of Film, Theatre & Television at the University of Reading. Thanks, as always, to our students past and present.

Introduction

Film noir's popularity with cinema audiences, film enthusiasts and film scholars has remained unabated since postwar French critics began discerning a new trend in American film with the release of such stylish and atmospheric crime features as *Double Indemnity* (1944) and *Murder, My Sweet* (1944). But what exactly *is film noir* and what makes it an object of such enduring appeal? This is a question that critics and historians have pursued with vigour, relish and no small amount of controversy over the years. We certainly hope users of this BFI Screen Guide, after reading our discussion of a representative selection of 100 titles, will be aided in coming to their own conclusions. This introduction aims to stake out some of the critical territory in relation to the question of *film noir*'s formation. It then surveys some of the more important trends in *film noir* criticism before concluding with some explanatory remarks outlining our selection criteria and the various formatting decisions we have taken in the preparation of the book.

In his important study of the phenomenon, James Naremore (1998) argues that *film noir* is 'an ideological concept with a history all its own, it can be used to describe a period, a movement, and a recurrent style'. Although American film critics noted a new tone of violent pessimism in films at the time, a key idea here is that *noir* should largely be seen as a retrospective category, deployed in the first instance by French critics such as Jean-Pierre Chartier (1946) and Nino Frank (1946) to describe the backlog of dark American films released in Paris immediately after the Occupation. Chartier, in particular, noted similarities between this cinema and aspects of the 'French school of *film noir*' from the 1930s (such as *Le Jour se lève* [1939]), but claimed that recent Hollywood titles were marked by a greater level of violence and despair. Later, in 1953, two French writers, Raymond Borde and Etienne Chaumeton, published their influential book on *film noir* – *A Panorama of American Film Noir 1941–1953* – that sought, for the first time, to propose a chronology for a form that was especially marked in their eyes by its dystopian conflation of screen violence, sexuality and narrative ambiguity. As Marc Vernet (1993) has astutely noted, the French thus initially invented *film noir* as an object of critical fascination because it served the specific purpose of allowing non-American cinephiles the pleasure of loving American culture while at the same viewing it through a negative lens.

Borde and Chaumeton's history dates the emergence of *film noir* from John Huston's *The Maltese Falcon* (1941). By the time Paul Schrader wrote his seminal article on the topic in 1972, he was able to suggest that by 1958 it had come to its natural end with the release of Orson Welles's *Touch of Evil*. Schrader defined classical American *film noir* in terms of a tripartite model, noting that initially it had had a polished studio phase, exemplified by films such as *This Gun for Hire* (Frank Tuttle, 1942) and *Laura* (1944), before turning to the streets of American cities, in films like *Call Northside 777* (1948) and *Force of Evil* (1948), to achieve a greater degree of narrative authenticity. Films such as *Kiss Me Deadly* (1955) marked *noir*'s final phase in their effort to rework conventions and address the new social realities of the 1950s.

More recently, this relatively neat teleology has been disrupted in a number of ways. If it can be agreed that *film noir* was not a stable film 'genre' in the sense of being, like the Western or musical, part of the way individual films were marketed and received as part of a preconstituted continuum, why not countenance the significance of elements already present in American cinema before the beginning of World War II? Michael Walker (1993), for example, has drawn attention to the correlation between elements of *film noir* and the cycle of hard-hitting social-problem and gangster films produced by Hollywood before 1934. Vernet has also argued that *noir*'s so-called 'expressionist lighting' was visible in numerous American detective and mystery dramas going back to the teens.

What then *are* the principal components of *film noir*'s narrative style? Frank Krutnik (1991), like many, has noticed the way in which many *film noir* titles particularly embody the expressive qualities of America's hard-boiled fiction tradition. Films such as *Side Street* (1950), *Cry of the City* (1948) and *The Dark Corner* (1946) suggest the significance of potentially perilous urban milieux while *Cornered* (1945) and *Criss Cross* (1949) convey a recurring sense of fatalism and despair. *Film noir*'s abiding interest in violence, death and sexuality is signalled by features like *Murder, My Sweet* and *Kiss of Death* (1947). For Schrader, these themes became directly translated into a readily identifiable narrative and visual grammar often marked by the deployment of a complex flashback structure and a distinctive sense of compositional tension. Janey Place and Lowell Peterson (1974), in a further influential article, developed this hypothesis by arguing that *film noir*'s visual style was specifically defined by a unique combination of framing and compositional strategies and lighting set-ups that, in turn, helped exemplify the psychological focus of the form. American *film noir*, they suggested, captured the malaise of American society through the way it looked. Thus, we see a prevalence of irregular camera angles, claustrophobic framings and disruptive mirror images to indicate the unstable background and subjectivity of the typical *noir* protagonist. *Film noir*'s marked use of low-key lighting added to the distilled sense of underlying menace and threat. For many critics, these elements have perfectly suited the underworld, lowlife locations of conventional *film noir* narratives with their recurring populations of small-time crooks, nightclub singers, prostitutes, casino owners and various corrupt politicians and/or police officers.

Looking at classical American *film noir* today, especially in the light of the films we have chosen for this BFI Screen Guide, it is clear that *noir* style is a far more heterogeneous phenomenon than these views on *film noir* style would imply. As Naremore has argued, elements of style noticed by Place and Peterson in fact occur across many different forms of Hollywood production and there is no single means of defining their attributes. As well as cinematographic aspects such as lighting and framing, it also makes sense to consider costume, set design and the relationship between *film noir* and the broader visual culture of the time. Several of the book's entries attempt to do just this.

Film noir's determinants are equally varied, pointing to a range of nationally specific and transnational factors. From a technological point of view, many of the characteristics defined by Place and Peterson were specifically enabled by changes in the quality of film production in the 1940s, ranging from the development of faster film stocks and coated lenses to more powerful lights and a more extensive use of wide-angle lenses. Importantly, as Sheri Chinen Biesen (2005) has also pointed out, 'the *noir* aesthetic derived from wartime constraints on filmmaking practices' as well as 'a response to an ... anxiety about war, shortages, changing gender roles and [the appearance of] "a world gone mad"'. Cities such as Los Angeles were literally 'blacked out' during night-time while urban populations at the same time found themselves encountering new sensations of the night with the advent of round-the-clock shift patterns in munitions factories. A further significant influence is the gradual change in censorship patterns, especially as the war progressed, permitting new and franker representations of mortality and violence in response to the personal experiences of many of the country's citizens (and filmgoers).

There is a transatlantic dimension to seeing the emergence of *film noir* as a reaction, in part, to the pressures of wartime conflict for it is undoubtedly true that many of *noir*'s most skilled practitioners, such as the directors Robert Siodmak, Fritz Lang, Curtis Bernhardt, Billy Wilder and Edgar G. Ulmer, and the cinematographers Eugen Schüfftan, Rudolph Maté and Franz Planer, all arrived as émigrés from Germany and Central Europe in the years following Hitler's coming to power. Whereas conventional *noir* history posits the idea that these film-makers simply imported something loosely termed 'German expressionism' to Hollywood, recent work in the field has argued that, much like the nature of *film noir* itself, the question of European influence is more dynamic, unstable and multifaceted than that. Certainly people like Siodmak brought the significant experience of working in the sophisticated German studios with them, but they also brought a temperamental disposition – what Thomas Elsaesser (2000) calls 'a double perspective on American society – one of admiration and the other a hyper-critical view, both *vying with one another*'. A film like Wilder's *Double Indemnity* is a perfect example of this kind of cultural force field in which a certain benign interest in popular American culture is matched by a wary, rueful distance from its many evident excesses. Once again here, *film noir* is as much about a state of mind as a single set of stylistic signs.

Over the years, since the emergence of a spate of important writings in the field in the 1970s, *film noir* has been subjected to continued intense critical scrutiny. Indeed, it is not too much of an exaggeration to claim that *film noir* has played a leading role in the development of ideas related to film criticism in general and contemporary Film Studies in particular. Perhaps the most significant topic that has been addressed is that of gender since often pernicious assumptions about the conventional codes of both masculinity and femininity permeate any number of key *film noirs* from *Dead Reckoning* (1947) and *Scarlet Street* (1945) to *Gilda* (1946) and *The Lady from Shanghai* (1947). In particular, critics from the 1970s onwards, influenced by the impact of second-wave feminism, have been fascinated with the unconventional figure of the *femme fatale*. On the one hand, some have seen *noir* being primarily a male fantasy in which femininity is exclusively defined in terms of straight male fears and desires. According to this logic, the figure of the *femme fatale* presents a dangerous threat to social stability that must be resolved by punishment so that the male hero may settle for stable heterosexual domesticity. On the other hand, others such as Elizabeth Cowie (1993), have sought to define the *femme fatale*, if only in limited terms, as a mildly progressive form of the liberated female. Her dominance of the film frame may, in this case, suggest a literal and metaphorical degree of cultural freedom permitting the notion that *film noir* might provide as much a feminine fantasy of dangerous sexuality as a masculine one. The point here though is that no matter how powerful it might be for the *femme fatale* to be designated excessively feminine, it still remains an ambiguous proposition. As Richard Dyer (1998) has neatly put it, 'If (some) women … participate in the construction and performance of femininity, is that seizing the opportunity afforded by male desire or colluding in it?'

As we have already seen, the concept of *film noir* – or 'dark film' – was initially largely defined as a foreign object of fascination. It is not surprising then that another important category underlying the critical discussion of Hollywood *film noir* is that of race. Just as *noir* problematised American cinema's 'usual generic or gendered distinctions', to use Naremore's phrase, so it also underlined many of the negative racial assumptions prevalent within the wider sphere of American culture at the time. From the very beginning, for example, *film noir* was unable to define a coherent and detailed African American social space that was inhabited by the same kind of immersive subjectivities afforded to white protagonists. Almost the only black characters we see in *Double Indemnity*, for instance, are the cleaners in the desperate opening pre-flashback scenes of the film. Perhaps following the implicit logic of the term, *film noir* instead favoured the construction of whiteness by aligning what Dyer (1997) calls the 'elimination of shadow' with the 'desire for visibility'. Hence, Eric Lott's (1997) fundamental perception that if subversive desires drive the narratives in *film noir*, it is by criminalising these desires 'and utilizing racial norms coded in moral terminologies and visual devices [that *noir* ultimately] preserves the idea of a whiteness that its own characters do not [fully] uphold'.

Having said this, it is also noticeable, as Naremore has pointed out, how unstable many of *film noir*'s narrative spaces actually are. Partly this must be due to the enormous influence of the generation of artists, writers and film-makers affected by the legacy of Roosevelt's New Deal culture in the 1930s who came into their own in Hollywood at the very time that *film noir* emerged as a major cultural form. Indeed, it was the prominence of liberal and left-minded personnel such as Edward Dmytryk (*Crossfire* [1947]) and Abraham Polonsky (*Force of Evil*) that led to the political censorship activities of the HUAC (House Un-American Activities Committee) in the latter part of American *noir*'s first decade. How then did *film noir* represent the contours of the American social landscape? As Mike Davis (1998) has observed, several of the early *noirs* such as *The Maltese Falcon*, *Double Indemnity* and *The Big Sleep* (1946) were based on crime novels and short stories that emerged during the Depression. Written by the likes of Dashiell Hammett, James M. Cain and Raymond Chandler, many of these tales tended to feature detectives struggling with the injustices of class amid a milieu of lazy, corrupt and idle wealthy West Coast suburbanites. In the postwar period, in films like *The Big Heat* (1953), attention shifted to a more oblique critique of social polarisation with a tougher and more vicious realism depicting a deeper level of collusion between official corruption and gangsterism.

The most important site of narrative action was, of course, the American city and one of the interesting aspects of this book is its coverage of a number of seminal New York and Los Angeles *noirs*. These include several undervalued films such as *Criss Cross* and *Odds against Tomorrow* (1959). In his definitive study of the relationship between the metropolis and American *film noir*, Edward Dimendberg (2004) notes the shift from the early 'centripetal' *noir* such as *Scarlet Street*, which presents a relatively reassuring fabric of local neighbour-hoods and familiar urban landmarks to the 'centrifugal' *noir* such as *Kiss Me Deadly*, where new urban locations are increasingly demarcated by the flow of images seen through the windscreen of an automobile.

An ancillary aspect of *film noir*'s urban setting is the recurring atmospheric iconography of its various faded boarding-houses, seedy bars, disreputable supper clubs and louche gambling dens. As Vivian Sobchack (1998) has pointedly demonstrated, these transitory, even criminal, spaces served the function of providing not just an allegory of the various economic and social crises of the time, but also a very real sense of what it was like to lose the emotional security of one's domestic life. *Film noir* is populated by characters who have lost direction and very often have no real place left to go. Many people have understood this quality of psychological dislocation as being an indication of the lasting trauma of the US's experience of World War II and, although this schema might seem overly deterministic, the figure of the war veteran nonetheless featured repeatedly in a number of *noirs*, such as *Crossfire* and *Cornered*, made just after the war.

So far this introduction has largely concentrated on the defining period of classical American *film noir* production lasting from the early 1940s through to the late 1950s. This is still the phase in *noir's* multifaceted history that most people call to mind when asked to visualise the qualities of *film noir* in their cultural imagination. One of the major arguments we wish to propose in this book, however, is that not only has *noir* continued to mutate and regenerate in the US – from modernist films in the 1970s such as *Night Moves* (1975) and *The Long Goodbye* (1973) through to the emergence of 'neo-noir' productions such as *Pulp Fiction* (Quentin Tarantino, 1994) – but that there is a still neglected international tale to be told. The attentive reader will therefore uncover accounts of various important European *film noirs* such as *Quai des Orfèvres* (1947) and *Brighton Rock* (1947) which, although made at exactly the same time as other films from the heyday of American *noir* production like *Out of the Past* and *Born to Kill* (also 1947), embody a different modality or sensibility more germane to locally specific traditions of cultural representation. With this in mind, we have also tried to diversify the field even further and include examples of *film noir* film-making from countries as wide apart as India, South Korea, Japan and Brazil. In other words, there is no such thing perhaps as *a film noir* but rather many forms and variations of a sensibility that alters and shifts according to culture, place and time. At the very least, there is a debate to be had. Read on and take part.

*   *   *

Given the wealth of material, and the relative breadth of the areas we have tried to cover, identifying 100 *film noir* or *noir*-related titles to write about for this BFI Screen Guide posed few problems. Indeed, it was much more difficult to agree on which titles *not* to include (which led, in part, to our decision to include an appendix of a further 100 titles, most of which we considered including at some stage of the preparation of the book).

What might constitute a representative list of 100 *film noir* titles? Inevitably, given the history of *film noir* and the nature of the debates that have circulated about the subject, the bulk of our entries are Hollywood studio – though not necessarily major studio – pictures. Similarly, the bulk of the entries – about two-thirds – come from the period 1940–58, generally regarded as the core period of *noir* production. However, to reflect the complex inheritance that *noir* draws on, we also include several pre-1940 European films. Similarly, to reflect classical *film noir*'s complex patterns of exchange and influence, we have included a significant number of post-1958 films from a broad range of national cultures. Overall, about a quarter of our entries are non-US in origin.

Availability on DVD (in one region or another) and/or regular circulation on terrestrial or cable television was an additional criterion for choice. It did not seem particularly useful to write about a lot of films that readers are unable to see. At the same time, there remain a few titles here that are not readily available to see or buy or rent. Perhaps this volume will encourage distributors to make some of these titles available. Fortunately, the growth in the popularity of *film noir* shows no sign of diminishing and DVD distributors seem happy to feed it, bringing all kinds of previously rare material, old and new, into distribution. Even during the period of preparation of this book, some titles we considered hard to see became available.

Our choices aim to reflect considerations of these various kinds rather than represent what we think might be the 100 'best' *film noirs*. Nevertheless, as will be clear from the contents, our 100 does include a fair sprinkling of films that have come to be considered by critics and spectators alike as 'classics' of *film noir*. 'Classics' inevitably implies some notion of 'best' even though both 'best' and 'classic' remain highly ambiguous concepts.

Each of the book's entries tries to identify what is distinctive about a particular film and relate it to some of the major debates about *film noir* discussed previously. At the same time, entries try to provide some historical context for the film and relate it to other films, whether they are included as entries in the book or not. Several entries make reference to later remakes. When entries make reference to other entries in the book they are marked with an asterisk to allow ease of cross-reference (although there are certainly more relationships to be made between films than those we highlight). As regards the titles cited for non-English-language entries, for the main entry we have used our – no doubt flawed – intuitive sense of the titles which most readers are likely to recognise, e.g. *High and Low* (Kurosawa Akira, 1963) or *La Bête humaine* (Jean Renoir, 1938). In the case of English-language titles of non-English-language films, the heading of the entry and the index also includes the film's original foreign-language title e.g. *The American Friend* (*Der Amerikanische Freund*) (Wim Wenders, 1977). Similarly, when English-language films made in the US have been released under more than one title, we have used the original US release title; when a film has been released under a different title in the UK, this information is generally included.

At the end of each entry we supply an agreed list of production credits. Inevitably, for reasons of space, these credits are very selective. Although there might have been a good case for a book on *film noir*, in particular, to provide credits for art directors or production designers, for example, we have generally kept to the reduced range of credits listed by other books in the series. We follow the Screen Guide convention of including the director's name directly under the entry title. However, this should not be taken to imply that we necessarily consider the director of a particular film to be the major, or only significant, influence on the way it turns out, as a number of our entries make clear.

The authors have debated how to deal with the fact that *film noir* was originally a French-language term coined by French critics to refer primarily to Hollywood cinema. Should we refer to *film noir* in italics to signal its French origin, or should we recognise that 'film noir' has passed into the English-language critical idiom and therefore use it without italics? (The same issue is raised, in a different context, by the French term *mise en scène*). Similarly, should we also refer to individual films in the *noir* idiom as *films noirs* – to preserve French grammatical usage – or as *film noirs*? In the vast literature on the subject, there are precedents for both. In trying to acknowledge the history of the form, we have agreed to use '*film noir*' to refer to both the general field of *noir* production and individual films, and '*film noirs*' to refer to more than one *film noir*, despite its potentially ugly grammatical construction.

The book includes three further sections.

References

This lists all books and essays that we refer to within the introduction and the individual entries. For the sake of readability, we decided against a formal academic annotation system, but this list of references should enable readers to readily locate all sources.

Further Reading

This overlaps with the References section, but offers a more extensive listing of important English-language books on *film noir*.

Another 100 Film Noirs

Given the many titles we considered for the book but had to reject for considerations of space and coverage, we wanted to register at least the titles, directors, countries and dates of another 100 *film noirs* which readers would probably find just as interesting as the 100 included in the book. Readers might consider these as subjects for further research.

36 (*36 Quai des Orfèvres*)
France, 2004 – 105 mins
Olivier Marchal

36, named like Henri-Georges Clouzot's *Quai des Orfèvres* (1947)* after
the central Parisian headquarters of the French police service, has been
likened by many critics to Michael Mann's landmark police thriller, *Heat*
(1995). While it is true that both films share a similar dramatic grandeur,
especially in their pitting of two leading screen actors against each other
– in this case Daniel Auteuil and Gérard Depardieu rather than Al Pacino
and Robert de Niro – it makes more sense to see Olivier Marchal's epic
tale of criminal treachery and professional duplicity in terms of its
successful contribution to the revival of the French *policier* (or *polar*). Like
earlier examples of the genre such as *La Balance* (Bob Swaim, 1982),
Police (Maurice Pialat, 1985) and *L.627* (Bertrand Tavernier, 1992), *36*
shares a firmly realist dramatic *modus operandi* in which the moral
complexities of the drama are articulated through an emphasis on the
various character similarities between the film's hardened criminals and
ruthlessly driven police officers.

Robert Mancini (André Dussollier), the current head of Paris's elite anti-
gang squad, is due for retirement and two officers are competing to be his
successor: the unconventional, angst-ridden Léo Vrinks (Daniel Auteuil)
and the slyly manipulative Denis Klein (Gérard Depardieu). Both men are
charged with arresting a gang responsible for carrying out a recent string
of violent robberies in the city. As the drama twists and turns, Vrinks's
initial attempt to arrest the criminals is foiled by Klein's drunken
intervention and a close associate is killed in the ensuing crossfire. The
force sides with Vrinks and the gang are eventually caught, but when
Klein subsequently discovers that Vrinks has covered up the murder of
Klein's main informer – by his own snitch – he has his successful rival
arrested and charged. Vrinks is jailed and Klein is cleared of his earlier
misconduct. Further events ensue and it is only years later that the
corrosive score between the two men is finally settled once and for all.

36 is marked by its distinctive combination of dramatic set-piece action sequences and pervasive sense of brooding melancholy. Its *mise en scène* alternates between a fast-moving, widescreen vision of the Parisian underworld and police departments – its use of architecture is especially sensational – and an intensely realised series of close-ups of Vrinks and Klein's initially separate, but then increasingly similar, psychological tics. The film's most obvious influence here is the cycle of gangster films directed by Jean-Pierre Melville, especially *Le Cercle rouge* (1970), that portrayed the voiceless solitude of those caught up on both sides of the French criminal *milieu*. Vrinks's informer, Silien, for example, must surely be named after Jean-Paul Belmondo's lead character in Melville's earlier *Le Doulos* (1962). Another aspect shared with Melville is the profound disengagement with the representation of women although *36*, despite its familiar repertoire of prostitutes and marginalised domesticated wives, does at least have one single female police agent.

There is a strong autobiographical element that underlines the film's surface appeal to authenticity. Marchal once served as a police officer and claims he only joined the force after seeing the French crime film director Alain Corneau's *Police Python 357* (1975). Much of the film is actually based on the real-life events that he experienced or that happened to Dominique Loiseau, a former police colleague (and subsequent script collaborator). It is these qualities, rather than its recourse to spectacular action aesthetics, that contribute to *36*'s significance as a French *film noir*. Superficially, it may appear to be in the mould of recent American crime cinema, but it also knowingly updates longer-standing French genre traditions that clearly still have enormous popular appeal. AP

Dir: Olivier Marchal; **Prod**: Franck Chorot, Cyril Colbeau-Justin, Jean-Baptiste Dupont; **Scr**: Olivier Marchal, Dominique Loiseau; **DOP**: Denis Rouden (colour); **Ed**: Hugues Darmois; **Score**: Erwann Kermorvant, Axelle Renoir; **Main Cast**: Daniel Auteuil, Gérard Depardieu, André Dussollier, Roschdy Zem, Valeria Golino; **Prod Co**: Gaumont, LGM Cinéma, TF1 Films Production, KL Productions.

The American Friend (*Der Amerikanische Freund*)
West Germany/France, 1977 – 127 mins
Wim Wenders

The American Friend intensified Wim Wenders's preoccupation with the ways in which postwar Germany's cultural imaginary was haunted by the United States with a number of intertextual elements informed by the legacy of *film noir*. Its geographical range from America to Germany to France neatly encapsulates the intercultural traditions suggested by the history of *noir* criticism and *noir* production, while the inclusion of such names as Sam Fuller (*Pickup on South Street* [1953]*) and Nicholas Ray (*On Dangerous Ground* [1952]*) recalls both the heyday of Hollywood *film noir* film-making and the subsequent inclusion of these directors in the European critical canon. Finally, key scenes from this intensely cinematic version of the American émigré crime writer Patricia Highsmith's *Ripley's Game* remind one of another major Highsmith film adaptation: the thriller, *Strangers on a Train* (1951), directed in the US by the British émigré, Alfred Hitchcock.

Bruno Ganz plays Jonathan Zimmerman, a Hamburg picture framer who is apparently dying of a blood disease. Befriended by his 'American friend', the mysterious Tom Ripley (Dennis Hopper), Zimmerman is introduced to an urbane French gangster (Gérard Blain) who persuades the German to become a mob assassin in return for the provision of a secure financial legacy for his wife and young son. The film traces the emotional architecture of their fleeting relationship against the backdrop of the atmospheric modern cityscapes of Hamburg and Paris.

Central to the film's distinctively melancholic emotional timbre is the bravura cinematography of Robby Müller who first captures the fleeting light conditions of the Northern port city then translates the tonal registers of its buildings, skies and rooms into a colour palette conveying an internalised feeling of unease. In this fashion, especially in its sense of suspended time and space, the film directly recalls another American

Caught despairingly between departure and arrival: the rootless Ripley (Dennis Hopper) in
The American Friend

influence: that of the paintings of Edward Hopper. The introspective
Zimmerman is caught in the present, unable to move forward, while the
rootless Ripley (bound to his cowboy hat and empty mansion overlooking
the city) is likewise trapped in the past, unable to engage in the future.
The compositions of the film reiterate this sense of stasis with an
emphasis on momentary spaces of transition. The recurring presence of
doorways, passageways and train stations suggests a world, much like
the cultural universe of *film noir*, caught despairingly between departure
and arrival. Only the regulated warmth of the female space of the

Zimmerman home with its parade of optical toys and childhood memorabilia offers seclusion.

Müller's sense of colour undoubtedly makes *The American Friend* one of the most beautiful European films of the 1970s. It now looks like a distilled period piece from the pre-digital era, just when the architectural skyline of the European city was under transition and when CCTV was beginning to infiltrate its streets and tunnels. Along with Jürgen Knieper's wary, urgent score the film suggests a very different take on the chameleon-like persona of Highsmith's Ripley, established previously in René Clément's *Plein Soleil* (1960). Here, there is none of Alain Delon's continental athleticism. Rather, Hopper's discernibly Americanised Ripley is even more mutable and unknowable. When Zimmerman aptly visits the American hospital in Paris, he is told that this is where Jean Gabin, famed for his French poetic realist crime films such as *La Bête humaine* (1938)* and *Le Jour se lève* (1939)*, died. *The American Friend* is full of these real and imagined *film noir* ghosts, but the specific inclusion of the theme of life-threatening illness ultimately produces a pervasive sense of mourning. Like the film's central protagonists, *film noir*, Wenders seems to be suggesting, now has nowhere left to go. AP

Dir: Wim Wenders; **Prod**: Joachim von Mengershausen; **Scr**: Wim Wenders from Patricia Highsmith's novel *Ripley's Game*; **DOP**: Robby Müller (colour); **Ed**: Peter Przygodda; **Score**: Jürgen Knieper; **Main Cast**: Dennis Hopper, Bruno Ganz, Lisa Kreuzer, Gérard Blain, Nicholas Ray, Sam Fuller; **Prod Co**: Filmverlag der Autoren, Les Films du Losange, Moli Films, Road Movies Filmproduktion, WDR, Wim Wenders Productions.

The Asphalt Jungle
US, 1950 – 112 mins
John Huston

Heist or caper movies show men – usually desperate and disparate men – coming together to work as a team then falling out as they come under pressure. *The Asphalt Jungle*'s team is an archetypal one: gently spoken mastermind Doc (Sam Jaffe), whose obsession with adolescent female sexuality proves his undoing; hunchbacked, loyal Gus (James Whitmore); safecracker Louis (Anthony Caruso), desperate to pay his sick child's health bills; and Dix (Sterling Hayden), forced by bankruptcy from his family horse farm in Kentucky to earning a brutal living as a petty thug in the alienating city. John Huston deliberately humanises his beleaguered criminals and contrasts their honour and loyalty with the crooked lawyer Emmerich (Louis Calhern) and bookie Cobby (Marc Lawrence) who finance (and cheat) them and the police (some of them corrupt) who hunt them. In the late 1940s/early 1950s, MGM was still mostly associated with musicals and comedies and MGM boss Louis B. Mayer found *The Asphalt Jungle*'s characters nasty and ugly, though Huston goes to considerable lengths to make them sympathetic and moral.

The fine opening credit sequence sets the tone. We see the grey, forbidding pre-dawn city, and a man (Dix) blending in, discreetly evading a police prowl car. This city – a composite of Cincinnati and Los Angeles – is a decaying, ugly, unfriendly place, despite the seductively silvery reflection of streetlights reflected on automobile bodies. Women – the lawyer's trophy mistress, Angela (Marilyn Monroe), and even Doll (Jean Hagen), who would like to save Dix – are marginal. This is a male world, where danger comes less from duplicitous women than from what Doc calls the 'blind accidents' which can change the course of events – like his own arrest after staying a moment too long watching a young girl dance instead of making good his escape.

The Asphalt Jungle offers two very different endings. In what would have been a suitably moral ending to a 1930s gangster film, the

Plotting the heist in *The Asphalt Jungle*: (left to right) Doc (Sam Jaffe), Dix (Sterling Hayden), Louis (Anthony Caruso) and Gus (James Whitmore)

avuncular – but unsympathetic – police commissioner (John McIntire) tells the press about people being robbed, murdered, raped twenty-four hours a day; without the police 'the jungle wins. The predatory beast takes over.' The remaining man at large, Dix, is labelled 'a hardened killer, a man without human feeling or mercy'. The film then cuts to Doll and the mortally wounded Dix driving desperately, half-conscious, through the Kentucky countryside to Hickory Wood Farm, where he stumbles into the field and collapses dead before he can reach the horses, which gather round his body.

MGM's best-known earlier *noir* – *The Postman Always Rings Twice* (1946)* – was not very moody in look, despite other *noir* qualities, but *The Asphalt Jungle* adopts *film noir*'s characteristic low-key lighting, particularly in interiors. Its detailed account of the meticulous planning and execution of the robbery, with its attendant suspense and the individualisation of those involved, may well have inspired many later heist movies, such as *Rififi* (1955)*. Burnett's novel and Huston's movie also inspired several remakes: the Western *The Badlanders* (Delmer Daves, 1958), the blaxploitation picture *Cool Breeze* (Barry Pollack, 1972) and the British thriller *Cairo* (Wolf Rilla, 1963), all distributed by MGM. (MGM Television also made a reputedly very good TV series titled *The Asphalt Jungle*, which ran for one season in 1961 on the ABC network, but there was no connection to the 1950 film). JH

Dir: John Huston; **Prod**: Arthur Hornblow, Jr; **Scr**: Ben Maddow, John Huston from W. R. Burnett's novel; **DOP**: Harold Rosson (b&w); **Ed**: George Boemler; **Score**: Miklós Rózsa; **Main Cast**: Sterling Hayden, Louis Calhern, Jean Hagen, James Whitmore, Sam Jaffe, John McIntire, Marc Lawrence, Anthony Caruso, Marilyn Monroe; **Prod Co**: MGM.

La Bête humaine
France, 1938 – 100 mins
Jean Renoir

Jean Renoir's passionate adaptation of Emile Zola's tale of hereditary violence opens with a close-up of a burning furnace. Slowly, the camera tracks back and we realise that we are in the fulcrum of a steam locomotive manned energetically by two men later named as Jacques Lantier (Jean Gabin) and Pecqueux (Carette). For the next few minutes, we cut furiously between the gestural excitement of the engine room and a series of purely visceral shots sensationally filmed from the edge or front of the train as it speeds through the passing French landscape. It is only much later that we realise that this gripping montage has captured the philosophical thrust of the film: that the transient vibrancy and momentum of human activity is ultimately subservient to the enduring force of predestination suggested by the railway's parallel tracks.

The film enacts this *noir*-related theme by dramatising the romance between Lantier and Séverine (Simone Simon), the glamorous wife of his lugubrious railway colleague Roubaud (Fernand Ledoux), that begins after Roubaud murders Séverine's lascivious godfather on the Paris–Le Havre train in revenge for the man's repeated sexual transgressions. Disgusted by her husband's actions, and knowing that Lantier has also witnessed the couple on the train, Séverine starts an illicit sexual affair with the gentle, roughly hewn engine driver. When Séverine begins to plot the murder of her husband, Lantier realises that he can no longer avoid the legacy of his family's drunken, violent past and the couple's fleeting but obsessive relationship ends finally in dark tragedy.

Central to Renoir's typically textured analysis of the class and emotional dimensions of Lantier and Séverine's romance are the repeated shots of the couple clasping each other, gazing up off screen left in an ambiguously defined combination of passion and despair. In one famous scene, set amid the night-time railway yards, dressed in near-identical black leather coats, they embody the archetypal doomed *film noir* couple. The atmospheric rendition of the sets, especially the dynamic use of mirrors and reflective surfaces, owes much to the input of cinematographer Curt Courant (*Le Jour se lève* [1939]*), who along with other German and middle-European émigrés then working in France, helped shape the look of French poetic realism.

As the film historian Charles O'Brien (1996) has pointed out, the term '*film noir*' first began to appear within French critical discourse in relation to such poetic realist films as *Le Quai des brumes* (Marcel Carné, 1938), *Le Puritain* (Jeff Musso, 1937) and *La Tradition de minuit* (Roger Richebé, 1939). Writing of Courant's cinematography in *La Bête humaine* in the French press, for example, the prominent critic, Emile Vuillermoz, specifically noted that '*noir* is currently the colour in fashion in our studios'. Poetic realism, as critics such as Ginette Vincendeau (1993) have also argued, is indeed the missing link in *film noir*'s intercultural history as not only was the atmospheric visual style of these films an influence in its own right, but several titles, including *La Bête humaine*, were then exported and remade in Hollywood in various English-language versions.

Fritz Lang's version of Renoir's film, *Human Desire* (1954), paired Glenn Ford and Gloria Grahame from Lang's *The Big Heat* (1953)* in the leading roles. It retains much of the original's intensity, but lacks Renoir's characteristic intricacy and fluidity when it comes to the depiction of personal and social relationships. *La Bête humaine* has an elemental quality – there are repeated shots of fire, water, earth and metal – but what saves it from mere abstraction is the consistency of its still astonishingly modern interest in the fragility of human lives. AP

Dir: Jean Renoir; **Prod**: Raymond Hakim, Robert Hakim; **Scr**: Denise Leblond (uncredited), Jean Renoir (uncredited) from Emile Zola's novel; **DOP**: Curt Courant (b&w); **Ed**: Suzanne de Troeye, Marguerite Renoir; **Score**: Joseph Kosma; **Main Cast**: Jean Gabin, Simone Simon, Fernand Ledoux, Jean Renoir, Carette, Blanchette Brunoy; **Prod Co**: Paris Film.

The Big Combo
US, 1955 – 89 mins
Joseph H. Lewis

The Big Combo merges several familiar *film noir* plots. Like *The Big Heat* (1953)* its dogged, slightly dull cop Leonard Diamond (Cornel Wilde) battles to bring down an organised crime boss, here Mr Brown (Richard Conte), and has a troubled relationship with a mob-attached woman who is instrumental in helping him. Like *Cry of the City* (1948)* it pits the cop against a more charismatic criminal figure, though the psychological 'doubling' of cop and gangster in *Cry of the City* is replaced here with envy or jealousy: Brown tells Diamond his problem is that 'you'd like to be me'. At the film's centre is Diamond's neurotic desire for Brown's mistress, Susan (Jean Wallace). Diamond wants her help but, more fundamentally, he *wants* her. His irrational obsession with both 'saving' and having her is what drives him, though 'drive' hardly describes his preoccupied, almost trance-like state during much of the story.

The enigmatic Susan is central to the film's take on criminality, violence and sexuality (issues approached equally powerfully, in Joseph H. Lewis's earlier *Gun Crazy* [1950]*). She is the focus of the film's strikingly shot opening: blonde, dressed in white, she tries to escape from a night-time boxing match but is stopped by Brown's minders. The sequence sets the film's visual and moral tone, with John Alton's low-key, deep-focus lighting and low angles of the dark, deserted, echoing stadium passageways powerfully complementing her headlong flight. Susan is attracted to Brown's power and charisma and unable to break with him despite her bourgeois, cultured background. She is sexually in thrall to him. For Brown, who insists that she dresses only in white, she is a class conquest and a trophy. In the film's most audacious sequence, Susan having declared her repugnance towards him, Brown kisses her violently, disappearing from the frame as his kisses move down her body to pleasure her, the camera resting on Susan's momentarily ecstatic expression before fading. In the far from conventional ending, Susan finally acts against Brown, and Susan and Diamond are left as silhouettes, shrouded in darkness and fog, tentatively moving toward each other.

Though raw sexuality is implied in many *film noirs*, few are as explicit as *The Big Combo*. Similarly, few present homoerotic subtexts as clearly as *The Big Combo* does with its pair of sadistic killers, Fante (Lee Van Cleef) and Mingo (Earl Holliman). The film is notable for its imaginatively perverse and violent scenes of torture and killing, on a par with *Kiss Me Deadly**, made in the same year. What keeps *The Big Combo* engaging is less its plot – decidedly creaky as Diamond searches for cracks in Brown's empire – than the fascination of the Diamond–Susan–Brown triangle and Alton's and Lewis's inventively expressive photography and *mise en scène* of a world in which almost everything is played out in dark interiors and night-time exteriors.

By the mid-1950s former B-movie studio Monogram had changed its name to Allied Artists and, as Chris Hugo (1993) suggests, was aiming higher with hybrid A/B films like *The Big Combo* to exploit new conditions in film exhibition. As in many crime films of the period, following the findings of the early 1950s Kefauver Senate Committee on organised crime, crime here is seen to hide behind a legitimate corporate front. Though this is 'the big combo', what we *see* here, no doubt because of the film's budget constraints, in fact looks like a rather small-time operation – just two bosses and two enforcers. JH

Dir: Joseph H. Lewis; **Prod**: Sidney Harmon; **Scr**: Philip Yordan; **DOP**: John Alton (b&w); **Ed**: Robert Eisen; **Score**: David Raksin; **Main Cast**: Cornel Wilde, Richard Conte, Brian Donlevy, Jean Wallace, Robert Middleton, Lee Van Cleef, Earl Holliman; **Prod Co**: Allied Artists.

The Big Heat
US, 1953 – 90 mins
Fritz Lang

Like *Fury* (1936), *You Only Live Once* (1937), *Beyond a Reasonable Doubt*, *While the City Sleeps* (both 1956), *The Big Heat* is a classic and concentrated instance of Fritz Lang's preoccupation with individual morality, justice and the law. As his 1952 Western *Rancho Notorious* has it, it's another tale of 'Hate, Murder and Revenge' in which basically honest cop Dave Bannion (Glenn Ford), investigating the suicide of a police officer, is pushed by systematic police corruption to become a rogue cop operating beyond the constraints of the law. In this sense, Bannion occupies a very different position from that of the *film noir* private investigator, whose relationship to the law is characteristically more ambivalent. *The Big Heat* is also one of several *noir* films, such as *The Enforcer* (Bretaigne Windust & Raoul Walsh [1951]), *The Big Combo* (1955)* and *Underworld USA* (Samuel Fuller, 1960), inspired by the early 1950s Kefauver Senate Committee, which exposed the extent of US organised crime and featured gangster syndicates organised along the lines of legitimate business.

What begins as an earnestly moral investigation by Bannion into police corruption soon becomes a more problematic individual crusade when the corrupt upper echelons of both police and mob try to curtail his activities. The quest turns towards personal revenge when his wife (Jocelyn Brando) is murdered by a car bomb intended for him. Though Bannion's moral position ensures a bedrock of spectator sympathy, as single-mindedness turns into virulent obsession, a certain distance is introduced. Bannion's crusade jeopardises the lives of the women whose support he depends on – his wife, the girlfriend of the corrupt cop whose suicide sets the plot in motion, the crippled woman who gives him a lead and, most powerfully, Debbie (Gloria Grahame), the girlfriend of crime boss Lagana's violent enforcer, Vince Stone (Lee Marvin). Debbie – half-dumb, half-worldly wise – has her fate sealed when she befriends Bannion. The two scenes between them in Bannion's anonymous hotel room – 'early nothing', as she memorably calls it – lit and staged to emphasise both their proximity and their separation, full of repressed desire and curiosity about each other, are crucial in bringing Bannion to a greater understanding of his anger and urge for violent revenge.

The *femme fatale* function here is split between the young, sexy Debbie, initially associated with criminality, and the hard, middle-aged widow of the police suicide, Bertha Duncan, who plans to benefit from her husband's corruption and death. In their extraordinary, mink-coated encounter – 'Sisters under the mink' as Debbie puts it – Debbie acts as a kind of proxy for Bannion when she kills Duncan, whose death will make corruption public and bring down 'the big heat'.

Lang, as usual, opts for studio artifice over location authenticity, and a claustrophobic, closed world in which almost everything takes place in interiors. However, the film's look of artifice sits uneasily with its representation of extreme violence, even though the actual violence – the car bomb, women burned with cigarettes, Debbie's scalding from boiling coffee – happens off screen. The film's world is not unrelentingly bleak – the crippled woman risks helping Bannion, his brother-in-law's World War II buddies rally round, honest cops voluntarily support him, and Debbie gives her life – but the extent of corruption and violence overshadows any prospect of social good. Lang undercuts a formulaic 'happy end', with Bannion restored to the police and corruption supposedly eradicated, when he is called out to a hit-and-run on South Street and, disturbingly, asks them to keep the coffee hot. JH

Dir: Fritz Lang; **Prod**: Robert Arthur; **Scr**: Sydney Boehm, from William P. McGivern's *Saturday Evening Post* serial; **DOP**: Charles Lang (b&w); **Ed**: Charles Nelson; **Score**: Daniele Amfitheatrof, Arthur Morton, Henry Vars (none credited); **Main Cast**: Glenn Ford, Gloria Grahame, Jocelyn Brando, Alexander Scourby, Lee Marvin, Jeanette Nolan; **Prod Co**: Columbia.

The Big Sleep
US, 1946 – 118 mins
Howard Hawks

In the early 1940s, Raymond Chandler was promoted as the hard-boiled literary successor to Dashiell Hammett and James M. Cain. The success of his Philip Marlowe novels – *The Big Sleep* (1939), *Farewell, My Lovely* (1940), *The High Window* (1942) and *The Lady in the Lake* (1943) – encouraged the production of a number of *noir* thriller films. As well as the movies adapted from his novels, Chandler made important script contributions to *Double Indemnity* (1944)* and *The Blue Dahlia* (1946)*.

The Big Sleep poses some problems of chronology. It *should* be an influential early *noir*, alongside *Murder, My Sweet** (from *Farewell, My Lovely*), *Double Indemnity* and *Laura** (all 1944), but it was not released until late August 1946, after *noir* had become fully established with *Fallen Angel** (1945) and the 1946 releases of *The Dark Corner**, *The Postman Always Rings Twice** and *The Killers**. In fact, *The Big Sleep* finished shooting in January 1945 and a version of the film was shown to US Pacific troops during summer 1945. However, Jack Warner believed that *Confidential Agent* (Herman Shumlin, 1945) (from Graham Greene's novel) – which only started shooting after principal photography on *The Big Sleep* had been completed – would provide a better Bacall vehicle to follow up her debut (with Bogart) in Howard Hawks's Hemingway adaptation *To Have and Have Not* (1944). When *Confidential Agent* failed to perform as hoped, Hawks was recalled for reshoots and re-editing designed to enhance the wisecracking, sexy dynamics of the Bogart–Bacall pairing (though this resulted in some loss of plot coherence). The eighteen-month postponement in release allowed the film to benefit from some easing of censorship, and the film subsequently proved a big box-office hit.

Much of the film's success derives from the spiky relationship between private investigator Marlowe (Bogart) and Vivian Sternwood (Bacall), whose wealthy, ailing father describes her as 'spoiled, exacting, smart and ruthless'. Though there are fewer detective protagonists in *film noir* than one sometimes imagines, the tough, sharp private eyes in films like *The Maltese Falcon* (1941)*, *Murder, My Sweet*, *The Big Sleep* and *Out of the Past* (1947)* contributed enormously to the representation of masculinity in the genre as a whole. Though Hammett's Sam Spade and Chandler's Marlowe are rather different, Bogart's star persona – established, essentially, between 1941 and 1945 – runs the characters together (Dick Powell's equally fine Marlowe in *Murder, My Sweet* is softer, more vulnerable). Though Marlowe here is probably less in control of events than Spade in *The Maltese Falcon*, his unflappability, informed guesswork, sense of humour and deep-seated moral sense stand him in good stead. That moral sense is crucial, because the world around him is mired in violence, corruption, blackmail, perversion and murder. Even the film's humour, sometimes verging on farce, has a very dark edge. Marlowe and Vivian, not yet quite tainted, need each other to survive – though the good-humoured sexual high jinks they embody somewhat compromise the film's overall darkness.

The plot of *The Big Sleep* is very complicated – famously, even Chandler did not know who had killed one of the characters – but its pleasures depend more on character and atmosphere. Though shot almost entirely on studio sets, the film superbly evokes the village-like Los Angeles topography of urban sprawl and canyons separated by the various car rides. Perversely, Michael Winner's 1978 remake, with Robert Mitchum as Marlowe, relocates the action to London. JH

Dir, **Prod**: Howard Hawks; **Scr**: William Faulkner, Leigh Brackett, Jules Furthman, from Raymond Chandler's novel; **DOP**: Sid Hickox (b&w); **Ed**: Christian Nyby; **Score**: Max Steiner; **Main Cast**: Humphrey Bogart, Lauren Bacall, John Ridgely, Martha Vickers, Dorothy Malone, Elisha Cook, Jr; **Prod Co**: Warner Bros.

Blast of Silence
US, 1961 – 77 mins
Allen Baron

Blast of Silence begins with an arresting shot (still vivid though unseen for years): a black screen and the roaring sound of a train hurtling towards a pinprick of light, then emerging from a tunnel into daylight. Over the train noise, birthing screams, and a voice-over recalling 'the black silence' and being 'born in pain … with hate and anger built in.' Frankie Bono (Allen Baron), solitary hit man, steps off the train at New York's (now vanished) Penn Station, where he has come, in the 'dead' days around Christmas, to execute a minor mobster.

This bleak, melancholic study of alienated criminality – set amid half-empty streets and Christmas street decorations – follows Frankie's preparations for the hit. He runs into an old girlfriend, Lori (Molly McCarthy), from his orphanage youth and begins to feel the – unfamiliar – need to relate to her. Later, Frankie's gun contact guesses his target, tries to blackmail him, and needs to be eliminated. These complications and signs of 'weakness' lead Frankie to try to cancel the contract but, forced to carry out the hit, he is then himself, almost offhandedly, executed at the end, when he goes for his pay-off.

Frankie himself says little, but the voice-over narration traces a short, violent, lonely life: 'You're alone. But you don't mind that – you're a loner. That's the way it should be.' This omniscient second-person narrator – unusual for a voice-over – is very disconcerting, not least because spoken with such gusto (by blacklisted actor Lionel Stander). The voice-over recedes during Frankie's awkward attempts at socialising – the film's clumsiest and least confident sequences – but almost relishes Frankie's watery, muddy death amid windswept marshes: 'God works in mysterious ways, they said. Maybe he is on your side, the way it all worked out … . You're home again, back in the cold black silence.'

Blast of Silence was made on a minimal budget with borrowed equipment, hustled film stock, nonprofessional actors, improvised camera

Noir naturalism: hit man Frankie Bono (Allen Baron) meeting his contact (Charles Creasap) on the Staten Island Ferry in *Blast of Silence*

movement, and without shooting permits – what Baron calls 'guerrilla shooting' and 'stolen shots'. As one might expect of an American early 1960s independent film, *Blast of Silence* looks and sounds – with its jazzy score – more like John Cassavetes's *Shadows* (1959) than a studio-made *noir* (indeed, Erich Kollmar was camera operator on both films). Like Cassavetes, Baron was working much like the *nouvelle vague* – though at the time neither knew much about the new French cinema. Unlike the silky monochrome of many studio *film noirs*, *Blast of Silence* is mostly grainy and grey – almost neo-realist in look. Shot largely on location, *Blast of Silence* offers a remarkable record of what New York City – not just Greenwich Village and Fifth Avenue but also Harlem, the Staten Island Ferry and Queens – looked like in 1960 in a way that studio films largely fail to do.

Baron worked for television before *Blast of Silence* and spent most of his career – into the 1980s – directing episodic television (*Dukes of Hazzard*, *Charlie's Angels*, *Cagney and Lacey*, among many others). *Blast of Silence* was barely distributed at the time and has hardly been seen since, though its – and Baron's – fate might have been a little different if it had not just missed the deadline for Cannes in 1961. *Blast of Silence* isn't the 'lost masterpiece' that some have claimed, but it's a fascinating *film noir* from the post-classical *noir* period. JH

Dir, Scr: Allen Baron; **Prod**: Merrill Brody; **DOP**: Merrill Brody (b&w); **Ed**: Peggy Lawson, Merrill Brody; **Score**: Meyer Kupferman; **Main Cast**: Allen Baron, Molly McCarthy, Larry Tucker, Peter Clume, (uncredited voice-over narrator: Lionel Stander); **Prod Co**: Alfred Crown, Dan Enright Production, Magla Productions.

The Blue Dahlia
US, 1946 – 96 mins
George Marshall

Encouraged by the success of *Double Indemnity* (1944)*, Paramount put hard-boiled novelist Raymond Chandler on contract where, with the support of producer John Houseman, he conceived this atmospheric and elaborately plotted film about a returning war veteran's fateful involvement in his wife's murder investigation. The original title for *Double Indemnity – Incendiary Blonde* – might well have also served for *The Blue Dahlia* as it is not long before Johnny (Alan Ladd) becomes involved with a mysterious blonde woman (Veronica Lake) who, as it turns out, is the estranged wife of the same nightclub manager with a criminal past (Howard Da Silva) that Johnny's dead wife has also been seeing. The film marked the third pairing of its two leads after *This Gun for Hire* (Frank Tuttle, 1942) and *The Glass Key* (1942)* had demonstrated Ladd and Lake's long-term appeal with Hollywood audiences.

The Blue Dahlia begins with a daytime shot of Johnny returning to LA with his two wartime buddies, Buzz and George, and as we see them descend from a bus into the Californian sunshine, we note that the bus's final destination is marked 'Hollywood'. It is a visual reminder, reinforced by Chandler's subsequent pithy and acidic script, that their homecoming might be as much marked by dreams and falsehoods as the promise of a new beginning. As the male trio say bleakly in their toast at a nearby bar, 'Here's to what was.'

Like *Mildred Pierce** (released the previous year), *The Blue Dahlia* paints a portrait of Los Angeles marked by criminal ghosts and the seedy glamour of the leisured classes. Only the constant sight of men in uniform in the background of street scenes and hotel lobbies suggests that America is a country still in the final throes of violent conflict. Alan Ladd spends most of the condensed time frame of the film wandering the bars, boarding rooms, private bungalows and nightclubs of the city in a kind of trance, thwarted in his efforts to solve his wife's murder by the constant impression that the city has fallen under the spell of a deep-seated moral inertia.

Chandler's original script had emphasised the ethical dimension of this scenario by underlining the returning soldiers' sense of fortitude and wronged victimhood. Although Buzz (played with considerable psychological intensity by William Bendix) was to have been the original murderer of Johnny's manipulative party-going wife, the script made it clear that he was driven to this crime by the disorientation caused by a permanent head injury. As it was, censors at the Navy Department intervened and another, rather more unlikely, killer was found. This rather weakens the dramatic impact of the narrative but what remains, partly due to the elegantly managed art direction of Hans Dreier (*Sunset Boulevard* [1950]*) and partly due to the pace and wit of Chandler's script is nonetheless an enduring classic of early American *film noir*.

The Blue Dahlia, named after the film's eponymous nightclub, subsequently became the inspiration of the title given to the violent and much-publicised Los Angeles 'Black Dahlia' murder that took place in the city the following year. These unresolved events were dramatised in Brian de Palma's film, *The Black Dahlia* (2006). AP

Dir: George Marshall; **Prod**: John Houseman; **Scr**: Raymond Chandler; **DOP**: Lionel Linden (b&w); **Ed**: Arthur P. Schmidt; **Score**: Victor Young; **Main Cast**: Alan Ladd, Veronica Lake, William Bendix, Howard Da Silva, Doris Dowling, Tom Powers; **Prod Co**: Paramount.

Body and Soul
US, 1947 – 104 mins
Robert Rossen

Renowned today for its profound influence on Martin Scorsese's *Raging Bull* (1980), Robert Rossen's magisterial boxing drama charts with sardonic precision the intersection between material gain and ethical decline as Charlie Davis (John Garfield), a working-class Jew from New York's Lower East Side, escapes his family poverty by signing up to the rackets. Like much of its scriptwriter Abraham Polonsky's work, such as *Force of Evil* (1948)*, *Body and Soul* is less about its ostensible subject – though the fight sequences are remarkably staged and won editor Robert Parrish an Academy Award – than about the moral corruption of American life due to the violent logic of untamed capitalism. For Polonsky, this vivid and relentlessly paced human drama could therefore justifiably be called 'a folk tale from the Empire city'.

Body and Soul came with an impeccable pedigree. Its director had worked in New York's left-wing theatre in the 1930s and had previously scripted such *noirs* as *The Strange Love of Martha Ivers* (Lewis Milestone, 1946) and *Johnny O'Clock* (Robert Rossen, 1947). Polonsky's own New York Jewish Communist background and previous wide-ranging writing career gave him an ear for the kind of sharp, clearly delineated dialogue that allows even the most minor characters to briefly shine. The film's emotional core is provided by John Garfield, another veteran of the city's Group Theater, whose vibrant portrayal of desire and ambition followed a recent leading role in *The Postman Always Rings Twice* (1946)*. All three were later implicated by the activities of the House Committee on Un-American Activities (HUAC) and suffered lasting damage to their promising careers as a result.

At the heart of *Body and Soul* lies the claim that one's life is shaped as much by the pressures of material circumstances as any abstract sense of destiny. Rossen and the cinematographer, James Wong Howe, instigate a dynamic and unstable visual field in order to display their perception of the play of social pressures within urban life. This is a film based on shifting, but always plausible and well-orchestrated, human compositions. The spaces around its characters also seem to possess a force of their own, leading to the staging of alternate channels of possibility or their opposite: an awareness that power lies beyond one single person's control. Only at the very end of the film does Charlie come up for air and assert his proper liberty, claiming defiantly: 'What're you going to do? Kill me? Everybody dies!'

The moral and political dimensions of Charlie's narrative trajectory are reinforced by the film's temporal organisation. Much of *Body and Soul* is recounted in flashback in order to display both progression and loss. It is important that we see as much what Charlie has to sacrifice as what he has gained. There is a chronological sweep to the storytelling that looks back to Hollywood's social dramas of the 1930s and forward to Scorsese's meditation on American violence, crime and masculine failure in *Mean Streets* (1973) and *Goodfellas* (1990). Like these films, but in a different ethnic context (that of working-class Jewish New York) it's a reminder of how much the vitality of the US's migrant history has sharpened the ability of mass culture, especially through the interstices of *film noir*, to condense the nation's troubled experience of modernity in the twentieth century. AP

Dir: Robert Rossen; **Prod**: Bob Roberts; **Scr**: Abraham Polonsky; **DOP**: James Wong Howe (b&w); **Ed**: Robert Parrish; **Score**: Hugo Friedhofer; **Main Cast**: John Garfield, Lilli Palmer, Hazel Brooks, Anne Revere, William Conrad, Joseph Pevney, Lloyd Gough, Canada Lee; **Prod Co**: Enterprise Productions.

Born to Kill
US, 1947 – 92 mins
Robert Wise

One of the virtues of B-movies was the meatier, more challenging roles that they offered to actors more often seen in supporting roles in A-features. Claire Trevor, fine in supporting roles in A *noirs* like *Murder, My Sweet* (1944)* was particularly good in major B *noir* roles like *Born to Kill* and *Raw Deal* (Anthony Mann, 1948). In *Born to Kill*, one of the darkest *noir* studies of untrammelled evil, Trevor plays cold-hearted, newly divorced Helen hooking up with psychopathic tough guy Sam (B-movie stalwart Lawrence Tierney, otherwise best known for *Dillinger* [1945] and *Reservoir Dogs* [1991]). Trevor's subtle performance contrasts with Tierney's somewhat wooden, one-track intensity – although, arguably, this suits the character's psychopathology. Confusingly, the working title of *Born to Kill* was *Deadlier than the Male* – the title of the source novel – and the film was retitled *Lady of Deceit* for UK release, but all three titles foreground the centrality of the *femme fatale* and her murderous intent.

The first ten minutes set the film's tone. In Reno, where Helen is boarding while awaiting her divorce, fellow boarder, Laury (Isabel Jewell), has a new man, Sam, who she describes as big and quiet but giving the impression that if you stepped out of line, 'he'd kick your teeth down your throat'. Housemother Mrs Craft (Esther Howard) comments approvingly, adding that her 'husbands was just turnips'. Helen agrees that 'Most men are.' Sam, however, certainly isn't: he exchanges meaningful glances with Helen at the casino but waits in the house's darkened kitchen and brutally murders a man he has seen with Laury, and then Laury too. Helen finds the bodies but makes plans to return to San Francisco rather than call the police. Sam's philosophical roommate Marty (Elisha Cook, Jr) takes news of the murders calmly but warns Sam (who has suffered previous nervous breakdowns) that he 'can't go round killing people when the notion strikes you. It's not feasible.' At Marty's suggestion, Sam leaves. Running into Helen on the train, they are attracted to each other and talk about knowing what you want and going out and getting it.

Though nothing in the rest of the film matches the darkness, matter-of-fact violence and elemental desire of this opening, *Born to Kill* combines being never less than riveting with being ever on the edge of tumbling into absurdity. Issues about class and wealth are central: Helen plans to marry into society wealth and Sam takes his chance to marry her socialite foster-sister, but they continue to lust after each other in something approaching an *amour fou*. Helen's respectable, wealthy fiancé represents security and goodness, but she craves Sam's 'strength, excitement and depravity'. Inevitably, their lust for wealth, power and each other precipitates their losing everything: in an ending of almost Shakespearian proportions, Sam shoots Helen and the police bring down Sam.

Robert Wise edited Orson Welles's *Citizen Kane* (1941) and *The Magnificent Ambersons* (1942) at RKO before directing two atmospheric horror movies for Val Lewton (*Curse of the Cat People* [1944] and *The Body Snatcher* [1945]). Welles's work and Lewton's low-budget horror movies were both important influences on *film noir*'s expressionist visual style, and Wise handles the film's *noir* set pieces – like the murders in the darkened kitchen or Sam's murder of Marty in the night-time sand dunes – very effectively. Wise's most striking *film noir*, however, remains the tough, bitter, superbly lit and shot boxing picture *The Set-Up* (1948). JH

Dir: Robert Wise; **Prod**: Sid Rogell; **Scr**: Eve Greene, Richard Macaulay from James Gunn's novel *Deadlier than the Male*; **DOP**: Robert De Grasse (b&w); **Ed**: Les Millbrook; **Score**: Paul Sawtell; **Main Cast**: Claire Trevor, Lawrence Tierney, Walter Slezak, Philip Terry, Audrey Long, Elisha Cook, Jr; **Prod Co**: RKO.

Brighton Rock
UK, 1947 – 92 mins
John Boulting

From Alberto Cavalcanti's *They Made Me a Fugitive* and Robert Hamer's *It Always Rains on Sunday* to Carol Reed's *Odd Man Out**, 1947 was a key year for British *film noir*. John Boulting's celebrated adaptation of Graham Greene's novel still shocks today in its graphic portrayal of gangland violence and thwarted sexuality set, as the film's opening section tells us, 'down the dark alleyways and festering slums' of 'another Brighton', a world away from the town's then popular image as a respectable holiday resort. Like its counterparts of the same year, *Brighton Rock* marries an attention to the seedy underbelly of everyday British life – what Andrew Spicer (2002) has termed 'a paranoid world of social and sexual corruption' – with a rich degree of shrewdly observed character analysis and local vernacular detail.

At the film's heart is the sinister, youthful character of Pinkie Brown (Richard Attenborough) who, following his predecessor's brutal death, has taken over as the leader of a local criminal gang. When a London journalist arrives under the name of 'Kolley Kibber' promising a reward to anyone recognising him from his photograph in the paper, Pinkie immediately identifies the man as his boss's killer, Fred Hale (Alan Wheatley). After killing Hale in a sensationally shot sequence on a ghost train, Pinkie gets Spicer (Wylie Watson), one of his accomplices, to temporarily take the victim's place. After Rose (Carol Marsh), a local tearoom waitress, also becomes involved, Pinkie is forced to take even more dramatic measures that set in chain a sequence of ultimately tragic events for all concerned.

The intensity of Richard Attenborough's performance reminds one of the same saturnine qualities that Peter Lorre brought to such European and Hollywood *film noirs* as *M* (1931)* and *The Maltese Falcon* (1941)*. Pinkie's cold-hearted relationship with the simple but devoted Rose is truly disturbing. His adversary in the film becomes the buxom and loquacious theatrical entertainer, Ida Arnold (Hermione Baddeley), who turns detective as she begins to realise that Hale may have died in suspicious circumstances. Their battleground is Brighton itself, which Boulting and his expert cinematographer Harry Waxman consistently paint with an atmospheric and richly textured verve. The film begins with a gripping chase sequence through the town's main streets that, through its mobile long shots and rapid cutting, establishes the spatial parameters of the subsequent action. Gradually, as we move from local hotels and

Local vernacular detail in *Brighton Rock*'s tale of gangland violence and thwarted sexuality

pubs to cheap and claustrophobic boarding-rooms, the drama closes in on itself and the film's main protagonists find themselves increasingly trapped in a series of ever tighter and more grotesque visual compositions. Central to all of this is the pier: by daylight a venue of light entertainment and casual promiscuity, by night a site of murderous desire and retribution.

Graham Greene's work played an important role in the development of *film noir* on both sides of the Atlantic. Robert Murphy (2007) has called the adaptation of his story, *The Green Cockatoo* (William Cameron Menzies, 1937) 'the first British film noir' and his novel, *A Gun for Sale*, was the basis of an influential early American *film noir*, Frank Tuttle's *This Gun for Hire* (1942). Further important Greene adaptations include *Ministry of Fear* (Fritz Lang, 1944) and *Confidential Agent* (Herman Shumlin, 1945) and the writer, of course, also collaborated himself with Carol Reed on the seminal *noir*-related *The Third Man* (1949), set in Vienna. For many though, *Brighton Rock* still remains the most successful and unsettling screen rendition of that elusive combination of menace, guilt and social unease that characterises that unique place (or state of mind) known simply as 'Greeneland'. AP

Dir: John Boulting; **Prod**: Roy Boulting; **Scr**: Graham Greene, Terence Rattigan from Graham Greene's novel; **DOP**: Harry Waxman (b&w); **Ed**: Peter Graham Scott; **Score**: Hans May; **Main Cast**: Richard Attenborough, Carol Marsh, Hermione Baddeley, William Hartnell, Wylie Watson, Alan Wheatley; **Prod Co**: Charter Film Productions, Associated British Picture Corporation.

Call Northside 777
US, 1948 – 111 mins
Henry Hathaway

Call Northside 777 followed on from Henry Hathaway's previously successful docudrama collaborations with the influential Fox producer Louis de Rochemont, such as *The House on 92nd Street* (Henry Hathaway, 1945), by recounting the investigation of a prominent Chicago newspaper journalist, McNeal (James Stewart), into the wrongful prosecution of Frank Wiecek (Richard Conte), a Chicago man convicted of murdering a policeman during the Prohibition era. A mysterious press advertisement, asking the reader 'to call Northside 777' with further information, leads McNeal to the prisoner's mother, who recruits him in her battle to prove her son's innocence. Based on real events, the film is now seen as one of the most important of the cycle of documentary *noirs* that marked a turn away from stylised studio melodrama towards a visual style which favoured a greater investment in notions of truthfulness and actuality and a closer proximity to life 'as it is'.

Hathaway's film evokes these principles in its opening credit sequence showing a sheaf of hand-typed sheets being turned so as to evoke what could either be a newspaper report or a shooting script. It continues with an introductory section that blends elements of real documentary footage and dramatic reconstruction, which are then linked together on the soundtrack by the controlling narration of an off-screen male voice. J. P. Telotte (1989) has argued in his analysis of the documentary *noir* tradition that there is a 'compromise' built into films such as *Call Northside 777* through 'their twin pull to both reveal and dominate truth, [and] to appear transparent while filtering reality through a traditional narrative mechanism'. This is especially true in two key sequences of the film in which the narrative investigation loses its prevailing sense of historicity. Instead, an appeal to 'liveness' is made through the 'real-time' representation of the uncovering of important evidence provided by a lie detector and a photographic facsimile machine. The spectator is invited to

witness these events 'as if they were there' in the room, but in order
to substantiate their dramatic significance, Hathaway also chooses to
repeatedly intercut between two concurrent narrative spaces so that, as
well as observing the neutral act of revelation, we are also invited to
identify with the psychologically and politically significant reactions on the
part of the film's fictionalised protagonists.

Another aspect of the documentary *noir* that features heavily within
the film's *mise en scène* is the vernacular realism engaged to portray
Chicago itself. *Call Northside 777* is saturated with now evocative local
signage for all manner of public and private institutions of the time that
works in conjunction with the depiction of important architectural
landmarks to anchor important narrative transitions. These elements are
often framed with a more emphatic mobile lens in order to suggest that
the film is honing in on a local everyday reality. Once again though, there
is an interesting linkage of what Steven N. Lipkin (1989) calls 'indexical
footage' with 'modelled footage'. The film, for example, links a detached
documentary perspective of Chicago's Polish migrant neighbourhood –
much of which is shot on actual location – with other more carefully
staged studio scenes characterised by highly mannered *noir*-like lighting
set-ups. The result is thus a remarkable tension that has a bearing on
how one finally reads the film. McNeal's shift in *Call Northside 777* from
hard-nosed sensationalist to moral citizen echoes documentary *noir*'s
own broader ethical revision of *film noir*'s conventional cynicism, but by
having the film's denouement based on the status of the visual document
– Wiecek is freed on the basis of a photograph – the spectator is still also
inevitably forced to consider the implications of the way in which the
film's very own claim to truth has, in fact, been managed and fabricated
by its makers. AP

Dir: Henry Hathaway; **Prod**: Otto Lang; **Scr**: Jerome Cady, Jay Dratler from newspaper
articles by James P. McGuire, Jack McPhaul (uncredited); **DOP**: Joseph MacDonald (b&w);
Ed: J. Watson Webb, Jr; **Score**: Alfred Newman; **Main Cast**: James Stewart, Richard Conte,
Lee J. Cobb, Betty Garde, Kasia Orzazewski, Helen Walker; **Prod Co**: Twentieth Century-Fox.

The Castle of Sand (*Suna no utsuwa*)
Japan, 1974 – 143 mins
Nomura Yoshitaro

Modern Tokyo and veteran cop Imanishi (Tamba Tetsuro) and his agile, younger sidekick Yoshimura (Morita Kensaku) have begun a labyrinthine investigation into the murder of a man found by the railway tracks in Kamata. Their only clue is the word 'Kameda' heard spoken in a northern Japan accent by the victim's recent drinking companion. As the detectives travel across Japan in their quest for the dead man's identity, they ponder whether the word refers to a family or a place before eventually discovering that the etymology of 'Kameda' in fact relates specifically to a remote rural region in the southwest of the main island, Honshu. Finally, they begin to trace the connections between the dead man, his adopted son – a successful classical music conductor – and an elderly leper, the boy's actual father. In so doing, they uncover a web of repressed emotion and wartime suffering that still resonates within the fragmented world of contemporary Japan.

The first three-quarters of *The Castle of Sand* are marked by an elaborate temporal and spatial structure that interweaves the process of the police investigation with separate revelations about the main protagonists and their past and present interrelationships. Gradually, through a combination of assiduous forensic work and improbable coincidence, the detectives piece together the clues and the final section of the film is largely based around Imanishi's lengthy exposition of the crime and its history to his colleagues. This is intercut with a live concert by the victim's adopted son and, now we also learn, killer and a set of flashbacks that detail how the boy and his true father were forced to leave their home village in the 1940s and wander the country because of the stigma of the man's crippling disease.

The Castle of Sand was the most commercially successful of a series of adaptations of the work of the best-selling crime novelist, Matsumoto Seicho, by the prolific genre director, Nomura Yoshitaro. Other titles include *The Chase* (*Harikomi*, 1958), *Zero Focus* (*Zero no shoten*, 1961) and *The Shadow Within* (*Kage no kuruma*, 1970). Despite its extended denouement, which dissipates into a rather ineffectual combination of professional self-congratulation and maudlin sentimentality, the film, like many *film noirs*, matches a sensational public crime with private trauma. An emphasis on travel and geography, in conjunction with echoes of the unresolved emotional legacy of the war years, suggests a narrative that can be plausibly read as a subtle social critique of the country's modern superficial 'false identity.' This link between the private and public realm is particularly conveyed by the film's recurring trope of a close-up shot (through a telephoto lens) that then zooms out to reveal the implicit connection between the current stage of the detectives' investigation and a set of broader shifting social contexts.

Nomura's interest in naming and origins relates to his ongoing attempt to meld together two different generic concerns: the professional exactitude of the police procedural and the messy psychological conflict of the family drama. The theme of paternity links the two with the travels of the two roving detectives appearing to echo those of the earlier nomadic couple. For contemporary viewers, the father–son relationship between the two police officers may turn out to be at least as affecting as the ostensible subject of the narrative, but there is no denying the film's underlying impulse to show how the bonds (as well as the sins) of the past return to haunt the present for all concerned. AP

Dir: Nomura Yoshitaro; **Prod**: Hashimoto Shinobu, Mishima Yoshihara, Sato Masayuki; **Scr**: Hashimoto Shinobu, Nomura Yoshitaro, Yamada Yoji from Matsumoto Seicho's novel; **DOP**: Kawamata Takashi (colour); **Score**: Kanno Mitsuaki, Sugano Kosuke; **Main Cast**: Tamba Tetsuro, Kato Go, Morita Kensaku, Shimada Yoko, Ogata Ken, Matsuyama Seiji, Ryu Chishu, Saburi Shin; **Prod Co**: Shochiku.

The Chase
US, 1946 – 84 mins
Arthur D. Ripley

Having produced some of the best Nero films of G. W. Pabst (*Pandora's Box* [1929], *The Threepenny Opera* [1931]), and Fritz Lang (*M* [1931]*, *The Testament of Dr Mabuse* [1933]), Seymour Nebenzal perhaps wondered what he was doing in Hollywood working on more or less pulp material like *The Chase*. Scripted by Philip Yordan from a Cornell Woolrich novel and with substantial stars and personnel, but on a low budget, *The Chase* fits the *noir* profile well: pill-popping returning war veteran gets involved with wealthy, recklessly sadistic criminals and finds himself embroiled in mayhem.

Unemployed and down on his luck but honest – a 'law-abiding jerk' as Peter Lorre's Gino puts it – Chuck Scott (Robert Cummings) returns a lost wallet to crime boss Eddie Roman (Steve Cochran) and is hired as his chauffeur. He becomes protective towards Roman's desperately unhappy wife Lorna (Michèle Morgan), who feels she has been 'bought and paid for' even though she's no *femme fatale*. Together they plot an escape to Cuba that goes terribly wrong. Pursued by the vicious Roman's equally vicious sidekick Gino, Lorna is killed. Chuck, falsely accused of murder, finds himself trapped – visually and narratively – in a quintessentially *noir* web of deceit and is also killed. At this point – further destabilising our relationship to the characters and narrative – the 'escape' is shown to have been a lengthy (and barely signalled) dream or psychotic incident, brought on by Chuck's shock-induced anxiety neurosis. Back in 'reality', Chuck seeks medical help for his memory loss and attempts to continue to rescue Lorna, succeeding when Roman and Gino are killed while pursuing them. Uncharacteristically for such a *noir*, the film seems to be ending happily, with Chuck and Lorna together in Havana, but, eerily, the apparently 'happy end' is audaciously undercut as images and action from the earlier dream are replayed, and dream and reality converge (just as they do in later David Lynch films like *Mulholland Dr.* [2001]*).

Director Arthur Ripley – a screenwriter since the 1920s and occasional director from the late 1930s – is a somewhat enigmatic figure. Little in his earlier work hinted at the *élan* of *The Chase* – a sign, no doubt, of how much the film depends both on its source novel and script and on German émigré cinematographer Franz Planer, responsible for the *noir* look of Robert Siodmak's *Criss Cross* (1949)*. Other than *The Chase*, Ripley is remembered for directing Robert Mitchum's personal, low-budget project *Thunder Road* (1958), written and produced by, and starring, Mitchum.

Cummings plays the same kind of 'honest Joe' caught up in events as he does in Hitchcock's *Saboteur* (1942). Michèle Morgan, the haunted face from Marcel Carné's and Jacques Prévert's *noir* poetic realist *Le Quai des brumes* (1938), has little to do here other than look haunted. This was her last film in a patchy American career since 1941 before returning to France, though she later appeared, more successfully, in Carol Reed's Graham Greene-scripted British *noir The Fallen Idol* (1948).   JH

Dir: Arthur D. Ripley; **Prod**: Seymour Nebenzal; **Scr**: Philip Yordan from Cornell Woolrich's novel *The Black Path of Fear*; **DOP**: Franz Planer (b&w); **Ed**: Edward Mann; **Score**: Michel Michelet; **Main Cast**: Robert Cummings, Michèle Morgan, Steve Cochran, Lloyd Corrigan, Peter Lorre; **Prod Co**: Nero Films.

Chinatown
US, 1974 – 131 mins
Roman Polanski

Based on an original and highly articulate screenplay by Robert Towne, the beguiling and cynical tone of Roman Polanski's *Chinatown* can be compared to other contemporaneous reworkings of the private-detective *film noir* such as *The Long Goodbye* (1973)* and *Night Moves* (1975)*. All three features share a similar disposition: an enthusiasm for unpicking the moral securities of their principal male protagonist and a distrust of any kind of authority associated with the supposed virtues of American capitalism. *Chinatown* similarly anticipates period *noirs* like *L.A. Confidential* (1997)* and *Devil in a Blue Dress* (1995)* in its exploitation of Los Angeles cultural history in order to recount a crime story whose ethical perspective explicitly depends on the audience's knowledge of what was still to happen to the city beyond the immediate time frame established within the film's narrative.

Jake Gittes (Jack Nicholson) is a private detective hired to spy on Hollis Mulwray (Darrell Zwerling), the chief engineer of the Los Angeles Water Department, by a woman claiming to be his wife. This sets up a sequence of events that results in a well-publicised sex scandal, the death of Mulwray and the discovery that the man's real wife (Faye Dunaway) is someone entirely different. Gittes now finds himself embroiled in a much wider investigation that interweaves the darkest elements of personal family history with the secret machinations of a powerful city businessman, Noah Cross (John Huston), to control the future development of the Los Angeles water supply. Based loosely on the real-life history of how William Mulholland and others successfully managed the irrigation and economic development of the San Fernando Valley at the expense of farmers further north – 'bringing the city to the water' in the words of one character – *Chinatown* speaks of the legacy of a political and moral corruption hitherto buried in the recent past.

Most of Polanski's film is shot in the ochre hues of the rural and suburban Californian sunshine. The natural beiges and watery blues (at dusk) of John A. Alonzo's cinematography, in combination with the film's effective use of widescreen composition, integrate the male detective within a novel parched environment that appears, in Paul Arthur's phrase (1996), to actually 'squeeze human movement'. Gone is the more human scale of conventional *film noir*'s night-time rain-soaked streets. Here, Gittes – who spends most of the film with a nose injury and one step behind his adversaries – remains permanently displaced and disorientated by the treacherous space that subtly envelops him. Repeatedly, figures either invade the frame to surprise him or he finds himself at odds with a protagonist placed in such a way within the image to thwart his command over the situation. As many critics have observed, this is a film of porous boundaries in which the dynamics of private conduct and public appearance, as well as private business and public good, are now cruelly reversed.

Chinatown never explicitly resolves the meaning of its title, though like *The Lady from Shanghai* (1947)* it includes action that takes place in its eponymous location. From Gittes's point of view it refers to an unresolved trauma – something that happened on his watch as a former police officer. From Polanski's perspective, as a fellow outsider, perhaps it also conveys the dark and buried contours of the city's migrant history, thus also providing a reminder of the orientalist assumptions that peppered classical American *film noir*. The first clue to understanding the word though comes through the haunting notes of Jerry Goldsmith's memorable trumpet-based score: its plangent melancholy and longing serving to condense the film's unique concern with both a past and a genre now long since vanished. From the vantage point of Nixon-era America, *Chinatown*, in its own despairing fashion, serves as a reminder of the corruption of innocence wherever this may occur.

Robert Towne originally devised *Chinatown* to be the first part of a trilogy involving Gittes's tangled relations with the Los Angeles authorities. The second, *The Two Jakes*, about the Californian oil industry, was directed by Jack Nicholson and released in 1990. The third, *Cloverleaf*, about the development of the city's freeway system, has never been made but elements of the narrative surface in the animated *noir* pastiche, *Who Framed Roger Rabbit* (Robert Zemeckis, 1988). AP

Dir: Roman Polanski; **Prod**: Robert Evans; **Scr**: Robert Towne, Roman Polanski (uncredited); **DOP**: John A. Alonzo (colour); **Ed**: Sam O'Steen; **Score**: Jerry Goldsmith; **Main Cast**: Jack Nicholson, Faye Dunaway, John Huston, Perry Lopez, Darrell Zwerling; **Prod Co**: Paramount Pictures, Long Road, Penthouse.

C.I.D.
India, 1956 – 140 mins
Raj Khosla

Director Raj Khosla learned his craft with master producer-director Guru Dutt and producer-star Dev Anand. Dutt's first feature as director was the crime story *Baazi* (1950), produced by and starring Dev Anand and one of the early features produced by new production company Navketan (founded in 1949 by brothers Dev and Chetan Anand and a major channel through which actors and directors associated with the leftist Indian Peoples' Theatre Association entered the movie industry).

Popular Indian cinema developed its own distinctive generic structures – very often a radical mixing up of genre forms which would usually be considered very separate in western cinema (which can make the films feel very different from US and European popular cinema). It also borrowed liberally, though idiosyncratically, from developments in western cinemas (and not just in the unauthorised stealing and hybridising of plots). In the 1940s/1950s, the influence of Italian neo-realism and American crime cinema, for example, was widespread. Guru Dutt admired John Huston's films, such as *The Asphalt Jungle* (1950)* and Navketan productions often combined elements from US crime pictures with elements of social realism. Indian cinema of this period often adopted a visual style very similar to the US *noir* look, but films like *Baazi* and *C.I D.* are also very close in the kinds of crime stories they tell.

Like *The Big Heat* (1953)*, *C.I.D.* features a cop forced into suspension who uses his own resources to fight official corruption and bring down the crime boss. Here, police inspector Shekhar (Dev Anand) is framed for the murder of a newspaper editor. Both films end in the – at least apparent – triumph of morality. Much of the action narrative of *C.I.D.*, such as the urban nocturnal car chase or the extended sequence of escape from the crime boss's mansion, would not look very out of place alongside US 1940s/1950s *film noirs*. Additionally, the film cultivates its modern urban Bombay location settings like Marine Drive with more flair – albeit in a musical sequence – than many other Hindi pictures of the period. However, the film's Indian-ness asserts itself in several ways: its moral framework is more upbeat and the more western generic elements sit next to strikingly Indian ones. The *noir* nocturnal car chase, for example, segues – disconcertingly for most western viewers – into a song-and-dance sequence featuring traditional village girls gathering water from a river in sparkling morning sunshine. Similarly, the broad comedy associated with Johnny Walker's petty thief is hardly to western tastes. Indian audiences, wholly used to – indeed, *expecting* – the mixing of *masalas*, would be unlikely to find anything odd about these juxtapositions.

This was the first Hindi picture with Waheeda Rehman, a Guru Dutt discovery and star of some of his finest 1950s melodramas, such as *Pyaasa* (1957) and *Kagaz ke phool* (1959) (as well as his mistress and muse). Here Rehman plays Kamini, an Indian version of the good-bad girl, who works with the crime boss but finally comes round to conventional morality and saves the cop, thus providing alternative romantic interest for Shekhar. Nevertheless, Shekhar ends up, unsurprisingly, with the less morally ambiguous – but also less interesting – daughter of the chief of police, Rekha (Shakila). JH

Dir: Raj Khosla; **Prod**: Guru Dutt; **Scr**: Inder Raj Anand; **DOP**: Anwar, V. K. Murty (b&w); **Ed**: Y. G. Chawhan; **Score**: O. P. Nayyar; **Lyrics**: Majrooh; **Playback singers**: Geeta Dutt, Asha Bhosle, Mohd Rafi; **Main Cast**: Dev Anand, Shakila, Johnny Walker, K. N. Singh, Bir Sakuja, Waheeda Rehman; **Prod Co**: Guru Dutt Films.

Collateral
US, 2004 – 120 mins
Michael Mann

Collateral is already looking like one of the great Los Angeles *film noirs*.
Its suspenseful narrative structure and incorporation of groundbreaking
high-definition colour DV technology provide both an intimate and
psychologically intense character study and a richly textured, almost
painterly, portrait of the contemporary city at night. Max (Jamie Foxx) is
a good-natured cab driver starting the evening shift. He briefly meets a
highly pressured female lawyer, Annie Farrell (Jada Pinkett Smith), and
the two compare notes about their line of work before she leaves his car
for the office. Max's world is shattered when his next customer, Vincent
(Tom Cruise), turns out to be a mob hit man about to start a night of
contracted assassinations. As the victims begin to fall across the city, the
police pick up the trail until after an explosive shoot-out in a Korean
nightclub, Max realises Vincent has just one more person left to kill: his
new acquaintance, Annie.

Despite its sensational modern veneer of mobile screens, reflected
glass surfaces, empty streetscapes and anonymous office towers and
highways, Michael Mann's film also retains a number of classical genre
elements. These include a detailed portrait of the empire of the gangland
overlord and the minutiae of the stakeout operations conducted by the
police detectives. In a curious fashion, *Collateral* can also be read as a
perverse 'buddy movie' in which the conventional camaraderie of the
male-centered *film noir* becomes displaced, rather like in *The Hitch-Hiker*
(1953)*, onto a hybrid form of the road film. In this sense, the fate of
Max becomes increasingly linked to the spectral, aggressively self-
contained figure of Vincent as the couple's increasingly fierce psychological energies feed off each other right up to their fatal showdown on
a dawn MTA train bound for LA airport.

Central to the film's success is its conception of space and colour.
Mann shoots the interiors of the cab, in which much of the action takes

place, from a variety of compressed camera set-ups. The film only opens up during these passages when we also glimpse the moving vehicle in a series of magnificent overhead aerial shots that look down directly at the city streets and architecture below. As the film progresses, and after we have traversed what is clearly a racially codified image of Los Angeles at night, Mann switches to a wider-angle lens and the editing quickens thus producing a new intensity and rhythm as the film reaches its denouement. The overall effect, as Mann has indicated in interview, is to establish an interstitial sense of the city in which the various dislocated ports of call are interspersed with journeys through a vividly rendered set of intermediary spaces denuded of any apparent human activity. The Viper FilmStream High-Definition Camera that records much of this action permits a far subtler tonal palette than conventional celluloid would ever achieve. Los Angeles's streetlamps, office building lights and skylines provide washes of petrochemical blues, reds and greys. At times, one hue predominates, almost to the point of abstraction, as if the material contours of the place – much like the case with traditional black-and-white *film noir* – can disappear without the stability of daylight.

New technologies are also inscribed into the film's *mise en scène*. Vincent navigates Los Angeles with the aid of a special memory stick and Max's eventual rescue of Annie is contingent on a mobile phone. In time this may date the film, but for now *Collateral*, like indeed Michael Mann's equally beautiful (if less comprehensible) follow-up, *Miami Vice* (2006), seems stationed at the vanguard of contemporary *film noir* aesthetics. AP

Dir: Michael Mann; **Prod**: Michael Mann, Julie Richardson; **Scr**: Stuart Beattie; **DOP**: Dion Beebe, Paul Cameron (colour); **Ed**: Jim Miller, Paul Rubell; **Score**: James Newton Howard; **Main Cast**: Tom Cruise, Jamie Foxx, Jada Pinkett Smith, Mark Ruffalo, Peter Berg, Bruce McGill; **Prod Co**: Paramount Pictures, Dreamworks SKG, Parkes/MacDonald Productions, Edge City.

Cornered
US, 1945 – 102 mins
Edward Dmytryk

Cornered is the second – and most underrated – of three important
RKO *film noirs* made by the team of director Edward Dmytryk, producer
Adrian Scott and screenwriter John Paxton, following *Murder, My Sweet*
(1944)* and preceding *Crossfire* (1947)*. Dick Powell's Canadian ex-POW
Laurence Gerard is investigating his French wife's death and what he is
convinced was her betrayal by French collaborators. Though not a private
eye, Powell is again an investigator, building on the hard-boiled, smart-
talking, often droll – quintessentially *noir* – persona developed in *Murder,
My Sweet*. At the same time he represents an early version of the
returning war veteran, so common in later *noirs*. Gerard's leads take him
to Buenos Aires, making *Cornered* the first of several distinguished *film
noirs* – notably Hitchcock's *Notorious* and *Gilda** (both 1946) – set in a
postwar Argentina bristling with unreformed Nazis.

    Like *Crossfire*, the film blends – somewhat unevenly – crime thriller
and political tract. Dogged though he is, Gerard, as master fascist Jarnac
(Luther Adler) says, is a 'fanatic without a purpose'. His quest is
essentially personal and about the past, whereas the émigré fascists
and democrats are engaged in a larger, long-term political struggle.
An 'amateur at intrigue', as private investigator Melchior (Walter Slezak)
puts it, he constantly bumps accidentally into and threatens the
democrats' carefully laid plans.

    Visually, *Cornered* is full of disconcerting shadows and threatening
night streets. An unsettling, dreamlike sequence takes place in a subway
station where Gerard meets a mysterious woman who tells a crazy story
which has to be suspended as trains roar past; they pass an eerily suspect
figure reading a newspaper and finally Gerard has one of his intermittent
dizzy spells, the result of a war injury. Indeed, what with blackouts and
being knocked out several times, Gerard spends a considerable amount
of time unconscious.

Cornered has a fearsomely complicated plot and frequently, Gerard, like the spectator, doesn't quite know what is going on or finds himself out of his depth. An isolated, vulnerable, deeply melancholic figure, Gerard depends on the sardonic dialogue afforded by John Paxton's script to maintain his equilibrium. In a funny but yet desperate hotel-room sequence in which Gerard knows he is being set up, a woman tries to seduce him; he asks what she uses for morals, and she replies that she thinks 'they're a little overrated'; invited to kiss her, he does so, and asks where her husband is; as they kiss again, she says she could make him forget, and he rejoins 'But not for long, and not enough – for that you'd have to have a heart.'

Duped time and again, Gerard finally succeeds when his quest and the democrats' plans coincide. At the denouement, the film's main characters gather and the crime thriller and the political tract come together. The elusive Jarnac, so far unseen and even now hidden in shadow, and the captive Gerard exchange views about fascism and democracy – a little self-consciously, but then this was 1945. Jarnac, asserting that democrats 'attack the evil in man, we accept it', viciously kills Melchior. Saved by the democrats, Gerard beats Jarnac mercilessly, as if possessed, before blacking out again, conceding later that he was 'a little kill-crazy'. As the police arrive, Gerard, droll to the end, says he'd 'better stick around – they may be confused by all the bodies'. JH

Dir: Edward Dmytryk; **Prod**: Adrian Scott; **Scr**: John Paxton, John Wexley; **DOP**: Harry J. Wild (b&w); **Ed**: Joseph Noriega; **Score**: Roy Webb; **Main Cast**: Dick Powell, Walter Slezak, Micheline Cheirel, Nina Vale, Morris Carnovsky, Steven Geray, Jack LaRue, Luther Adler; **Prod Co**: RKO.

Criss Cross
US, 1949 – 88 mins
Robert Siodmak

Criss Cross begins with a dramatic, mobile aerial view of the Los Angeles skyline at night. Slowly, the camera descends towards a parking lot and in the course of a brief succession of shots we see a couple caught in a passionate embrace by the headlights of a reversing car. Steve (Burt Lancaster) and Anna (Yvonne de Carlo) are the tragic pair whose desperate, illicit romance forms the emotional core of one of Robert Siodmak's greatest *film noirs* (remade by Steven Soderbergh as *The Underneath* in 1995). We soon learn that Steve and Anna are in fact divorced from each other, but after wandering and drifting in the margins of the American oil and construction industries, Steve has returned to his native city and has started seeing his former wife again. Anna's new husband, the weak but pugilistic local gangster Slim Dundee (played with typical verve and menace by Dan Duryea), becomes involved in a heist with Steve, now a security guard for an armoured delivery company, but the two rivals' plans to double-cross each other unravel with fatal consequences. The film ends with a powerful rhyming image to that seen in the film's opening: Anna and Steve lie dead in each other's arms, shot point blank by Slim in the confines of a deserted beach cottage. Once more, the camera is the only witness.

This sense of passionate detachment framing the narrative is undercut throughout the film by an emphasis on Steve's prolix, troubled subjectivity. As in many *film noirs*, including *The Killers* (1946)*, with which *Criss Cross* may be fruitfully compared, much of the information we gather is in fact from an internalised system of point-of-view flashbacks. Heady, woozy dissolves are also deployed to suggest key moments of dramatic tension. It is likely that this may not have been the case if the film's original producer, Mark Hellinger, had not suddenly died, leaving the project to be sold to Universal along with its leading star and director. Elements of a different film nonetheless surface, especially in the

Anna (Yvonne de Carlo) and Steve (Burt Lancaster) embrace as they are threatened by Slim (Dan Duryea) at a deserted beach cottage in *Criss Cross*

fascinating documentary-like portrait of working-class Los Angeles that emerges in the family sequences set around Bunker Hill. The daytime scenes of Union Station in its heyday are also finely judged and evocative of what David Thomson (1990) has described as 'the dusty sheen of an LA that John Fante wrote about'.

Criss Cross is thus a film of multiple visual surfaces that are masterfully managed by a combination of Franz Planer's evocative control over tonal registers in his lighting set-ups and Siodmak's consistently dynamic and revealing framing of group compositions. It looks backwards to Siodmak's European heritage in a number of ways. The film's theme of fatalistic desire and criminality remind one, for instance, of his earlier success, *Stürme der Leidenschaft/Tumultes* (1932), and as Michael Grost (2008) has also observed, up to and during the heist at an oil refinery, Siodmak dramatises events with unusual recourse to the canted, geometric compositional style of the Soviet modernist photographer, Alexander Rodchenko.

As throughout Siodmak's career, *Criss Cross* also uses aspects of the decor to further narrative meaning. In a key scene in the hospital where Steve is laid up after the raid, he (but especially the spectator) tracks the sinister events in the corridor outside through the aid of a carefully positioned dressing-table mirror. Indeed, the whole film is blocked in this fashion: at times compressing space and people into the frame and elsewhere opening up a sequence to illustrate the force of events beyond the control of the central protagonist. Steve then is a character who is finally doubly crossed: both by the thugs and police officers in his life and by the ways in which the film's visual style conveys, but finally circumscribes, his desires. In this fashion, this is thus one of the bleakest, if also most visually rich, *film noirs* of the 1940s. AP

Dir: Robert Siodmak; **Prod**: Michael Kraike; **Scr**: Daniel Fuchs, William Bowers (uncredited) from Don Tracy's novel; **DOP**: Franz Planer (b&w); **Ed**: Ted J. Kent; **Score**: Miklós Rózsa; **Main Cast**: Burt Lancaster, Yvonne de Carlo, Dan Duryea, Stephen McNally; **Prod Co**: Universal.

The Crooked Way
US, 1949 – 87 mins
Robert Florey

Although there were plenty of major studio A-picture *film noirs*, the cycle did lend itself to the lower production values of the B-picture. Urban locations were easily available, while darkness and a tendency to abstraction could cover up a lack of elaborate sets. Lower budgets meant lower expectations, which often led to an unusual degree of artistic freedom in finding creative solutions to economic constraints. The remarkably similar plots of the independent B-picture *The Crooked Way* and the Joseph L. Mankiewicz Fox A-picture *Somewhere in the Night* (1946) make an instructive comparison.

Amnesia, allowing all kinds of narrative confusion, was a popular 1940s *noir* subject. In films like *Crack-Up* (Irving Reis, 1946), *Black Angel* (Roy William Neill, 1946), *The High Wall* (Curtis Bernhardt, 1947) and *Dark City* (William Dieterle, 1950), memory loss resulting from military service strikingly dramatised the disorientation and confused identity of war veterans returning to civilian life.

The amnesiac protagonists of *The Crooked Way* and *Somewhere in the Night* – Eddie Rice (John Payne) and George Taylor (John Hodiak) respectively – learn that before enlisting they were criminals, pursued by both criminal associates and the police. Both have been re-socialised by war experience but must undergo a violent ordeal at the hands of former partners – Vince Alexander (Sonny Tufts) and Mel Phillips (Richard Conte) – to establish new, respectable identities. Both rely on the support of women they 'wronged' in the past, Nina (Ellen Drew) and Christy Smith (Nina Guild).

Both films begin by establishing the characters' amnesia, demobilisation and discovery of their old identity. *Somewhere in the Night* – though by no means an uninteresting film – manages its exposition rather cumbersomely, with an elaborate field-hospital sequence employing subjective camera and voice-over. Mankiewicz's more literary credentials may explain the impression of too much plot needing to be worked through. By contrast, *The Crooked Way* – twenty-three minutes shorter overall – cuts to the chase with great economy: a minimal documentary-style opening is followed by a scene, strikingly lit and shot by cinematographer John Alton, in which Eddie, about to be demobilised, is briefed by his doctor in a darkly shuttered room dominated by an X-ray of his skull. His face remains in shadow, any optimism about his future belied by the enveloping darkness. Arriving in Los Angeles, Eddie *does* find people who knew him – cops, who caution him, and former criminal associates. Very quickly it is established that Eddie is trapped by his past.

As well as its laboured storytelling, *Somewhere in the Night* was made entirely on elaborate studio sets, whereas *The Crooked Way*, always intelligently and precisely lit by Alton, makes greater use of location shooting – including some stunning location shots of 1940s Los Angeles. John Payne, in mid-passage from minor 1940s musical comedies to minor 1950s Westerns, is very good as the bewildered but tough Eddie, and *looks* just right, while John Hodiak in *Somewhere in the Night* never looks quite comfortable (though both films benefit from fine minor-role performances).

French-born director Robert Florey made some sixty mostly routine B-movies, often crime stories, but also some experimental films, such as *The Life and Death of 9413 – A Hollywood Extra* (1928) (and he also wrote extensively about Hollywood). He could clearly rise to the occasion of good material and collaborators, as with *Murders in the Rue Morgue* (1932) and *The Beast with Five Fingers* (1946). His last film, before moving into television, was another *film noir*, *Johnny One-Eye* (1950). JH

Dir: Robert Florey; **Prod**: Benedict Bogeaus; **Scr**: Richard H. Landauer from Robert Monroe's radio play *No Blade Too Sharp*; **DOP**: John Alton (b&w); **Ed**: Frank Sullivan; **Score**: Louis Forbes; **Main Cast**: John Payne, Sonny Tufts, Ellen Drew, Rhys Williams, Percy Helton; **Prod Co**: La Brea Productions.

Crossfire
US, 1947 – 86 mins
Edward Dmytryk

Washington at night and, according to one character in Edward Dmytryk's atmospheric war veteran *noir*, 'the snakes are loose'. *Crossfire* is a film that embodies Vivian Sobchack's notion (1998) of *film noir's* 'lounge time'. Its combination of hallucinatory, fragmented temporal structure and unstable milieu largely comprised of anonymous boarding-rooms, bars, clip joints and other transitory public spaces perfectly evokes the loss of social, spatial and psychological integration that Sobchack argues characterises *film noir's* take on American society in the early postwar period. Here, there is no sense of 'home' or familial 'security'. Instead, the soldiers in this classic RKO *noir* are still coming to terms with their recent past with no firm indication of a promising future life ahead.

Crossfire was one of the last socially conscious dramas such as *Cornered* (1945)* produced by Edward Dmytryk's unit at RKO before its Roosevelt-era ideals were finally extinguished by the impact of the HUAC on American public life. The story of a group of male veterans, one of whom, Montgomery (Robert Ryan), murders a Jewish civilian called Samuels and sets up another soldier, Mitchell (George Cooper), as the fall guy, was adapted from Richard Brooks's novel *The Brick Foxhole* with the source text's focus on homophobia shifted to the more politically acceptable topic of anti-Semitism. In this sense, the film itself is clearly caught 'in the crossfire' between being a *film noir* and a standard problem picture with the bridge between the two elements being the emphasis placed on the role of the investigating legal authorities. Like *Mildred Pierce* (1945)*, a film that similarly blends two competing genre elements, it ends with a new day dawning from the windows of the police office, as if the private shadows of the *noir* city have been finally dispelled by the convenient assertion of the light of public moral authority.

It is hard though to sustain a reading of the film that argues its ending is all that unconditional. Undoubtedly, it succeeds as a progressive

Washington at night and 'the snakes are loose' in *Crossfire*

film in outlining the dangerous legacy of anti-Semitism – in this sense the character of Samuels is himself caught 'in the crossfire' of a clearly delineated moral conflict – but what remains is also an unsettling portrayal of despair and urban anomie. Like other 'war-veteran *film noirs*', such as *Dead Reckoning* (1947)*, *Crossfire* is closely interested in the construction of a complex, damaged masculine subjectivity which is pictured still floundering 'in the crossfire' of the impact of previous battles on the psyche. The men's return to America is largely characterised by a lack of any kind of emotional settlement hence, in part, the recourse to disruptive camera angles, abrupt cutting patterns, harsh low-key lighting and provocative extreme close-ups within a *mise en scène* that has been likened by James Naremore (1998) to 'an expressionistic, militarized locker room'. This is a film as much about a state of mind as the state of a body politic. In this sense, to return to Sobchack, *Crossfire* perfectly captures that moment when America, like many *film noir* characters, 'was fixed in a transitional moment looking back toward a retrospectively idyllic world that could not historically be recuperated [and] looking forward with a certain inertial apprehension of a probable dead end'. AP

Dir: Edward Dmytryk; **Prod**: Dore Schary, Adrian Scott; **Scr**: John Paxton from Richard Brooks's novel *The Brick Foxhole*; **DOP**: J. Roy Hunt (b&w); **Ed**: Harry W. Gerstad; **Score**: Roy Webb; **Main Cast**: Robert Mitchum, Robert Ryan, Gloria Grahame, Robert Young, Sam Levene, George Cooper; **Prod Co**: RKO.

Cry of the City
US, 1948 – 91 mins
Robert Siodmak

Fox initially conceived *Cry of the City* as a Victor Mature follow-up to their successful *Kiss of Death* (1947)*. Mature would play another tortured gangster figure in a film which would again marry a documentary approach with something more expressively *noir* (though there is no interest here in documenting police procedures). In the event, Mature took the role of police lieutenant Candella, while Richard Conte was assigned to play the gangster, Martin Rome.

When *film noirs* used the device of doubling two characters, they gave it a new psychological and expressive twist (see also, for example, Siodmak's own *The Dark Mirror* [1946]). Candella and Rome are childhood friends from a shared Italian American community but on different sides of the law. Candella is clearly at home with Rome's family, which seems as much Candella's as Rome's, with Candella as a kind of 'good son'. Both men suffer major injuries and leave hospital beds to continue their quests. Though Candella, poor but moral, tells Rome he should have settled down and married, in fact he himself has no woman or family. Though Rome, outside the law, is clearly doomed, Candella too has few options other than to pursue and destroy Rome.

Siodmak plays on the doubling theme at both narrative and visual levels, exploiting Conte's and Mature's physical characteristics. Smart, lean, tough, charismatic Rome is initially more sympathetic, more the 'hero', despite his criminality, and we are invited to empathise with his secret love affair with the angelic Teena (Debra Paget), his dealings with the bent lawyer and his efforts to avoid capture. Gradually, though, Rome's amoral, egocentric character emerges and our sympathies shift towards the heavier, dour but dogged Candella. Apparently against type, Rome dresses in light clothes and Candella in black, but Rome is less a moral figure than a ghost or lost soul. The film begins with the wounded Rome receiving the last rites and throughout he is living on borrowed time, with nowhere to rest – as Candella says, 'run, run, run, till he can't run any more; he's a dead man'.

As befits the film's setting, religious motifs play an important role. Rome and Candella battle for the 'soul' of Rome's younger brother Antonio/Tony (Tommy Cook), who aspires to be like Rome until he sees him for what he is. In the final shoot-out in the dark street, the tearful Tony stumbles from Rome's body towards the badly injured Candella,

Law and crime bound together until the end: Rome (Richard Conte) and the wounded Candella (Victor Mature) in the closing sequence of *Cry of the City*

pausing briefly midway between them. As the film ends, we see Candella take over the role of Tony's 'brother' and mentor.

Robert Siodmak was still under contract to Universal, where he made *The Killers* (1946)* and *Criss Cross* (1949)*. His preference for the artifice and expressive possibilities of studio shooting was more welcome there, but here he successfully combines an almost neo-realist rendering of Little Italy street life – the film's trailer places great emphasis on both day and night New York City locations – with a highly expressive use of both locations and studio settings. Rome's escape from the hospital jail, for example, derives maximum tension from the location's long tunnels and traffic that Rome must navigate, but Siodmak also engages the expressive possibilities of *mise en scène* to emphasise both the doubling of the protagonists and their entrapment. JH

Dir: Robert Siodmak; **Prod**: Sol S. Siegel; **Scr**: Richard Murphy from Henry Edward Helseth's novel *The Chair for Martin Rome*; **DOP**: Lloyd Ahern (b&w); **Ed**: Harmon Jones; **Score**: Alfred Newman; **Main Cast**: Victor Mature, Richard Conte, Fred Clark, Shelley Winters, Debra Paget, Rose Given, Tommy Cook; **Prod Co**: Twentieth Century-Fox.

The Dark Corner
US, 1946 – 99 mins
Henry Hathaway

As Lawrence Alloway (1971) has pointed out, one of the most symptomatic figures of 1940s *film noir* – central to some its best films, like *Out of the Past* (1947)*, *The Lady from Shanghai*, (1947)*, *D.O.A.* (1950)* – is the 'fall guy'. This – invariably male – figure is framed by shadowy forces in ways he can't understand for reasons he can't readily fathom. *The Dark Corner* is one of the most effective films of this type. Its protagonist's anguished, existential cry – 'I feel all dead inside. I'm backed up in a dark corner and I don't know who's hitting me' – epitomises the condition of the fall guy, and the *noir* victim-hero in general.

Bradford Galt (Mark Stevens), just released from wrongful imprisonment on the west coast (which could be read metaphorically as the common *noir* plot situation of demobilisation from the armed forces), returns to New York to try to resume life as a private eye. However, his apartment and stripped-down office are shadowy, hostile spaces, and he finds himself staked out by a mysterious, menacing investigator known to him only as 'White Suit' (William Bendix) (after the rather anachronistic white suit he wears). Galt's off-kilter, violent encounter with White Suit is a triumph of *noir* visual style and atmosphere (though the film's essentially studio look doesn't sustain claims for it as one of Fox's documentary-style *noirs*). Sullen and embittered, Galt figures out that the frame he finds himself in has something to do with his former partner Tony Jardine (Kurt Kreuger), who had been responsible for Galt's jailing. Foppish, sharp-tongued, devious art collector Henry Cathcart (Clifton Webb, reprising his character from *Laura*, [1944]*) is targeting Jardine because his younger wife Mari (Cathy Downs) is having an affair with him. In a further echo of *Laura*, Cathcart has married Mari for her

(*Next page*) Incomprehension and despair on the faces of Kathleen (Lucille Ball) and Galt (Mark Stevens) in *The Dark Corner*

resemblance to a prized and worshipped portrait in his collection. The vicious Cathcart gets White Suit to kill Jardine and frame Galt. In an extraordinary scene, Cathcart then kills White Suit by backing him out of a window.

Galt, tough private eye though he is, is mothered – with obvious implications for his already battered masculinity – through his despair by his secretary Kathleen (Lucille Ball, in one of her few dark dramas before being lost forever to *I Love Lucy*). Kathleen's upbeat faith in Galt and her practicality – and her firm focus on nothing less than marriage – make her a rather odd character in the *noir* world. She and Galt present a sympathetic, ordinary, classless couple, at home with colourful slang and sports metaphors – very different from the film's murderously amoral and paranoid wealthy, society characters.

Typically, the *noir* fall guy is denied proper closure because the discovery or defeat of the forces framing him comes about less by his own efforts than by auto-destruction. Here, Mari finally shoots Cathcart before he can dispose of Galt. Galt's desperate situation for most of the movie makes the supposed happy ending – Galt and Kathleen united as a couple – feel somewhat perfunctory and unsatisfying, though Mark Stevens's performance is excellent throughout (as it was in *The Street with No Name* and *The Snake Pit*, both 1948). JH

Dir: Henry Hathaway; **Prod**: Fred Kohlmar; **Scr**: Jay Dratler, Bernard Schoenfeld from Leo Rosten's short story; **DOP**: Joe MacDonald (b&w); **Ed**: J. Watson Webb; **Score**: Cyril Mockridge; **Main Cast**: Mark Stevens, Lucille Ball, Clifton Webb, William Bendix, Kurt Kreuger, Cathy Downs; **Prod Co**: Twentieth Century-Fox.

Dark Passage

US, 1947 – 106 mins

Delmer Daves

Dark Passage was the second of Bogart and Bacall's three *film noirs* together (after *The Big Sleep* [1946]* and before John Huston's *Key Largo* [1948]), and their partnership is central to its appeal and effect. Bogart's character, Vincent Parry, is edgier and more bitter than his Marlowe in *The Big Sleep*, or his Rip Murdock in *Dead Reckoning** (released in January 1947, as *Dark Passage* completed shooting). He is more a victim-hero than a seeker-hero: the film's 'epilogue' apart, the fates are against him throughout, leaving him with no apparent way out.

The film begins with Vincent, wrongly convicted of murdering his wife, making a daring escape from San Quentin prison. He is picked up by Irene Jansen (Bacall), who takes him back to her apartment and hides him. Irene has followed Vincent's case because her father, though innocent, was convicted of the same crime (against Irene's stepmother). While taking all this in, viewers are wrestling with the film's inventive use of subjective point-of-view camera (*The Lady in the Lake**, released in the same month as *Dark Passage*, January 1947, also used subjective camera). Although we glimpse Vincent after about thirty minutes, we do not see his (i.e. Bogart's) face until over an hour into the film. Vincent undergoes plastic surgery – triggering a hallucinatory sequence as the paranoid protagonist succumbs to sedation – which provides reasons for us not to see his features. However, the lengthy withholding of the outcome of the operation until the removal of the 'Invisible Man'-style bandages and the revelation of Vincent's (diegetically new) face as Bogart's (non-diegetically familiar) face, makes for a very curious scene – not least because from the film's opening, we have heard Vincent's voice-over in Bogart's instantly recognisable voice. The 'revelation' evokes a powerful mix of emotions in the spectator that spills beyond the story moment – not least when Irene/Bacall comments, smiling, that she likes the new/old look.

Somewhat oddly for a *film noir*, Vincent is redeemed by Irene's unquestioning love. Insofar as there is a *femme fatale*, Agnes Moorehead's characteristically acerbic Madge Rapf, the actual murderer of Vincent's wife, fulfils the role. Her unnerving death – half-accident/half-suicide (backing away from Vincent, she falls through an open window) – removes the major witness who could prove his innocence. In what could serve as a bleak *noir* ending, Vincent, all his leads and witnesses gone and no way out, is forced to flee into San Francisco's threatening night streets – a very fine, quintessentially *noir* sequence. The film's breathtakingly implausible epilogue – Vincent and Irene reunited by the moonlit beach in Peru, a perfect example of a *deus ex machina* ending – was perhaps demanded by the Bogart–Bacall coupling. It enables the audience to feel good but simultaneously not believe a word of it.

David Goodis's source novel, an important ingredient in the film's success, left the future of the couple in considerable doubt. Perhaps the film ending's implausibility reflects this. Goodis's work is generally characterised by a fine sense of place, and one of the film's strengths is its precise rendering of the San Francisco cityscape's different levels, like Irene's notable Malloch Apartment Building. JH

Dir: Delmer Daves; **Prod**: Jerry Wald; **Scr**: Delmer Daves from David Goodis's novel; **DOP**: Sid Hickox (b&w); **Ed**: David Weisbart; **Score**: Franz Waxman; **Main Cast**: Humphrey Bogart, Lauren Bacall, Agnes Moorehead, Bruce Bennett, Tom D'Andrea, Clifton Young; **Prod Co**: Warner Bros.

Dead Reckoning
US, 1947 – 100 mins
John Cromwell

Writing on the release of John Cromwell's engrossing investigative thriller, *Dead Reckoning*, the *New York Times* remarked that 'For those with a taste for rough stuff, *Dead Reckoning* is almost certain to satisfy. All others are hereby cautioned to proceed at their own risk.' This neatly points to the issue lying at the heart of this hard-boiled veteran *noir* (and indeed so many other *film noirs* of the period): an anxiety over the supposed virtues of male virility and the threat of femininity that this concurrently suggests.

Rip (Humphrey Bogart) and his close friend, Johnny, are two returning paratroopers from war-torn Europe. On learning that they are to be unexpectedly presented with medals at a ceremony in Washington, Johnny suddenly disappears. Rip travels to Gulf City in search of Johnny and soon discovers that his army colleague is actually wanted for murder. In an attempt to uncover the truth behind the affair, Rip becomes embroiled with Johnny's former lover, Coral Chandler (Lizabeth Scott) – also wife of the deceased – and finds himself exposed to the machinations of the corrupt local nightclub owner, Martinelli (played with assured menace by Morris Carnovsky).

As Frank Krutnik (1991) has observed, the real topic of the film's investigation though is the search for a return to the same emotional plenitude experienced by Rip and Johnny during their time in the theatre of war. This impossible quest forces Rip to constantly 'test' Johnny's former lover who becomes at once a false substitute for Johnny himself and a constant reminder of the vexed ways in which women in *film noir* seem to constantly circumvent male understanding through the irreducible logic of sexual difference. Rip, unable to accept the promise of feminine knowledge and thwarted in his quest for uncomplicated male bonding is thus doomed to remain alone on the same 'lonely street' that all male *noir* hard-boiled types seemingly spend their lives wandering down.

A tale of two cities: John Cromwell's oneiric *Dead Reckoning* advertised on the streets of London

In this sense, *Dead Reckoning* may be usefully compared to *Gilda* (1946)*, a film that it was at one stage designed to follow up and to which it still bears some superficial similarities. Had the vibrant Rita Hayworth also appeared in Cromwell's film, there might have been less recourse to the more conventional tropes of Bogart's male loner persona, but, as it is, the largely unexplored character of Coral is simply reduced to being one more 'problem' Rip has to solve. The difficulty he even has with naming her is symptomatic of his problems with sexual difference: she ends up being 'Mike'; her deathbed scene being visualised in Rip's imagination as a final forlorn parachute drop into unconsciousness.

Like *Gilda*, *Dead Reckoning* offers a splendidly louche nightclub environment that presents a similar image of decadence and corruption in counterpart to the conventional heroism of the American war effort. To reinforce this, Martinelli and his henchman, Krause, are identified with nationalities that the Allies fought against and their own apparent attraction to each other is conveyed more through psychosexual intrigue than the quick-witted banter of heterosexual male camaraderie.

Dead Reckoning's vivid Southern setting, with its constantly referred-to motif of 'sweet-smelling jasmine', suggests an oneiric space apart from the real concerns of postwar 'civvy street' (and indeed the conventional geography of *film noir*). This air of a seductive dream is apt for a film that, for the most part, is told in breathless flashback (Rip confessing to a local priest). It loses some of its dramatic tension once the narrative shifts back to the present, but there is no denying the final pessimistic take that *Dead Reckoning* has on conventional male desire. AP

Dir: John Cromwell; **Prod**: Sidney Biddell; **Scr**: Oliver H. P. Garrett, Steve Fisher, Allen Rivkin from Gerald Drayson, Sidney Biddell's story; **DOP**: Leo Tover (b&w); **Ed**: Gene Havlick; **Score**: Marlin Skiles; **Main Cast**: Humphrey Bogart, Lizabeth Scott, Morris Carnovsky, Charles Cane, Marvin Miller; **Prod Co**: Columbia.

Death Is a Caress (Døden er et kjærtegn)
Norway, 1949 – 88 mins
Edith Carlmar

Edith Carlmar's pioneering Norwegian *film noir* (and directorial debut) begins with an imprisoned murderer recounting the desperate recent events that have led to his incarceration in an Oslo jail. Speaking to his lawyer, Erik Hauge (Clause Wiese) speculates about the role either destiny or individual choice have played in relation to his final fate. The first-person narrative then turns to the recent past, adopting, if only in a limited sense, the confessional mode that Maureen Turim (1989) suggests is one of the traditional means by which *film noir* flashbacks are conventionally deployed. Erik is a former car mechanic who has abandoned his fiancée, Marit, after being seduced by Sonja Rentfort (Bjørg Riiser-Larsen), the bored and wealthy wife of a local businessman. The couple had an illicit affair, spiked with more than a hint of violent sexual passion, but when Sonja's husband presses for a successful divorce – there is no need for murder – they are forced together as man and wife and grinding domestic routine, as well as transparent class differences, lead to their eventual demise.

In many ways, *Death Is a Caress* appears to take on aspects of its immediate counterpart, the American *film noir*. Its narrative logic is determined by the downfall of a passive but desiring male protagonist who falls prey to the apparent machinations of a scheming *femme fatale*. It ruthlessly questions the role of predestination when it comes to the act of crime and its uncovering of the stench of immorality behind the polite façade of urban middle-class society recalls such obvious influences as the portrayal of the fractured Dietrichson household in *Double Indemnity* (1944)*. Edith Carlmar's picturing of Oslo however bears no relation to Billy Wilder's Los Angeles despite a similar scepticism about the materialist trappings of modernist life. The landscapes are relatively sunlit and tranquil and, in this sense, along with its pervasive undertow of pulp-like sexual perversity, the film may be best compared, as Audun

Engelstad (2006) has argued, to Tay Garnett's more intense and obsessive James M. Cain adaptation, *The Postman Always Rings Twice* (1946)*.

For a film so despairing of the potential of heterosexual relations, it is interesting that *Death is a Caress* was adapted from Arve Moen's source novel by the successful husband-and-wife team of Edith and Otto Carlmar. The film is particularly marked by the singularity of Carlmar's directorial style, which combines lengthy individual takes with a variety of inventive graphic montage elements. Carlmar's increasingly limited depiction of Erik's subjectivity is also noteworthy, given that the emotional terrain of the film is supposedly entirely recounted within his own flashback. It becomes ever harder to engage with Erik's taciturn and passive demeanour as the film turns more and more to soliciting an empathetic comprehension of Sonja's private desperation. In part, this is due to Bjørg Riiser-Larsen's bravura portrayal of an older woman lost in a fatal quest for an idealised version of her former self. In this sense, not least for her pronounced physical similarities, she appears to be a more social democratic (and thus less satirical) precursor to Gloria Swanson's Norma Desmond in *Sunset Boulevard* (1950)*. 'One day closer to death' goes the refrain of Erik's boss at the garage, speaking to his errant colleague. It is a peculiar measure of this quietly spoken film that, even though it ends with a form of direct address on the part of Erik to the audience, this phrase has as much to say about the nature of Sonja's plight as the general lot of those in ordinary work. AP

Dir: Edith Carlmar; **Prod**: Otto Carlmar; **Scr**: Otto Carlmar from Arve Moen's novel; **DOP**: Kåre Bergstrøm (b&w); **Score**: Sverre Bergh; **Main Cast**: Clause Wiese, Bjørg Riiser-Larsen, Ingolf Rogde, Gisle Straume; **Prod Co**: Carlmar Film.

Death of a Cyclist (*Muerte de un ciclista*)
Spain, 1955 – 88 mins
Juan Antonio Bardem

A lonely and desolate stretch of road in the wet and windswept gloom
of a wintry late afternoon somewhere outside Madrid. A well-to-do
couple in a motor car accidentally run down a passing cyclist, but after
stopping to check that the man is still breathing, Maria (Lucía Bosé)
persuades her adulterous lover Juan (Alberto Closas) to drive on and
keep the accident a secret. Juan Antonio Bardem's now classic feature
film from the repressive Franco era charts the moral decline of the two

The turmoil of private guilt for a public crime: Maria (Lucía Bosé) and her adulterous lover
Juan (Alberto Closas) in *Death of a Cyclist*

protagonists as they re-enter the stifling milieu of Spanish urban upper-class society only to find themselves under threat of blackmail from one of their most odious associates, the duplicitous art critic 'Rafa' (Carlos Casaravilla).

As Rob Stone (2007) has argued, with very few exceptions, there was no genuine tradition of Spanish *film noir* up to the 1970s because of the lack of any indigenous hard-boiled urban crime fiction, the pressures of moral censorship and the politically motivated desire of the Spanish authorities to render any *policíaca* (urban police thriller) serviceable to the authoritarian interests of the state. Despite this, many critics now argue that *Death of a Cyclist* nonetheless possesses many of the attributes of conventional *film noir*, in terms of both aspects of its narrative construction and its evocative *mise en scène*. Taken from an original story by Luis Fernández de Igoa, itself based on Tolstoy's novel *Resurrection*, the film explores the turmoil of private guilt for a public crime in a setting that encourages the spectator to draw analogies between the individual couple's fraudulence and the corruption of a society that seems explicitly riven by material division. Juan's redemption at the end of the film, when he persuades Maria to return to the scene of the crime before they are due to confess to the police, also opens up the legacy of the Civil War when he reveals that the surrounding fields were ones he fought in as a soldier in the 1930s.

Bardem's conception of the film relies much on Alfredo Fraile's moody cinematography and Margarita Ochoa's sharp and revealing editing. As Marsha Kinder (1993) suggests, he solved the problem of making a genre film relevant to its time by constructing an internal structure that relies on an analytically based alternation between melodrama and neo-realism. Hence the segueing between harshly lit and claustrophobic interior scenes – at times suggesting a Wellesian intensity – and more dispersed location sequences largely composed of extended revelatory long takes that depict the impoverished background of the dead cyclist. Bardem often sets one narrative moment against the other by linking scenes through sound, graphic element or psychological theme. Elsewhere, he adapts a Hitchcockian awareness of the mechanics of suspense. In one startling sequence set during a lascivious private flamenco party for some visiting American businessmen, for example, we cut ever closer to the central protagonists as 'Rafa' appears to be divulging the guilty couple's secret but the more we see, the less we hear as the sound of the music drowns out the words on the individual characters' lips.

It is telling that much of the immoral energy of *Death of a Cyclist* becomes displaced onto the female figure rendering Maria, for critics such as Jo Evans (2007), a plausibly transgressive *femme fatale* (despite obvious censorship restrictions of the time). Undoubtedly, she looks the part and her demise in a brutal car crash, shortly after killing Juan, has echoes of the fate of Jane Greer's character in *Out of the Past* (1947)*. Lucía Bosé had previously appeared in Michelangelo Antonioni's *Story of a Love Affair* (1950)* and the two films are worth comparing for their subtle ability to fuse riveting emotional conflict with revealing social critique. AP

Dir, Scr: Juan Antonio Bardem from Luis Fernández de Igoa's story; **Prod**: Manuel J. Goyanes, Georges de Beauregard; **DOP**: Alfredo Fraile (b&w); **Ed**: Margarita Ochoa; **Score**: Isidro B. Maiztegui; **Main Cast**: Alberto Closas, Lucía Bosé, Otello Toso, Carlos Casaravilla, Bruna Corrà, Julia Delgado Caro; **Prod Co**: Guión Producciones Cinematográficas, Suevia Films, Trionfalcine.

Detour
US, 1945 – 68 mins
Edgar G. Ulmer

A wandering male figure comes out of the night-time darkness into a roadside diner. Listening to a banal show tune he dislikes on the jukebox, he slumps over the counter and retreats into himself. The camera tracks forward and the lighting set-up shifts so that shadows gather over his face and we only see the haunted rims of his sullen, tired eyes. Al Roberts (Tom Neal) begins to tell his story.

Detour is a film recounted through unreliable flashback. We learn that Roberts had been hitching to Los Angeles to meet up with his former girlfriend when he met a man, Haskell (Edmund Macdonald), who gave him a ride. Unexpectedly, Haskell dies and Roberts assumes the man's identity. On the road again, Roberts meets Vera (Ann Savage), a sharp-tongued drifter who 'looked like she'd just been thrown off the crummiest freight train in the world' and who contrives to exploit the situation when she unexpectedly announces that she knows the truth about Haskell's fate. As Andrew Britton (1993) has pointed out, none of what Roberts tells us may be factually accurate since it is impossible to divine whether the film is in fact visualised through his eyes. Both the shifty, cynical patter of the voice-over and the fragmentary nature of the film's *mise en scène* conspire to produce a sense of 'a palimpsest beneath which we may glimpse the traces of the history [Roberts] has felt compelled to write'.

Ulmer had been a set designer for Max Reinhardt and worked as assistant director for Fritz Lang and Ernst Lubitsch in Berlin before moving to Hollywood in the 1930s. Best known for a string of low-budget genre features, by the mid-1940s he was employed by the small independent studio, PRC, where he had his own production team. *Detour* was famously shot in six days on a two-to-one shooting ratio and very minimal resources. These constraints undoubtedly contributed to the hallucinatory, pulp qualities of the film and force

A roadside diner and the haunted rims of Al Roberts's (Tom Neal) sullen, tired eyes: *Detour*

attention onto its two remarkable central performances. Tom Neal conveys a listless melancholic passivity as Roberts while Ann Savage's acerbic portrayal of Vera surely means that her character qualifies as the most vital, toughest-minded *femme fatale* of the classical *film noir* cycle.

Like his fellow Viennese émigré, Billy Wilder, Ulmer used *film noir* as a means to examine the numerous false promises of American capitalism. *Detour* is the antithesis of the archetypal Hollywood road movie that celebrates the promise of renewal in conjunction with the freedom of the open road. It reveals, as Britton (1993) again remarks, a desperate, thwarted sense of transit 'where the real logic of advanced capitalist civil society is acted out by characters who have completely internalized its values, and whose interaction exemplifies the grotesque deformation of all human relationships by the principles of the market'. Hence the film's desperate opening image from the rear of a moving car watching the space left behind rather than the space gained upon. Hence also the way that the film ends so memorably – almost where it began – with Vera dead and Roberts, now trapped without a name, forced onto the road once more with literally nowhere left to go. AP

Dir: Edgar G. Ulmer; **Prod**: Leon Fromkess; **Scr**: Martin Goldsmith, Martin Mooney (uncredited) from Martin Goldsmith's novel; **DOP**: Benjamin H. Kline (b&w); **Ed**: George McGuire; **Score**: Leo Erdody; **Main Cast**: Tom Neal, Ann Savage, Edmund Macdonald, Claudia Drake; **Prod Co**: PRC.

Devil in a Blue Dress
US, 1995 – 102 mins
Carl Franklin

Is *film noir* a specifically white phenomenon? This, as Manthia Diawara (1993) reminds us, is a question that goes back to Borde and Chaumeton's seminal book (2002, first published in the 1950s) where *film noir* was defined as 'black' 'because [its] characters have lost the privilege of whiteness by pursuing lifestyles that are misogynistic, cowardly, duplicitous, that exhibit themselves in an eroticization of violence'. It is also an issue that pervades Carl Franklin's evocative and highly entertaining adaptation of Walter Moseley's novel, exploring as it does the period of the heyday of classical *film noir* from the vantage point of its central protagonist, a black, unemployed aircraft engineer named Easy Rawlins (Denzel Washington).

From its opening wide-angle scenes in the predominately black neighbourhoods of 1948 Los Angeles, *Devil in a Blue Dress* visualises all that conventional *film noir* disavowed when it came to black American representation. Instead of the familiar repertoire of peripheral porters, janitors, cleaners, shoeshine boys, maids and nightclub singers, located only within the perimeters of a central white character's gaze, we observe a densely realised panorama of black American daily life that is striking in both its novelty and, of course, its transparent ordinariness. Franklin maintains this dual perspective throughout a complex narrative, which, like Roman Polanski's *Chinatown* (1974)*, involves a disturbing interaction between political corruption and private immorality. *Devil in a Blue Dress* is indebted to many of the conventions of *film noir* (and is thus intrinsically familiar), but by inserting race at its moral centre, it also forces one to reassess the previous ethical qualities of a form now made strange.

Like many *noir* male protagonists, Rawlins is a war veteran whose home in the growing suburbs of Los Angeles, although favourably situated, remains a tentative place of refuge. When invited to help locate

Daphne Monet (Jennifer Beals), the missing fiancée of Todd Carter (Terry Kinney), a local mayoral candidate, his explicit motivation is to secure his fragile transition from inner-city ghetto life. Rawlins soon becomes immersed in a labyrinthine murder mystery involving city politics and the transparently racist brutality of the city's police force. In the course of his investigation, he makes the dramatic discovery that Monet is, in fact, not white but bi-racial and that this is being used against Carter as an aspect of the spiralling blackmail chain underpinning the impending city elections.

In addition to Washington's charismatic star performance, our allegiance to the character of Rawlins is maintained by the familiar trope of a retrospective voice-over. Rather than evoking *film noir*'s more traditional fatalistic tone, however, this particular voice helps articulate the fear of being an investigator in a world that conventionally imagines the black protagonist to be the perpetrator of the crime, rather than the agent that instigates its resolution. That's not to say that *Devil in a Blue Dress* is a straightforward revisionist text. Rawlins's voice, and indeed the wider terrain of the film, still work to contain the threat of femininity that its title announces by displacing that other common *film noir* trope, an existential anxiety over male identity, onto the over-determined figure of the *femme fatale*. In his now classic book on the phenomenon, James Naremore (1998) argues that the most fascinating thing about *film noir* in its heyday was the way in which it 'both repressed and openly confronted the most profound tensions in the society at large'. Carl Franklin's elegant and textured film is a perfect example of how this still remains the case.   AP

Dir: Carl Franklin; **Prod**: Jesse Beaton, Gary Goetzman; **Scr**: Carl Franklin from Walter Moseley's novel; **DOP**: Tak Fujimoto (colour); **Ed**: Carole Kravetz; **Score**: Elmer Bernstein; **Main Cast**: Denzel Washington, Tom Sizemore, Jennifer Beals, Don Cheadle, Terry Kinney; **Prod Co**: Clinica Estetico, Mundy Lane Entertainment, Tristar Pictures.

D.O.A.
US, 1950 – 83 mins
Rudolph Maté

A man turns up at police headquarters to report his own murder, having discovered that he has been slipped a poison for which there is no antidote, and that he will be dead within a matter of days. The ingenious premise of *D.O.A.* is also archetypically *noir*: the character does not know who killed him or why, thus embodying a world in which people are at the mercy of unknown forces they cannot understand or control. Whereas characters like Galt in *The Dark Corner* (1946)* achieve some understanding and closure – if by chance as much as their own efforts – Frank Bigelow (Edmond O'Brien) in *D.O.A.* succeeds only to the extent of discovering who murdered him and why. He derives little comfort from learning that his poisoning turns out to have been unnecessary, almost arbitrary and, having told his story to the police, he collapses and is declared 'Dead on Arrival'.

The film begins impressively with Bigelow striding purposefully through the endless corridors of Los Angeles police headquarters to report his murder and tell his story, in flashback. Bigelow, a small-town public accountant reluctant to commit to his clinging fiancée/assistant, takes off to San Francisco to have some fun – perhaps we should read his torment partly as a kind of punishment. San Francisco offers frenzied activity, best summoned up in a jazz-club sequence, but by the time Bigelow comes to his senses and declines to follow up an amorous encounter, it is already too late. Confirmation that he has imbibed the toxin leads to an extended sequence in which Bigelow, in long tracking shots, runs desperately, at a furious pace, through the crowds and traffic of San Francisco's Market Street in a hopeless attempt to escape the inescapable. Indeed, Bigelow spends half the movie frantically running, partly out of sheer panic, partly to find his murderer in the limited time left to him. The over-complicated and sometimes clunky plot involves illegal sales, business corruption and marital infidelities, but the fact that the poisoning is by radiation – a wonderful shot shows the luminous poison glowing in a dark medical examination room – also suggests a Cold War perspective to the out-of-joint world in which Bigelow is the fall guy.

Rudolph Maté had a distinguished career as a cinematographer in Europe – working with Carl Dreyer, Fritz Lang, René Clair and Jean Grémillon – before moving to Hollywood in 1935 and doing distinguished work on Hitchcock's *Foreign Correspondent* (1940) and Charles Vidor's *Gilda* (1946)*, among others, before directing his first film in 1947. Here, Maté expertly uses extensive day and night location shooting to root Bigelow's nightmare and paranoid quest in both empty or busy San Francisco and Los Angeles urban spaces – streets, office buildings, stores, warehouses, buses.

Later Russell Rouse–Clarence Green story concepts could be merely gimmicky – like the absence of dialogue in Rouse's *The Thief* (1952) – but their ingenious story for *D.O.A.* inevitably attracted (unfortunately not very good) remakes: the Australian *Color Me Dead* (aka *D.O.A. II*) (Eddie Davis, 1969) and *DOA* (Rocky Morton & Annabel Jankel, 1988). JH

Dir: Rudolph Maté; **Prod**: Leo C. Popkin; **Scr**: Russell Rouse, Clarence Green; **DOP**: Ernest Laszlo (b&w); **Ed**: Arthur H. Nadel; **Score**: Dimitri Tiomkin; **Main Cast**: Edmond O'Brien, Pamela Britton, Luther Adler, Beverly Campbell, Neville Brand; **Prod Co**: Harry M. Popkin.

Double Indemnity
US, 1944 – 106 mins
Billy Wilder

By common consent, *Double Indemnity* is one of the most important
early *film noirs* and one of the most influential 1940s Hollywood films.
In particular, it helped propel the *film noir* cycle forward by pushing the
limits on representing sex and violence, with its relationship between a
thoroughly sexualised, ruthless *femme fatale* and a male protagonist
who, though guilty of premeditated murder – and punished accordingly
– remains, if not likeable, then at least sympathetic at some level.
Visually, *Double Indemnity*, like *Laura**, also 1944, mostly opts for a
softer look than the sharp *chiaroscuro*, low-key lighting effects of 1944's
*Murder, My Sweet** or *Phantom Lady**. However, it very successfully
creates a claustrophobic sense of place, using omnipresent Venetian
blinds to develop an intricate motif of bars of shadow which dog the
protagonist throughout.

Insurance salesman Walter Neff (Fred MacMurray, playing both with
and against his 'nice guy' screen persona) is often viewed as an almost
innocent victim in thrall to Barbara Stanwyck's Phyllis Dietrichson.
However, his sexual attraction to Phyllis – and what David Thomson
(2002) calls his 'lazy moral inertia' – allow him to set about both murder
and fraud with both eyes open, no matter how much he is later undone
by an existential sense of guilt. Motivated by a desire to beat the system
in which he is a lowly cog, and seeing the insurance business as akin to
gambling, he wants to 'crook the house'. Phyllis is perhaps not as
beyond redemption as generally assumed. During her first visit to Walter's
apartment, as he talks about women serving sentences for murdering
their spouses, Phyllis murmurs that 'Perhaps it was worth it to her.'
Wistfully dissatisfied, ready to contemplate murder to escape a kind of
domestic and marital imprisonment, she evokes the classic situation
of the *femme fatale* whose sexuality is their only access to any kind of
power. And there is no reason to suppose that Phyllis's final declaration

'Straight down the line': Walter Neff's (Fred MacMurray) car about to jump the lights in the opening sequence of *Double Indemnity*

of love for Walter – usually taken as a final, flagrant example of her duplicity – is not genuine: clearly, she has nothing to gain by lying at this point.

Billy Wilder and Raymond Chandler made several important changes in adapting Cain's novel (though Cain liked what they did). They introduced the voice-over flashback/confession structure, which, by showing Walter fatally wounded at the start, gives the film its powerful sense of predetermination, while Walter himself becomes a more 1940s wise-cracking character. They also significantly deepened the relationship between Walter and his boss Barton Keyes (Edward G. Robinson), so that it figures as a deeply felt male 'love' bond to parallel the sexually charged, unstable Walter–Phyllis relationship. The novel concludes with a switch to almost *Grand Guignol* melodrama – Walter and Phyllis on a ship heading south, preparing to feed themselves to the sharks. In many ways, the film's ending – Walter and Phyllis shooting each other, and Walter nursing his wounds as he confesses to Keyes via Dictaphone – is more satisfying. As is well known, Wilder shot an ending in which Walter, watched by Keyes, is executed in the gas chamber. Most critics feel Wilder was right to reject this ending, though James Naremore (1998) argues persuasively that it would appropriately conclude the film's 'straight down the line' motif and its critique of Fordist American culture's drive-in restaurants, supermarkets, bowling alleys and rows of office desks.

Lawrence Kasdan's *Body Heat* (1981) featured very similar characters (William Hurt and Kathleen Turner) and plot in a steamy Florida setting. Exploiting new freedoms in representing sex, it also allowed the devious *femme fatale* to evade punishment and prosper.   JH

Dir: Billy Wilder; **Prod**: Joseph Sistrom; **Scr**: Raymond Chandler, Billy Wilder from James M. Cain's novel; **DOP**: John F. Seitz (b&w); **Ed**: Doane Harrison; **Score**: Miklós Rózsa; **Main Cast**: Fred MacMurray, Barbara Stanwyck, Edward G. Robinson, Jean Heather, Tom Powers, Byron Barr; **Prod Co**: Paramount.

The Driver
US, 1978 – 91 mins
Walter Hill

Alain Silver and Elizabeth Ward (1993) claim *The Driver* as 'one of the earliest and most stylized examples of conscious neo-noir'. Thirty years ago it seemed like Robert Bresson with car chases, with its almost ascetic narrative style combined with spectacular automotive action. Walter Hill insists that he did not know Jean-Pierre Melville's French takes on the American crime film, but there are extraordinarily striking similarities between *The Driver* and *Le Samouraï* (1967)*: *Le Samouraï* involves a hit man, a dark lady and the cops; *The Driver* involves three unnamed characters – a getaway driver (Ryan O'Neal), a beautiful young gambler, The Player (Isabelle Adjani), and a detective (Bruce Dern) – playing cat and mouse in a largely nocturnal Los Angeles and barely lit interiors.

The film's start juxtaposes The Driver stealing a car with The Player gambling, both as enigmatic as each other. As The Player leaves the casino, a robbery takes place; she sees The Driver's face clearly but refuses to identify him for the police. The Driver seems to exist only to drive (which he does superlatively), live by his code and defend his reputation. Like the other characters, he has no backstory to speak of: he rarely betrays any emotions; among the few things we know about him is that he has a liking for country music; he lives in a cheap, sparsely furnished room, and has no obvious interest in money. The Player lives in a smart, modern apartment, as anonymous as a hotel room. Although The Detective hints at her having a dark past, we know almost nothing about her either; she too barely betrays any emotion. The Detective is more animatedly obsessive and garrulous, but only ever seen in a working context. It's all 'just a game' – 'Winners, losers, how it happened, score' – to The Detective, who has a single objective: 'I'm gonna catch me the cowboy that's never been caught.' Hill's early scripts and films were all strenuously pared down. As Hill put it, 'the way you find out about these characters is by watching what they do'.

The film's overall impression of mind-games and individual isolation is punctuated by three spectacular, extended high-speed car action sequences. Near the start, The Driver escapes from a mass police high-speed pursuit; in the middle, challenged about his driving skills, he systematically deconstructs the gang's Mercedes in a deserted underground car park; at the end, he pursues and catches the gangsters who have stolen his money. These sequences, shot with great verve, have a life and energy almost separate from the rest of the film but, paradoxically, they are not 'exciting' in any conventional sense, because The Driver remains wholly impassive.

Although The Driver is an isolated, existential figure, totally focused on his work – as The Detective tells him, he's 'got it down so tight there's no room for anything else' – the attractions and needs of the 'dark lady', though barely acknowledged, distract him. Although he knows he is being set up, The Driver begins to take uncharacteristic risks. In the denouement at Union Station, The Driver appears to have been caught with the money, but in a final twist the film ends with The Detective's defeat – perhaps the film's one false note. The Driver and The Player survive to drive and play another day. The outlaw characters retain our sympathy and win. JH

Dir, Scr: Walter Hill; **Prod**: Lawrence Gordon; **DOP**: Philip Lathrop (colour); **Ed**: Tina Hirsch, Robert K. Lambert; **Score**: Michael Small; **Main Cast**: Ryan O'Neal, Bruce Dern, Isabelle Adjani, Ronee Blakely; **Prod Co**: Twentieth Century-Fox, EMI.

Fallen Angel
US, 1945 – 98 mins
Otto Preminger

Preminger's atmospheric follow-up to his successful New York *film noir*, *Laura* (1944)*, begins with fleeting images of the Californian highway at night. Neon road signs announcing the film's major credits enter the frame before we see an intercity bus pull to a halt and the driver evict a sleeping drifter, Eric Stanton (Dana Andrews). Stranded halfway between Los Angeles and San Francisco, unable to pay his way to his destination, Stanton, an archetypal *film noir* loner, has arrived in the sleepy coastal town of Walton.

The film briskly paints a portrait of Walton society. Within the hour, Stanton has met the denizens of the local seaside diner, including the surly but alluring waitress, Stella (Linda Darnell). He soon falls in with a couple of grifters and through them also meets two well-to-do town ladies, including the hospitable but mildly repressed June Mills (Alice Faye). Preminger's characteristically artful mobile camera, along with Joseph LaShelle's careful and attentive lighting set-ups, portray a world riven by class and suppressed desire. Initially the shadowy, seedy milieu of the diner and the brightly lit domestic respectability of the Mills home seem at odds with each other, but as the narrative progresses, more similarities than differences are revealed, especially in the ways in which the emotions of the two female protagonists become enmeshed in Stanton's seemingly guileless machinations. The former New York press agent hatches a plan with Stella to briefly marry June in order to access her fortune. He'll then divorce her and run off with Stella who's fatally seduced by the thought of 'a real home' and furs. However, the night of the marriage Stella is found murdered and Stanton immediately becomes one of a number of plausible suspects. Only June is convinced that this artful wanderer is not the actual killer.

Fallen Angel achieves its particular qualities through a combination of different tonal registers. These are displayed in the film's *mise en scène* through the wide-ranging use of location cinematography, as well as studio set, and the way in which Preminger's camera relentlessly fails to settle on one particular character's point of view. This denial of spectatorial identification, as Chris Fujiwara (2008) has argued, constitutes an image of Stanton, especially, as both agent and onlooker. We are never given the full means of understanding what makes Dana Andrews's typically impassive protagonist tick. Indeed, *Fallen Angel* often seems to prefer the partial examination of his actions from a slightly less restricted female perspective. In one key shot, in which the town's different social worlds collide, we see Stella and Stanton outside the diner at night. The camera reverse-tracks as Stella leaves screen right. Still on Stanton, the camera then starts moving forward as if to capture his reaction more directly, but as he moves to follow angrily it simply passes him and stops instead on the blank emptiness of the building's corner. Slowly, out of the darkness, June's anxious older sister emerges, looking balefully onto what we are now explicitly denied full sight of.

Critics have observed that the production history of *Fallen Angel* was a somewhat troubled one. There are certainly clear signs of Darryl F. Zanuck's interfering editorial control in the uneven plotting of the later sections of the film. Despite these problems Fuijwara has suggested that *Fallen Angel* should still be seen a 'a key Preminger work for the way it addresses the problem of self-knowledge in terms of the difficulty of knowing any human being'. This may be true but, for exactly the same reasons, it can also be argued that this revealing and surprisingly poignant treatment of Marty Holland's source novel should now be seen more generally as an important *film noir* of the period. AP

Dir, Prod: Otto Preminger; **Scr**: Harry Kleiner from Marty Holland's novel; **DOP**: Joseph LaShelle (b&w); **Ed**: Harry Reynolds; **Score**: David Raksin; **Main Cast**: Dana Andrews, Alice Faye, Linda Darnell, Charles Bickford, Anne Revere; **Prod Co**: Twentieth Century-Fox.

Fear in the Night
US, 1947 – 71 mins
Maxwell Shane

Many *film noirs* or *noir* sequences embody a sense of the dream state, often dream states that the characters cannot shake off. Setting the overwhelmingly oneiric mood of the film as a whole, *Fear in the Night* begins with blurry, shifting images of light and shadow and a half-glimpsed, confusing struggle – is it murder? – in an octagonal mirrored room. The main character, Vincent (DeForest Kelley), then wakes from a 'dream' with thumb marks on his neck, blood on his hands and a button and key that figured in the drama. Unsurprisingly, he asks himself, in voice-over, 'Am I going insane?' Outside his window, the mundane street is bathed in sunlight. 'I had to get out of my room, into the sunshine,' he continues, 'I had to stay out of the shadows. I knew that tonight, I'd be afraid of the dark.'

Vincent belongs to that strain of weak-willed *noir* protagonists who find themselves – like Edward G. Robinson's characters in Fritz Lang's *Woman in the Window* (1944) and *Scarlet Street* (1945)* – in circumstances beyond their understanding or control. Vincent has 'an honest man's conscience in a murderer's body', but is helpless to do anything about it. The feminised, suggestible, passive Vincent, who cannot even drive a car, is contrasted with the no-nonsense masculine practicality and decisiveness of his cop brother-in-law Cliff (Paul Kelly – Ginny's enigmatic 'boyfriend' in *Crossfire*, made the same year), who does most of the work figuring out the complicated murder-and-hypnotism plot.

Like *Detour* (1945)*, *Fear in the Night* epitomises the inventive qualities of 1940s low-budget *film noir*. Maxwell Shane's script and direction manage to retain the attractively pulp feel of Cornell Woolrich's story (written under the name of William Irish) via plot contrivances, cheap look and variable performances. Kelley's somewhat blank performance style gives the impression – appropriately enough – that he

is sleepwalking through most of the movie. This was lead actor DeForest
Kelley's screen debut; after a journeyman career in film and television in
the 1950s/1960s, Kelley became a cult figure playing Dr McCoy in the
Star Trek television series and films, from the late 1960s onwards.

Maxwell Shane, in an otherwise undistinguished career, knew when
he had a good property: *Fear in the Night* has the odd distinction of
being the only *film noir* remade by the same director, with the same
script (despite different character names), for the same producers –
though it reverted to the title of Woolrich's original story. *Nightmare*
(1956), starring Kevin McCarthy as the protagonist/victim and Edward G.
Robinson as the cop brother-in-law, had a bigger budget and enhanced
production values but considerably less invention than the original.   JH

Dir: Maxwell Shane; **Prod**: William H. Pine, William C. Thomas; **Scr**: Maxwell Shane, from
William Irish's (Cornell Woolrich) short story *Nightmare*; **DOP**: Jack Greenhalgh (b&w); **Ed**:
Howard Smith; **Score**: Rudy Schrager; **Main Cast**: DeForest Kelley, Paul Kelly, Ann Doran,
Kay Scott, Robert Emmett Keane; **Prod Co**: Pine-Thomas.

Force of Evil
US, 1948 – 78 mins
Abraham Polonsky

After artistic and commercial success as screenwriter for Robert Rossen's *Body and Soul* (1947)*, Abraham Polonsky was encouraged by the film's producer and star, John Garfield, to direct a follow-up project for Enterprise Productions. The result – *Force of Evil* – is now widely acknowledged to be a lasting monument to the left-leaning film-making talents extinguished in the anti-Communist maelstrom of the HUAC investigations in the late 1940s and early 1950s. Enterprise Productions went under shortly after completion and Polonsky was eventually blacklisted. Today, for Martin Scorsese and the many others it has subsequently inspired, *Force of Evil* is undeniably a major work of twentieth-century American art, comparable in terms of its aesthetic complexity, political concern and humanist vision to the work of Arthur Miller or Orson Welles.

Force of Evil was adapted by Polonksy and Ira Wolfert from Wolfert's novel, *Tucker's People*, and reinvigorated the allegorical tale of Cain and Abel by recounting the conflict between two working-class brothers caught up in the machinations of New York gangland's numbers rackets. Joe (John Garfield) is the wisecracking, unscrupulous lawyer to a gangster chief who has plans to muscle in on the small operators in town, including Joe's weaker, but nonetheless principled, older brother, Leo (played with memorable verve and intensity by Thomas Gomez). Polonsky's film begins with majestic plunging views looking down on the teeming masses on the streets far below. It's a vision of 'an office in the clouds' that Joe wants Leo to share. It ends in tragedy with a now conscience-stricken Joe searching for his murdered brother amid the flotsam on the Hudson River. The densely plotted sequence of images charting Joe's forlorn descent to the bottom reaches of the city forms a perfect allegorical counterpoint to the film's opening.

Like many socially driven *film noirs* of the period, *Force of Evil* melds a highly dramatised *noir* style with an extraordinary amount of graphic detail picturing the everyday textures and realities of New York life. George Barnes's cinematography – strongly influenced by Polonsky's insistence that he immerse himself in the paintings of Edward Hopper – vividly captures the ways in which social surroundings help determine the nuances of character. The film is consistently alert to a sense of wider destinies, moral conflicts and political betrayals.

In part, this is also due to the verbal sparring and tensions of Polonksy and Wolfert's script and the way it is then enacted by the cast and interpreted by Barnes; especially in the cinematographer's consistently innovative two-shots depicting the exchanges between the brothers and between Joe and other leading characters. This is not surprising. Polonsky grew up in a Jewish immigrant neighbourhood and retained a feeling in this quintessential New York film for what William Pechter (1962) has called 'the sound of city speech, with its special repetitions and elisions, cadence and inflection, inarticulateness and crypto-poetry'. Indeed, Polonsky later commented that one of his aims in

Force of Evil was to 'use the succession of visual images, the appearances of human personality in the actors, and the rhythm of words in unison or counterpoint'. 'I varied the speed, intensity, congruence and conflict for design, emotion and goal, sometimes separating the three elements, sometimes using two or three together,' he stated. This is the measure of the film. It is one of the very few, and certainly the most politically astute, examples of the American *film noir* when word and image are correlated together in such a complex fashion so as to depict a human universe utterly bankrupted by greed and financial gain. AP

Dir: Abraham Polonsky; **Prod**: Bob Roberts; **Scr**: Abraham Polonsky, Ira Wolfert from Ira Wolfert's novel *Tucker's People*; **DOP**: George Barnes (b&w); **Ed**: Art Seid; **Score**: David Raksin; **Main Cast**: John Garfield, Thomas Gomez, Beatrice Pearson, Roy Roberts, Howland Chamberlain, Marie Windsor; **Prod Co**: Enterprise Productions.

Foreign Land (*Terra estrangeira*)
Brazil/Portugal, 1996 – 100 mins
Walter Salles, Daniela Thomas

Walter Salles is best known for *The Motorcycle Diaries* (2004) and *Central Station* (1998) but also produced notable Brazilian productions like *City of God* (2002) and *Lower City* (2005). These films, like many other recent Latin American productions, combine engaging stories and characters with the impulse to explore socio-economic realities. This is equally the case with *Foreign Land*, Salles's second feature, co-directed with frequent collaborator Daniela Thomas. Although not conventionally *noir* in appearance, *Foreign Land* uses a high-contrast, black-and-white photographic style, with bleached-out or inky black effects in many shots. Its deep-focus compositions in often very striking landscapes are reminiscent of *cinema nôvo* films like Glauber Rocha's *Barravento* (1962), and hand-held camera sequences and jump cuts proliferate. Among the many strengths of this location-shot film is its acute sense of time and place.

Aspiring actor Paco (Fernando Alves Pinto) lives in straitened circumstances with his doting mother in São Paulo, 1990. The new, democratically elected government's decision to freeze private savings causes chaos; the shock kills the ageing mother, destroying her dream of returning to her Basque origins in San Sebastian, Spain. Paco's life collapses but, determined to see San Sebastian on his mother's behalf, he becomes involved in smuggling a supposedly antique violin to Lisbon. Meanwhile, in Lisbon, intercut with Paco's story, expatriate Brazilian Alex (Fernanda Torres) has her own problems (with work, growing old, and her drug-taking boyfriend Miguel, involved in a shady gems deal) and wants to return home to Brazil. Paco's and Alex's minor criminal paths cross in Lisbon, which, as Paco is told, 'isn't the right place to find anyone – it's the ideal place to lose someone, or get lost'. When Miguel is killed, Paco's and Alex's fates come together in this 'foreign land' where, as the tagline says, 'love and danger meet', and, as befits *noir* paranoia, the plot takes off in unexpected directions.

Alex is a sort of enigmatic *femme fatale* – though she looks more like Maribel Verdú in *Y tu mamá también* (Alfonso Cuarón, 2001) than Rita Hayworth – by turns put upon, hard as nails, grieving, loving, while Paco is a sort of innocent out of his depth, a fall guy surviving on his instincts. His realisation about the fix he is in comes in a club scene where *fado* – bleak songs about fate, destiny – is being sung. Alex and Paco, increasingly attracted to each other, become a 'couple on the run'. At the end of the film they flee to Spain, where they fight off their pursuers and escape. Alex drives on towards San Sebastian with Paco dying in her lap, sobbing/singing to him the 'Honey Baby' song ('Vapor Barato') which the soundtrack takes up for the concluding aerial shot of them on the road. This fine sequence is perhaps weakened by what feels like an unnecessary epilogue in which the smuggled violin – the 'MacGuffin' – being played on a metro station, spills its diamonds, which scatter, unseen, among passing feet.

Foreign Land explores Lusophone identities and tensions: Paco wants to leave Brazil, Alex wants to return (although, as she says, looking across the Atlantic from 'the very edge of Europe', 'they thought paradise was somewhere over there. Poor Portuguese – they ended up discovering Brazil'). The black Angolans in Paco's hotel, for whom whites spell trouble, provide a colonial dimension: as Paco's friend Loli, says, looking out over the Tagus, forget about discovering the new world, 'it takes [the Portuguese] three hours to cross that fucking bridge'. JH

Dir: Walter Salles, Daniela Thomas; **Prod**: António da Cunha Telles, Flávio R. Tambellini; **Scr**: Marcos Bernstein, Millor Fernandes, Walter Salles, Daniela Thomas; **DOP**: Walter Carvalho (b&w); **Ed**: Felipe Lacerda, Walter Salles; **Score**: José Miguel Wisnik; **Main Cast**: Fernando Alves Pinto, Fernanda Torres, Alexandre Borges, João Lagarto, Luis Melo, Laura Cardoso, Tchéky Karyo; **Prod Co**: Videofilmes Produçoes Ltda, Animatógrafo.

Get Carter
UK, 1971 – 112 mins
Mike Hodges

Mike Hodges's bleakly atmospheric Tyneside gangster film has steadily grown in stature over the years and is now rated by a younger generation of (largely male) fans and critics as one of the greatest British crime films ever made. Its strengths rest in the quality of all its main performances, its acute sense of location and, above all, its modernist tone and visual style that seems to effortlessly combine the candid observational style of British social realism with the more oblique precision of European art cinema.

London gangster Jack Carter (Michael Caine) has returned to his hometown of Newcastle to attend the funeral of his brother Frank, who has recently died in mysterious circumstances. He reacquaints himself with his old haunts and soon begins to suspect that Frank was murdered. Carter finds himself embroiled in an internecine web of underworld rivalries set against a backdrop of gambling, drugs and local town-hall corruption. On discovering the role of Doreen (Petra Markham), his niece – or maybe daughter – in a related vice-ring, he sets about ruthlessly planning his violent revenge.

For anyone watching *Get Carter* today what strikes one most powerfully is its evocation of a now bygone era. The émigré cinematographer, Wolfgang Suschitzky, dramatically captures Tyneside life in the early part of the 1970s when ordinary fashions still carried echoes of the 'Swinging Sixties' and the coal- and shipyards of the city had yet to fall into their terminal decline of the 1980s. At the geographical heart of the film lies the ugly concrete austerity of the Trinity Centre multistorey car park where Jack meets the local gangland enforcer, Cliff Brumby (Bryan Mosley). The building's lack of human scale and the fraudulent complicity of its owners and designers make it an emblem of the moral bankruptcy that surrounds it. Indirectly, it also links the gangsters' contemporary criminal empires with relics of the older British Empire evoked by the corroding docks and factories that populate the Newcastle skyline.

Caine plays Carter as a cold-blooded psychopath in a London pinstriped suit with just enough banter and sexual charisma to leaven his cynical and brutal encounters with the locals. He's seen on the train north reading Raymond Chandler's *Farewell, My Lovely* and spends the film working his way through a packet of Gitanes cigarettes. Steve Chibnall (2003) relates *Get Carter* to a cycle of films at the time such as *The Reckoning* (Jack Gold, 1970) that took 'a jaundiced view of the relationships between metropolitan and provincial life'. Undoubtedly, much of the film's underlying psychological tension comes from the central relationship between Caine's established southern 'spiv' persona and the parade of northern types played by Britain's leading working-class character actors of the time. This conflict, however, is also articulated within the *mise en scène*. The everyday realities of Newcastle life are captured with a detached and even sociological precision lending the film, at times, a visible semi-documentary aesthetic. This contrasts with the more dramatically stylised sequences that place Carter directly in the centre of the action. Here, the framings are more geometrical and fluid and the control over space and time less illusionistic and more fragmentary. In this way, and along with his clearly problematic sexual politics, Carter is clearly a vintage *film noir* protagonist who, by the time of his unexpected and violent demise, has been left bereft of any meaningful place to go.

Stephen T. Kay's remake (2000) cast Sylvester Stallone as a Las Vegas gangster who returns to Seattle. In a nod to his by then iconic performance in the infinitely superior original, Michael Caine starred as Cliff Brumby. Mike Hodges has continued to make a significant contribution to British *film noir* with *Croupier* (1998) and *I'll Sleep When I'm Dead* (2003)*. AP

Dir: Mike Hodges; **Prod**: Michael Klinger, Michael Caine; **Scr**: Mike Hodges from Ted Lewis's novel *Jack's Return Home*; **DOP**: Wolfgang Suschitzky (colour); **Ed**: John Trumper; **Score**: Roy Budd; **Main Cast**: Michael Caine, Ian Hendry, Britt Ekland, John Osborne, Rosemarie Dunham, Tony Beckley, Petra Markham, Bryan Mosley; **Prod Co**: MGM.

Gilda
US, 1946 – 106 mins
Charles Vidor

Gilda revolves around two love triangles. In the first – barely disguised homoerotic – relationship, down-on-his-luck gambler (and, it's implied, war veteran) Johnny Farrell (Glenn Ford) is 'picked up' in Buenos Aires by mysterious Ballin Mundson (George Macready) and put in charge of his casino (the triangle is completed, rather unconventionally, by Mundson's vicious, phallic 'little friend', his sword stick). They agree to exclude women, but Mundson returns from a trip with Gilda (Rita Hayworth) in tow, setting up the second triangle and creating havoc, since Johnny and Gilda have been lovers and remain passionately bitter and confused about each other. Why Mundson wanted a wife is not clear: he likes to 'buy' pretty things like Johnny and Gilda but hate is the only emotion that genuinely excites him. Johnny's and Gilda's rekindled love/hate relationship drives the narrative forward through a combination of jealousy and misogyny.

Gilda prompted Richard Dyer's observation (1998) that *film noir* 'is characterised by a certain anxiety over the existence and definition of masculinity and normality'. Johnny's voice-over begins the film but then fades away, as if his control of the storytelling cannot be sustained. Spectator sympathies shift to Gilda as we watch Johnny tortured by unrealised desire for Gilda and her apparent infidelity. When Ballin disappears, presumed dead, Johnny marries Gilda, but only to take masochistic pleasure in confining and humiliating her. As Gilda puts it, 'You wouldn't think a woman could marry two insane men in one lifetime.'

Gilda did not fit easily into 1940s movie stereotypes: the *New York Times* reviewer was baffled by Gilda's 'perplexing lack of motive' but apparently blind to the psychosexual hangups of the male characters. Perhaps, as Sheri Chinen Biesen (2005) suggests, the film's women producer (Virginia Van Upp) and writers (Marion Parsonnet and Jo

Eisinger) were a factor in the film's sexual politics. The film's trailer implied that Gilda was more *femme fatale* than wronged woman, and Gilda does fulfil some of the functions of the *femme fatale*. Her sexualised appearance and overt sexuality unsettle the male characters, but she is far from the dangerous, duplicitous Kathy in *Out of the Past* (1947)* or Coral in *Dead Reckoning** (1947)* – or Hayworth's own *The Lady from Shanghai* (1947)*. Gilda's rendition of 'Put the Blame on Mame' is less a provocation – except to Johnny – than a desperate plea for help and release. Hayworth was Columbia's biggest star, at the peak of her idealised glamour in *Gilda* (the impoverished billsticker in *Bicycle Thieves* [1948] is pasting a poster for the film when, calamitously, his bike is stolen). Looking back over the wreckage of her private life, Hayworth rued that men 'went to bed with Gilda and woke up with me'.

Though much of the film is lit in high key, cinematographer Rudolph Maté (later the director of *The Dark Past* [1948] and *D.O.A.* [1950]*) devises some elaborately *noir* compositions which are strikingly expressive of characters' power relationships. There are also some extraordinary shots in which characters' barely visible faces suggest dark and confused emotions.

Gilda was one of several 1940s *film noirs*, including *Cornered* (1945)* and *Notorious* (1946), set in a Nazi-infiltrated Argentina. Only the philosophical minor character locals see what is really going on in the characters' twisted private lives and in Mundson's Nazi-linked, secret tungsten cartel. Appropriately, it is they who preside over the non-*noir* 'happy end': Mundson returns and is killed and Johnny and Gilda are reunited and leave to go 'clear home' – as if all their troubles were some foreign intrigue. JH

Dir: Charles Vidor; **Prod**: Virginia Van Upp; **Scr**: Marion Parsonnet, Jo Eisinger from a story by E. A. Ellington; **DOP**: Rudolph Maté (b&w); **Ed**: Charles Nelson; **Score**: Morris Stoloff; **Main Cast**: Rita Hayworth, Glenn Ford, George Macready, Joseph Calleia, Steven Geray; **Prod Co**: Columbia.

The Glass Key
US, 1942 – 85mins
Stuart Heisler

This Dashiell Hammett adaptation reprised the Alan Ladd/Veronica Lake partnership in *This Gun for Hire* released six months earlier, and can be defined as an early *film noir* less for its visual style than for its repertory of themes about corruption and wealth and the ambiguous morality of its main character. Ed Beaumont (Alan Ladd) is the taciturn, loyal sidekick and aide to Paul Madvig (Brian Donlevy), a good-humouredly corrupt political boss backing a reform candidate for governor because he fancies his daughter, Janet (Veronica Lake). Madvig's manoeuvres provoke trouble from his former racketeer partner Nick Varna (Joseph Calleia), who Beaumont has to take care of.

Donlevy's Madvig is a somewhat awkward figure, combining a reprise of Donlevy's comic, dumb-lug governor-by-accident in Preston Sturges's *The Great McGinty* (1940) and a 1930s style mobster. By contrast, Ladd's character seems strikingly modern – isolated and inward-looking, some way from the damaged, smiling killer of *This Gun for Hire*. Perhaps most modern is the ambiguity surrounding his sexuality. Although there is immediate chemistry between Ladd's and Lake's characters, Lake is clearly more up for it, and Ladd's attraction to her remains less obvious. Certainly, Ladd's scenes with Lake contrast sharply with the brief but tender and playful scenes with the nurse (Frances Gifford) when Beaumont is laid up in hospital. Beaumont seems willing, coldly, to sacrifice Janet at the end (like Spade at the end of *The Maltese Falcon* [1941]*, another Hammett adaptation) by having her convicted for her father's crime, with Janet incredulous that neither her social position nor her feminine charm are able to protect her ('I was getting worried … we'd have to hang the girl to make the old man crack'). Only at the very end does Beaumont confess that he 'has it bad' for her.

An essential counterpoint to the halting, cool Ladd–Lake relationship is the sexual ambiguity most startlingly implied in the homoerotic undertow of the sado-masochistic beating of Beaumont by Varna's heavy, Jeff (William Bendix): 'He likes it, don't you baby?' Almost equally painful to watch are Beaumont's coldly cynical seduction of the corrupt newspaper publisher's wife in front of her husband, his theft of the man's will shortly after he kills himself and his standing by as Jeff strangles Varna. As Lawrence Alloway (1971) has suggested, this is the movie in which, following *This Gun for Hire*, Ladd 'moved from anti-hero to hero, though of an amoral sort'. Ultimately, though, Ladd's character is to a large extent unreadable, not helped by the cop-out happy ending which finally unites Ladd and Lake but fails to resolve the film's many ambiguities.

Like *The Maltese Falcon*, *The Glass Key* was first made – pretty successfully – in the mid-1930s, directed by Frank Tuttle (who later directed *This Gun for Hire*), with George Raft and Edward Arnold in the Ladd and Donlevy roles. *Miller's Crossing* (Joel Coen [1990], with Gabriel Byrne, Albert Finney and Marcia Gay Harden in the Ladd, Donlevy and Lake roles) is an ironic cocktail of motifs from various crime/gangster films, but owes a considerable debt to Hammett in general and *The Glass Key* in particular. JH

Dir: Stuart Heisler; **Prod**: Fred Kohlmar; **Scr**: Jonathan Latimer from Dashiell Hammett's novel; **DOP**: Theodor Sparkuhl (b&w); **Ed**: Archie Marshek; **Score**: Victor Young; **Main Cast**: Brian Donlevy, Veronica Lake, Alan Ladd, Bonita Granville, Joseph Calleia, William Bendix, Richard Denning, Moroni Olsen, Frances Gifford; **Prod Co**: Paramount.

Gun Crazy
US, 1950 – 87 mins
Joseph H. Lewis

Gun Crazy, though largely rural in setting and using little low-key or *chiaroscuro* lighting, is a key *film noir* for its representation of crime, violence and eroticism. Like Joseph H. Lewis's other major *noir*, *The Big Combo* (1955)*, it is also a supreme example of what could be achieved within the limited means of the B-picture – precisely the kind of film which inspired French *nouvelle vague* films such as Jean-Luc Godard's *Breathless* (1960). Unlike couple-on-the-run crime pictures like Fritz Lang's *You Only Live Once* (1937) and Nicholas Ray's *They Live by Night* (1948)*, *Gun Crazy* refuses any emphasis on the essential innocence of protagonists caught up in a world beyond their control. Rather, Bart (John Dall) and Annie Laurie (a wonderful performance by the British actor Peggy Cummins) are bound together by their mutual obsession and expertise with guns and by unbridled sexual attraction bordering on *amour fou*, that passion beyond reason beloved by the surrealists for its rejection of more domesticated 'love' and romance.

Bart meets Laurie at a carnival sideshow featuring her sharp-shooting skills. Laurie challenges spectators to a shooting contest and Bart beats her. They look at each other 'like a couple of wild animals', their raw sexual attraction bristling alongside their shooting skills. Bart is warned that 'she ain't the type that makes a happy home' but they take off together and get married, Laurie torn between 'wanting to be good' and wanting to 'kick back' at life. When they run out of money, Laurie wants to take to violent crime, but the essentially gentle Bart is reluctant. However, when Laurie confronts him, seductively, with losing her or joining her, he greedily kisses her, and they take on something of the classic *femme fatale* and compromised hero roles. The film's original release title (January 1950), *Deadly Is the Female*, reflects this aspect of the film, but the re-release title (August 1950), *Gun Crazy* (the original story title) better reflects its enigmatic, irrational spirit.

Lewis orchestrates their life of crime and passion to enhance the visceral thrill of danger and violence, in the meat-packing factory heist, for example, and most famously in the small-town bank robbery, shot in one long take. The hand-held camera remains in the car's backseat as they excitedly approach the town, stays with Laurie in the car when Bart enters the bank, waits with her for his return and their getaway. The tension generated by the action sequences is skilfully mixed with the

A life of crime and passion: Bart (John Dall) and Annie Laurie (Peggy Cummins) in mid-bank robbery in *Gun Crazy*

pair's different responses to violence: Laurie gets high on it, while Bart is conscience-stricken. Although their elemental attraction to each other constantly brings them together – superbly realised when a getaway plan involving separate cars and different directions is quickly abandoned because they just can't leave each other – they are of course fated to die, together, by the gun. The film's strange finale – a return to Bart's childhood, the claustrophobic studio set of a mist-enshrouded swamp, a final pledge of love – is hard to read. As Bart's childhood friends, now representing the law, close in, Bart shoots Laurie before being shot down himself beside her. Should we take this as a conventionally moral ending – Bart protecting his childhood friends? Jim Kitses (1996) insists that 'Bart dispatches his love to protect her from herself, and the shedding of more blood.'

Though not a precise remake, *Guncrazy* (Tamra Davis, 1992), a love-on-the-run/obsession-with-guns/crime-spree movie, counts *Gun Crazy* – as well as *They Live by Night**, *Pretty Poison* (1968) and *Badlands* (1974) – among its inspirations.   JH

Dir: Joseph H. Lewis; **Prod**: Frank King, Maurice King; **Scr**: MacKinlay Kantor, Millard Kaufman, Dalton Trumbo (uncredited) from Kantor's *Saturday Evening Post* story *Gun Crazy*; **DOP**: Russell Harlan (b&w); **Ed**: Harry Gerstad; **Score**: Victor Young; **Main Cast**: Peggy Cummins, John Dall, Berry Kroeger, Morris Carnovsky; **Prod Co**: King Brothers.

He Ran All the Way
US, 1951 – 77 mins
John Berry

Not quite coincidentally, the height of *film noir* in the late 1940s/early 1950s was also the period when Hollywood's anti-Communist witch-hunt was at its fiercest. *He Ran All the Way* is a good example of the type of film leftist film-makers – writers and actors as well as directors – were trying to make within the system. Films like Joseph Losey's *The Prowler* (1951), Abraham Polonsky's *Force of Evil* (1948)*, Cy Endfield's *The Sound of Fury* (aka *Try and Get Me*, 1951) were *noir* thrillers but also character studies which opened out to social critique. By 1952, as a result of HUAC investigation and blacklisting, Berry had relocated to France, Losey and Endfield to Britain. Berry's and the screenwriters' names were initially removed from the credits of *He Ran All the Way*, which Garfield also produced. The film was ready for release in 1950 but rumours about Garfield's Communist sympathies led to theatres refusing to book the film, until he appeared before HUAC and denied allegations against him. It was Garfield's last film: he died of a heart attack in 1952, many said as a result of stress and blacklisted neglect by the industry.

Garfield plays Nick Robey, a troubled, confused, unemployed, working-class, petty criminal punk with a dysfunctional home life. In this sense he is like Bowie and Keechie in Nicholas Ray's *They Live by Night* (1948)*, 'never properly introduced to the world we live in'. Dragged into a factory payroll robbery which goes wrong, Nick runs off with the money. He befriends Peg (Shelley Winters), slightly dull, almost pretty, but loyal, the perfect foil for Nick's desperate toughness. She takes him home to her family's apartment, where Nick and Peg become increasingly attracted to each other and Nick enjoys the family's strong ties. However, suspecting they know the truth about him, he holds them hostage, terrorising them yet wanting at the same time to be part of the ordinary, solid, working-class family values they represent. Director John Berry superbly evokes the working-class ambiance of the public swimming pool where Nick meets Peg, and Peg's family's modest, cramped apartment, where privacy is almost impossible.

The film ends very powerfully as Peg and Nick, overcome by despair and self-loathing, descend the apartment block stairs to the street and what Nick hopes is his escape. At the street door, confronted by Peg's father (Wallace Ford), ferociously defending his family, Peg is forced to choose between her father and Nick. Barely hesitating, she shoots Nick, who staggers into the dark, wet street and slumps to the kerb. In disbelief, he watches the arrival of the car that Peg has bought for his escape, representing both the possibility of freedom and a consumer good, both beyond his reach. He crawls towards it and touches it, then collapses dead in the gutter. Peg, her father and bystanders look on, contemplating the waste.

Garfield's tough, smart, sympathetic persona, often in working-class roles, was integral to several important *film noirs*, including *Force of Evil*, *Body and Soul* (1947) and *The Postman Always Rings Twice* (1946)*. Often referred to as the American Jean Gabin, Garfield's role here is comparable with Gabin's in *Le Jour se lève* (1939)*. Berry had earlier directed *Casbah* (1948, with Yvonne de Carlo and Tony Martin), a curious, musical remake of Julien Duvivier's French *noir Pépé le Moko* (1936). JH

Dir: John Berry; **Prod**: Bob Roberts; **Scr**: Guy Endore, Hugo Butler, Dalton Trumbo (uncredited) from Sam Ross's novel; **DOP**: James Wong Howe (b&w); **Ed**: Francis D. Lyon; **Score**: Franz Waxman; **Main Cast**: John Garfield, Shelley Winters, Wallace Ford, Selena Royle; **Prod Co**: Bob Roberts Productions.

He Walked by Night
US, 1948 – 80 mins
Alfred Werker

He Walked by Night is essentially a police procedural movie ('From the Homicide Files of the Los Angeles Police', as the poster put it) and can be linked to the growing influence at the time of the more documentary-inspired, realist *film noir* in films such as *The House on 92nd Street* (1945), *Call Northside 777* (1948)* and *The Naked City* (1948), associated with producers like Louis de Rochemont. These qualities are strongly suggested by the use of a narrator and the montage of police and crime activity in Los Angeles, as well as by the overall amount of screen time devoted to the detailing of technical aspects of vital police work. We see, for example, the dogged, quietly spoken forensics expert Lee's work with Photofit technology and the analysis of shell casings, which provide essential information leading to the identification of the thief/killer. There is also an early use on film of the word 'dragnet', set up to corner the villain. Lee is played by Jack Webb, a radio star appearing in his first film, who went on to set up the radio police drama series *Dragnet*, with Webb as lead detective Joe Friday, which then became one of the most successful and influential US 1950s television series (as well as a 1954 feature film, directed by Webb).

In truth, *He Walked by Night* is a somewhat split film. More than just being a police procedural, and thus almost documentary in tone, it is also a lively and intriguing action thriller with strongly *noir* visual characteristics. It is well known that Anthony Mann worked on the film and shot many of its action and location sequences, effectively replacing Alfred Werker as director. The look and pace of Mann's other Eagle-Lion Film releases with John Alton as cinematographer (and other crew) – *Raw Deal* (1948) and *T-Men* (1947)* (both with similar semi-documentary elements) – certainly suggest that the pair's influence on the film was crucial.

At this thriller level, one of the most intriguing aspects of the film is the characterisation of Roy Martin (Richard Basehart), who kills a policeman

Forensic *noir*: (left to right) Jones (Jimmy Cardwell), Brennan (Scott Brady) and Lee (Jack Webb) in the lab in *He Walked by Night*

when disturbed while trying to rob an electronics store. While Martin is clearly steely intentioned and single-minded, he remains almost completely enigmatic, a true *noir* protagonist – an absolute loner, alienated from all social contact other than that with his dog. We never know why he does what he does, but several elements in his make-up are suggestive. There is something unsettling about the objects of his theft and inventiveness having to do with electronics. The inclusion of ex-service equipment and the man's military background in radio – along with the paranoid anti-Communism of the period – suggest espionage. Quite different, though, is the way in which Martin 'disappears' several times, evading police pursuit by sliding smoothly under the pavement into the drain system, suggesting something subterranean or furtively animal, certainly something 'other'.

Mann and Alton come into their own in set-piece *noir* action sequences like the failed police trap at the electronics company or the police ambush of Martin's Hollywood bungalow, with Martin alone inside in the darkness, wary and uneasy, his figure cut into ribbons by the light from the shutters. And the film's finale – Martin in the storm drains pursued by the police, with the gyrating torches of the pursuers and the water creating an exciting play of light and shadow – is tremendous stuff. JH

Dir: Alfred Werker, Anthony Mann (uncredited); **Prod**: Bryan Foy, Robert T. Kane; **Scr**: Crane Wilbur, John C. Higgins, Harry Essex from Wilbur's story; **DOP**: John Alton (b&w); **Ed**: Alfred De Gaetano; **Score**: Leonid Raab; **Main cast**: Richard Basehart, Scott Brady, Roy Roberts, Whit Bissell, Jimmy Cardwell, Jack Webb; **Prod Co**: Bryan Foy Productions, Eagle-Lion Films.

High and Low (*Tengoku to jigoku*)
Japan, 1963 – 143 mins
Kurosawa Akira

Kurosawa's gripping investigative thriller begins with a panoramic landscape view of the modern Japanese city. Although the film is ostensibly a blend of kidnap drama and *noir* police procedural – it was based on Ed McBain's American crime novel, *King's Ransom* – it is thus immediately clear that postwar Japanese urban society is as much under investigation as the elusive kidnapper sought by the local police.

Having said this, *High and Low* only really begins to unravel spatially after a lengthy examination of the secluded hilltop home of Gondo (Mifune Toshiro), the wealthy industrialist whose son has been the victim of a failed kidnap attempt. Instead, the son of Gondo's humble chauffeur has been taken and Gondo and the police are suddenly faced with the ethical and professional dilemma of how to counteract the demands of a mysterious male voice speaking by telephone from somewhere in the sweltering depths of the townscape below. Through a combination of relatively static, deep-space long takes and intensive close-ups that survey the anxious expressions of the main protagonists, Kurosawa's representation of the businessman's geometric modernist cage steadily evokes a domestic world set apart from ordinary life.

The hatching of the plan to hunt the criminal down is therefore as much a release from this social and emotional claustrophobia as a coherent attempt to foil the kidnapper. Crucially, a key part of the opening up of the film takes place on one of Japan's new high-speed bullet trains. Instead of the stately vistas from the windows of Gondo's mansion, we have a succession of fluid screens within screens. The addition of recorded 8mm film footage shot by the police adds to the growing dispersal of space and time, and we now begin to see the presence of the modern in the form of toll-roads, bridges, new housing developments and wider emblems of a heavily industrialised, media-saturated urban economy.

The revelation to the audience of the figure of the disgruntled
kidnapper, Takeuchi (Yamazaki Tsutomu), long before the police catch up
with him, sets up a system of psychological counterpoint between his
native intelligence and the lack of social awareness demonstrated
by Gondo. His isolation and relative young age (suggesting a figure
symptomatic of Japanese cinema's then new figure of rebellious male
youth) also marks him differently from the all-male teams of older
professionals (police, business executives and newspapermen) on his case.

Eventually, in a key scene before the eventual capture of Takeuchi,
coherent narrative and social space begins to fragment altogether. In an
extended sequence set in a Yokohama nightclub, the port city to the

Surveillance, professionalism and modernity: Chief Detective Tokura (Nakadai Tatsuya) (left)
leads the investigation in *High and Low*

south of Tokyo, reflective surfaces and confusing light patterns play off each other as we see a world apart from the polite surfaces of contemporary Japanese society. The vibrant, cosmopolitan mix of music and people works in ambiguous contrast to the committed, group-centred professionalism of the film's main narrative agents, with the visible evidence of drug dealing clearly denying any sense that this milieu could be an admissible alternative to the pressures of modern life.

Regardless of the film's detailed investigation of both the act of crime and the tensions of modernisation, *High and Low* refuses any conclusive reading as a *film noir*. Despite their emphasis on surveillance, for example, the police emphatically fail to see the social divisions revealed in the course of their work and when Gondo and Takeuchi actually come face to face in prison – no longer high and low but horizontal partners – we're still not really sure what has motivated the men to come to this. The film's politics thus remain opaque, with only the telling devastating long shot seen earlier of Gondo's Norman Bates-like mansion high above, reflected in a river full of pollution low below, remaining any kind of viable clue to the literal translation of the film's title: 'heaven and hell'. AP

Dir: Kurosawa Akira; **Prod**: Kikushima Ryuzo, Tanaka Tomiyuki; **Scr**: Hisaita Eijiro, Kikushima Ryuzo, Kurosawa Akira, Oguni Hideo from Ed McBain's novel *King's Ransom*; **DOP**: Nakai Asakazu, Saito Takao (b&w); **Ed**: Kurosawa Akira; **Score**: Sato Masaru; **Main Cast**: Mifune Toshiro, Nakadai Tatsuya, Kagawa Kyoko, Mihashi Tatsuya, Sada Yutaka, Yamazaki Tsutomu; **Prod Co**: Toho, Kurosawa Production Co.

A History of Violence
US, 2005 – 92 mins
David Cronenberg

Violence, or the threat – and even allure – of violence, often in ingenious or exotic forms, is integral to US crime pictures and *film noir* in particular, but rarely is it the central concern. Its centrality to *A History of Violence* is what makes this largely rural neo-*noir* so interesting. From the start, Cronenberg plunges us into extreme violence – the more effective for being so casual – as two psychotic, small-time gunmen leave mayhem behind them at a motel, in a scene which evokes – though with significantly greater violence – the prologue to *The Killers* (1946)*.

Deceptively, these two killers are not the story's focus; alongside them, the film introduces the small town of Millbrook, Indiana, and the Stall family. Tom Stall (Viggo Mortensen), to all appearances ordinary and neighbourly, runs the town's diner. The earlier killers brutally hold up the diner and set in train the film's narrative dynamic: acting intuitively, Stall skilfully kills both men. Tom becomes a hero, his story splashed across news media. Neither the townspeople, nor we spectators, have any reason as yet to doubt Tom, but both they and we begin to doubt appearances when one-eyed mobster Carl Fogarty (Ed Harris) arrives at Tom's diner and insists on calling him Joey (or 'crazy fucking Joey' – since Fogarty claims Joey took his eye out with barbed wire). Our understanding begins to shift as we recognise the not unfamiliar *noir* scenario of the figure with a shadowy past who tries to hide and lead a quiet, mainstream life but is dragged back, against his will, to deal with unfinished business (for example, *Out of the Past* [1947]*, which could have been a good title for this film too).

The mobsters' threat to Tom's family – his wife, Edie (Maria Bello) and two children – precipitates a further demonstration of his ruthless violence, and hence a family crisis about his true identity. This in turn pushes Tom to return alone to his mob past. He drives his pickup through small towns and countryside to Philadelphia – the familiar *noir* journey into the night, the city and the past – to confront his wealthy mobster brother Richie (William Hurt), a creepy figure in his vulgar mansion. Richie appears to welcome Tom but, more concerned about his place in the mob, and incapable of seeing 'the upside' of the straight life, casually orders his garrotting. Tom's deadly skills enable him to fight off and kill his attackers, including Richie.

Tom may not be doomed by his past, as many 1940s *noir* protagonists were, but nothing is resolved, neither his identity as husband, father and citizen, nor the possibility of further repercussions from the darkness of his previous life. Cronenberg gives nothing away in the final scene depicting Tom's return home. The family is having dinner, but there is no welcome; his young daughter sets his place and his teenage son passes the meat loaf, but his wife does not look at him and no-one speaks; the screen goes black.

As the title suggests, this is both a story about violence and the story of a character with 'a history of violence' (adapted from a graphic novel, though Cronenberg denies having known this), but the question of violence is not restricted to Tom. Earlier, his son Jack (Ashton Holmes) responds to bullying with violence, and his wife seems both attracted and repelled by Tom's potential for violence. But Tom remains central to the film: as his brother asks of Tom's/Joey's identity and double life, 'When you dream, are you still Joey?' JH

Dir: David Cronenberg; **Prod**: Chris Bender, J. C. Spink; **Scr**: Josh Olson, from John Wagner's & Vince Locke's graphic novel; **DOP**: Peter Suschitzky (colour); **Ed**: Ronald Sanders; **Score**: Howard Shore; **Main Cast**: Viggo Mortensen, Maria Bello, Ed Harris, William Hurt, Ashton Holmes; **Prod Co**: BenderSpink.

The Hitch-Hiker
US, 1953 – 71 mins
Ida Lupino

Renowned for her intense and gutsy performances in tough Warner Brothers' action films like Raoul Walsh's *They Drive by Night* (1940), Ida Lupino turned to independent production with her husband, Collier Young, at the end of the 1940s. She directed this taut and brutal road *film noir* for their company, The Filmmakers, the year after she appeared as the female lead in *On Dangerous Ground* (1952)* (to which she also reputedly contributed one or more scenes behind the camera).

The Hitch-Hiker was based on a story by Daniel Mainwaring (*Out of the Past* [1947]*), who had borrowed elements from the true-life account of the notorious hitch-hiker killer, Billy Cook, captured on the run in Mexico a few years previously. Roy Collins (Edmond O'Brien) and Gilbert Bowen (Frank Lovejoy) are two friends on a fishing holiday who inadvertently pick up a wanted killer named Myers (William Talman) who holds the men violent hostage as they travel south of the border to evade the police. Talman plays Myers with threatening menace as he manipulates every situation on the road in order to ensure the pair neither escape nor draw attention to their desperate plight.

Lupino and the esteemed RKO cinematographer, Nicholas Musuraca, work effectively to integrate the two essential elements of the road *noir*: the claustrophobic intensity of the scenes depicting the car interiors and the expansive qualities of the exterior landscapes signalling the freedom the film's narrative constantly elides. As with his elegant and atmospheric rendering of light in the driving scenes of *Out of the Past*, Musuraca demonstrates that he is a master of illuminating the pressurised psychological intimacy of the car at night. Irregular lighting set-ups further distort the intense, damaged features of Myers's face as he sits in the backseat with his gun. By day, the light and arid textures of inland California (standing in for Mexico) evoke a harsh poetry similar to that of Walsh's earlier crime thriller with Lupino, *High Sierra* (1941).

Wanted killer Myers (William Talman) threatens Gilbert Bowen (Frank Lovejoy) (left) and Roy Collins (Edmond O'Brien) (right) in *The Hitch-Hiker*

The Hitch-Hiker relies as much on sound elements as visual style in order to convey narrative tension. Again, these relate either to the car or the natural world outside its temporary confines. The car radio is the means by which Myers tracks the progress of the police on his tail. At night, by the roadside, coyotes are heard wailing in the darkness beyond. When the car horn becomes trapped, the two elements become fused as the machine dispenses a macabre blare over the empty expanse of the dry plains. Importantly, the radio also becomes the device by which the plot opens up as we cut intermittently to the American and Mexican police colluding to send false signals to Myers about their search. Without the aid of any retrospective voice-over as in the other great road *noir* of the classical period, *Detour* (1945)*, this thus sets up a chain of moral expectations which obviates the film's otherwise penetrating bleakness.

Ida Lupino famously resisted any attempts to categorise her as a woman director but it is worth pointing out that *The Hitch-Hiker is* the only American *film noir* in this book directed by a woman. It is worth noting too that there are no female characters to speak of in the film, giving it an intensely homosocial quality. This may suggest a potentially queer reading but rather, as Lauren Rabinovitz (1995) has argued, Lupino's work more starkly conveys 'a vision of hell that is masculinity fragmented into neurotic components of maladjustment in a world that orders adjustment'. AP

Dir: Ida Lupino; **Prod**: Collier Young; **Scr**: Ida Lupino, Collier Young, Robert L. Joseph, Daniel Mainwaring (uncredited); **DOP**: Nicholas Musuraca (b&w); **Ed**: Douglas Stewart; **Score**: Leith Stevens; **Main Cast**: Edmond O'Brien, Frank Lovejoy, William Talman, José Torvay; **Prod Co**: The Filmmakers.

I'll Sleep When I'm Dead
UK/US, 2003 – 103 mins
Mike Hodges

Mike Hodges established himself as a master of the British crime film with *Get Carter* (1971)* and has returned to it most obviously in *Croupier* (1997) and this film. Inevitably, critics compared *I'll Sleep When I'm Dead* with *Get Carter*, whose plot is similar (and whose closing beach sequence may be being invoked here), and found it too loosely plotted and, fatally, more self-consciously an 'ideas' film. Certainly, the film is more neo-*noir* than gangster film in its tendencies, with its great title evoking both pulp crime fiction – Charles Willeford, say – and existential anguish. *I'll Sleep When I'm Dead*, less self-conscious than the more cerebral, European art movie-like *Croupier* (a cult hit in the US), is an excellent example of British *film noir*'s preoccupation with what Andrew Spicer (2002) terms 'a critique of male prowess, potency, sexuality and criminality'.

I'll Sleep When I'm Dead begins with the surreal image of a golfer teeing off balls into the sea from a darkening, empty beach, watched by a smartly dressed figure in the dunes who disappears and reappears walking towards his parked car. A voice-over suggests flashback: 'Most thoughts are memories. And memories deceive. The dead are dead, they're gone. What's left to say he was here at all? Not much.' The film then crosscuts between the bearded, unkempt figure of Will (Clive Owen) living a solitary life in a camper van in remote Welsh countryside, and a younger, sharply dressed, confident young Londoner, Davey (Jonathan Rhys Meyers), a petty thief and drug dealer, on a round of casual dealing and seduction. Davey is followed, subjected to a brutally humiliating rape by Boad (Malcolm McDowell) – consumed by bitter disgust at Davey's lifestyle – and later commits suicide. Failing to make phone contact with Davey, Will returns to his former London stamping ground to investigate, evoking the not unfamiliar *noir* tale of the former criminal living a reclusive life but compelled to return to his former milieu.

Gradually, we learn that Will is Davey's older brother, formerly a feared South London gang boss, who disappeared suddenly. Following some kind of 'breakdown', Will is out of touch with his former associates and has become a recluse. As he articulates it to former lover Helen (Charlotte Rampling), he is 'living in grief – for a life wasted'. Defeating everyone's expectations about his return, Will uncovers the circumstances of Davey's death, takes on some of his former identity and lifestyle and finds and kills Boad.

The film's pleasures include its look and its scripting. The *noir*-ish nocturnal London sequences superbly render a decaying South London, in much the same way that Newcastle is pictured in *Get Carter*. Hodges and scriptwriter Trevor Preston – who share the credit 'A Mike Hodges– Trevor Preston film' (just as *Croupier* is a 'A Mike Hodges–Paul Mayersberg film') – do not spell out plot connections or character motivations. Instead, the film centres on Will's enigmatic state of mind and intentions, with Owen giving a superb performance that combines stillness with power. The enigmas continue to the end: why does Will promise to take Helen away but never turn up, leaving her waiting with a villain ready to take him down? Where will Will go and what will he do now? The conclusion reveals the flashback structure – the golfer on the beach observed by someone we now know is Will. As he drives away and disappears, the opening voice-over is repeated, clearly now speaking for Will himself as much as for Davey. JH

Dir: Mike Hodges; **Prod**: Michael Corriente, Mike Kaplan, Roger Marino; **Scr**: Trevor Preston; **DOP**: Michael Garfath (colour); **Ed**: Paul Carlin **Score**: Simon Fisher-Turner; **Main Cast**: Clive Owen, Charlotte Rampling, Jonathan Rhys Meyers, Malcolm McDowell, Jamie Forman; **Prod Co**: Mosaic Film Group, Revere Pictures, Will & Co.

I Married a Communist
US, 1949 – 73 mins
Robert Stevenson

One of several late 1940s/early 1950s *noir* thrillers, including *I Was a Communist for the FBI* (Gordon Douglas, 1951) and *Pickup on South Street* (1953)*, incorporating anti-Communist sentiments, *I Married a Communist* is another *film noir* in which the dark past comes back to haunt the protagonist and ultimately cause his death. The difference here is that that dark past has less to do with criminal or romantic transgressions than with former membership of the Communist Party.

The San Francisco-set story intertwines personal relationships, waterfront labour relations and Communist Party machinations. Brad Collins (Robert Ryan) and Nan (Laraine Day), having met and been married all within a week, concede they know nothing about each other. Brad has working-class roots and worked the docks but is now employed by the shipowners. Union leader Jim (Richard Rober) had expected to marry Nan, and Brad had an earlier relationship with glamorous Party member Chris (Janis Carter). When Brad suggests compromise in a labour dispute, Party boss Vanning (Thomas Gomez) – who throughout calls Brad by his Party name of 'Frank Johnson' – summons Brad. Their night-time meeting in a dark warehouse is carefully orchestrated by Vanning so that Brad witnesses the torture and murder of a renegade Party member. Vanning tries to blackmail Brad into working for the Party, insisting that the Party will decide 'who's out and when'. Vanning arranges the murder of both Nan's idealistic young brother and Chris, who has fallen for him, and prepares to eliminate Brad. Nan, avenging her brother's death and trying to protect Brad, joins him in the dark warehouse to confront Vanning. Brad is shot trying to protect Nan, but survives long enough to kill Vanning with – appropriately – a longshoreman's hook, evoking his dock-worker past. Brad confesses his mistakes to Nan and recommends her previous beau, Jim, as the right man for her.

As this summary makes clear, there is very little that is 'ideological' about Vanning and his comrades. As in *Pickup on South Street* Party members are, really, just racketeers – though Vanning makes reference to Brad/Frank being part of the 'embittered, lost generation of the 30s' that sought solutions in socialism. Even so, Gomez is very chilling as the ruthless *apparatchik* denying Party members private lives or emotional entanglements that get in the way of the Party's needs, destroying the movie's two central romantic relationships and arranging murders with no qualms. Robert Ryan plays Brad with his usual ambivalence and sense of barely contained violence; though the 'hero', he remains far from sympathetic. *I Married a Communist* is a curiosity rather than a great movie. Much of the film is shot in bland high key, but *noir* specialist cinematographer Nicholas Musuraca renders the night-time, deserted waterfront warehouse as a treacherous, threatening space and the two sequences which take place there are excitingly staged and lit.

The movie was made just before the second phase of the HUAC investigations, when paranoia about Communists in Hollywood remained intense. Screenwriter Daniel Mainwaring claimed that RKO boss Howard Hughes used the film's script to get rid of a lot of writers, directors and actors: anyone who refused to work on it was fired. The film was known in the US as both *I Married a Communist* and *The Woman on Pier 13*, the latter being used for its UK release (presumably to disguise its anti-Communist plot). *The Woman on Pier 13* is the more evocative title, though Nathaniel Rich (2005) tells us there *was* no Pier 13 on the San Francisco waterfront – and it is far from clear which 'woman' that title had in mind. JH

Dir: Robert Stevenson; **Prod**: Sid Rogell; **Scr**: Charles Grayson, Robert Hardy Andrews from George W.George's & George F. Slavin's story; **DOP**: Nicholas Musuraca (b&w); **Ed**: Roland Gross; **Score**: Leigh Harline; **Main Cast**: Robert Ryan, Laraine Day, John Agar, Thomas Gomez, Janis Carter; **Prod Co**: RKO.

I Wake Up Screaming
US, 1942 – 82 mins
H. Bruce Humberstone

Released just a few months after *The Maltese Falcon* (1941)*, which
established many of the early *noir* detective conventions, *I Wake Up
Screaming* shares with *Stranger on the Third Floor* (Boris Ingster, 1940)
the distinction of being one of the earliest in that strain of *noir* movies in
which the suspect needs to turn detective to prove his innocence.

Superficially brash, sophisticated New York promoter Frankie (Victor
Mature) and his smart friends wager that they can turn attractive 'hash-
slinger' Vicky Lynn (Carole Landis) into a celebrity. They succeed, but when
she is murdered Frankie becomes prime suspect. In alternating flashbacks,
Frankie and Vicky's feet-on-the-ground sister Jill (Betty Grable, excellent in
a rare dramatic role) tell the story to police interrogators. The police are
led by heavy, brooding detective Ed Cornell (Laird Cregar), determined
to put Frankie in the electric chair, or 'hot spot'. (*Hot Spot* was the US
working title and the film was first shown to critics under this title, which
was retained for the UK release, though *I Wake Up Screaming* – the
source novel's title – became the official US title.) In a famously menacing
scene, Frankie, tossing and turning in his sleep, wakes up in his darkened
apartment to find Cornell watching him and telling him that he will nail
him. To prove his innocence, Frankie enlists Jill's help. Though attracted to
him, she is also suspicious, until he shows himself to be as honest and
straightforward as she is. Cornell knows who murdered Vicky but wants
to punish Frankie for putting Vicky – the object of Cornell's voyeuristic
fantasy – out of his reach. Turning the tables on Cornell and confronting
Cornell in *his* apartment, Frankie – in shades of Fox's later *Laura* (1944)* –
finds an obsessive shrine to Vicky. Exposed, Cornell poisons himself before
he can be arrested. In the original novel, set in Hollywood, the situation of
the cop – supposedly based on pulp novelist Cornell Woolrich – was given
added poignancy by his being terminally ill with TB; here, though corrupt
and crazy, Cornell nevertheless arouses some sympathy.

Though Humberstone was a Fox contract director with an otherwise unremarkable career (directing several *Charlie Chan* films in the late 1930s), *I Wake Up Screaming* looks good and works well. Cregar's distinctive presence gives the film an eerie effectiveness and the film's overall darkness gives strong credence to Frankie's desperate predicament. After a blandly, high-key-lit opening, Frankie's and Jill's interrogations plunge us into a powerfully *noir* world, with high-contrast lighting and deep shadows, in which Cornell is often pictured in semi-darkness or with Venetian blind shadows across his face. The scene in which the unstable switchboard operator (an archetypically Elisha Cook, Jr role) reveals himself as the murderer is particularly atmospheric. Most of the film is set at night or in dark interiors, but two well-lit scenes – Frankie and Jill swimming at a local lido and emerging from an all-night cinema into bright morning light – effectively suggest the pair's essential straightforwardness. The script's smart humour reinforces their status as regular guys: dismissing Frankie's warning about marrying a hunted man, she quips that 'most married men have a hunted look anyway'; hiding out in the all-night cinema, the movie that bores them both silly is called – some years before *Brief Encounter* (1945) – *Flames of Passion*.

Fox used the same script, somewhat insipidly, for *Vicki* (Harry Horner, 1953), with Jeanne Crain as Jill, Jean Peters as Vicki, Elliott Reid as Frankie (renamed Steve) and Richard Boone as Cornell. JH

Dir: H. Bruce Humberstone; **Prod**: Milton Sperling; **Scr**: Dwight Taylor from Steve Fisher's novel; **DOP**: Edward Cronjager (b&w); **Ed**: Robert Simpson; **Score**: Cyril J. Mockridge; **Main Cast**: Betty Grable, Victor Mature, Carole Landis, Laird Cregar, William Gargan, Elisha Cook, Jr; **Prod Co**: Twentieth Century-Fox.

I Walk Alone
US, 1948 – 98mins
Byron Haskin

This underrated *noir* gangster film was an early example of the postwar trend for showing corporate crime organised as legitimate business – as in Don Siegel's 1964 version of *The Killers*, Sam Fuller's *Underworld USA* (1960) and *Point Blank* (1967)*. The film's central interest is the ways in which the world of crime had changed from the 1930s to the postwar world. Frankie Madison (Burt Lancaster) refused to squeal on his 1930s bootlegging partner Noll Turner (Kirk Douglas) and now emerges from fourteen years in prison determined to claim his half of the fortune that Noll's apparently legitimate nightclub has amassed in his absence. Driving along Broadway with his brother Dave (Wendell Corey), now Noll's accountant, Frankie comments that '14 years and it's still the same'; Dave replies that 'It only *looks* the same.' The film traces Frankie's bewilderment faced by the postwar world he encounters and his determination to get his due.

Despite Frankie's criminal past and willingness to continue his criminal activities, he is a sympathetic figure: he is the disadvantaged one and he still operates with a code of loyalty and honour. Noll, by contrast, though accepted by society, operates with corrupt and ruthless self-interest, his viciousness masked by charm and sophistication. In an extended scene, Frankie has managed to assemble only four, barely useful, old mob cronies to force Noll to hand over his share. Guns drawn, they confront Noll, who explains, grinning, that 'This is big business. We deal with banks and lawyers and a Dun and Bradstreet rating … . The old days are gone and you've gone with them.' Frankie, flummoxed, ends up throwing the company books across the office and impotently ripping up the accounts.

This key sequence about the new realities of crime as business is counterposed by two finely realised old-style brutally violent gangster scenes, both very *noir* in look – dark, urban, seedy. Frankie is beaten to a pulp in a dark back alley and collapses into the garbage, before being rescued by Dave. Dave, who switches sides and explains to Frankie how the business really works, is then targeted and murdered on the street at night and found dead on the sidewalk. Dave is not the only one to 'switch sides': Kay (Lizabeth Scott), a chanteuse in Noll's club and supposedly romantically attached to – though also exploited by – him, shows that she is not the *femme fatale* she first appears by joining forces with Frankie and Dave. After Dave's death, Frankie and Kay trick Noll – in a neatly metaphorical turnaround, Frankie pretends that a pen in his pocket is a gun – and Frankie gets the $2900 he was owed from the bootlegging days. In a shoot-out in the club, Noll is killed by the police and there is a romantic happy end for Frankie and Kay, freed from their pasts.

The film's two male stars are central to its effect. Burt Lancaster's role has echoes of his roles in *The Killers* (1946)* and *Criss Cross* (1949)*, while Kirk Douglas plays his character in similar vein to his role in *Out of the Past* (1947)*. Lawrence Alloway (1971) suggests that the predominant influence on the film was probably producer Hal Wallis, who also produced, between 1945–50, *The Strange Love of Martha Ivers* (1946), *The File on Thelma Jordon* (1949), *Desert Fury* (1947) and *Dark City* (1950). These films, made by different directors, all dealt with similar thematic material. JH

Dir: Byron Haskin; **Prod**: Hal B. Wallis; **Scr**: Charles Schnee, Robert Smith, John Bright from Theodore Reeves's stage play *Beggars Are Coming to Town*; **DOP**: Leo Tover (b&w); **Ed**: Arthur Schmidt; **Score**: Victor Young; **Main Cast**: Burt Lancaster, Lizabeth Scott, Kirk Douglas, Wendell Corey, Kristine Miller, George Rigaud, Marc Lawrence, Mike Mazurki; **Prod Co**: Paramount.

In a Lonely Place
US, 1950 – 94 mins
Nicholas Ray

In a Lonely Place was produced by its star Humphrey Bogart's
independent production company, Santana Pictures, under the terms of
a deal with Columbia Pictures, whereby the senior company provided
studio shooting facilities and distribution. This arrangement undoubtedly
accounts for the film's distinctive timbre as it hovers between the
promising uncertainty of the wider world and the restrictive topoi of
studio sets that largely contain the desire, longing and eventual romantic
estrangement within the narrative to the uneasy glamour of a Hollywood
nightclub, the taciturn banality of a police office and the conventional
domesticity of a series of Los Angeles apartments. Nicholas Ray's film,
one of the most emotionally complex *film noirs* of the classical period,
studies these spaces with infinite precision. His characters' gestures,
language, glances are choreographed to the point that singular
allegiance between character and spectator becomes impossible.
As V. F. Perkins (1993) succinctly notes, for a film about a murder
investigation, *In a Lonely Place*

> is interested neither in creating mystery nor in following the process of
> detection. … Above plot it promotes character and both psychological
> and social portraiture, using the suspicion of murder as a pressure to
> dramatise the course of a romance from the discovery of love to its
> disintegration.

The plot revolves around three intersecting narratives: the adaptation
of a cheap novel by the troubled screenwriter, Dixon Steele (Humphrey
Bogart); the police investigation of the murder of a hat-check girl,
Mildred Atkinson, who was last seen at Dixon's home the night she died
'in a lonely place' out of town; and the blossoming romance between
'Dix' and his neighbour, Laurel (Gloria Grahame), whose feelings are

called into question when she comes to doubt whether 'Dix' is really innocent of the violent crime. These elements all allude to disparate notions of truth and fiction and it is a testament of the film's emotional complexity that neither 'Dix' nor Laurel remain unscathed as Ray's agile camera and Solt's discriminating script compassionately scrutinise the revealing analogies that can be drawn between detection, romance and storytelling.

It is not surprising, therefore, that critics have found *In a Lonely Place* hard to define in terms of genre. In some ways, its interest in violent male psychology and unsolved crime, not to mention its occasionally vivid moments of *noir* film style, define it clearly as a *film noir*. For others, the title of the film refers rather to the anguished emotional hinterland of the gothic woman's film in which we must assume the central protagonist is the emotionally conflicted Laurel. It is also possible to imagine the correlation between the title and the compromises and treacheries of the film industry thus marking Ray's film as a less self-reflexive counterpart to *Sunset Boulevard* (1950)*, Billy Wilder's oneiric 'Hollywood on Hollywood *noir*' of the same year. Dana Polan (1993) even argues for consideration of parts of the film in the light of the American screwball-comedy tradition.

No matter, the ambiguities and the strengths of *In a Lonely Place* also lie in the quality and suggestiveness of its two lead performances. Bogart's 'Dix' exemplifies a weary, unresolved romanticism broken by extreme bouts of temper and violence. His character supersedes the generic template of the *noir* male loner, partly defined by Bogart himself in films such as *Dead Reckoning* (1947)*. Grahame gives a marvellously astute performance – perhaps her career best – as, in Perkins's words, 'a woman who hates to be taken by surprise and not to have her performance under control'. We are allowed to see the flaws in both *and* to see how each character discovers these faults in the other. As the

(*Next page*) Detection, romance and storytelling: Laurel (Gloria Grahame) and 'Dix' (Humphrey Bogart) 'in a lonely place'

story of the film within the film, the police inquiry and the romance draw ever closer by the end, the couple draw ever further away until, in the final shot in which they become permanently separated, they are left to discover again what it is like to live with the unwished-for disappointment of being 'in a lonely place'. AP

Dir: Nicholas Ray; **Prod**: Robert Lord; **Scr**: Andrew Solt, Edmund H. North from Dorothy B. Hughes's short story; **DOP**: Burnett Guffey (b&w); **Ed**: Viola Lawrence; **Score**: George Antheil; **Main Cast**: Humphrey Bogart, Gloria Grahame, Frank Lovejoy, Carl Benton Reid; **Prod Co**: Santana Pictures.

Le Jour se lève
France, 1939 – 93 mins
Marcel Carné

From its opening caption – 'imprisoned, trapped in a room, [a man] remembers the circumstances which made him a murderer' – the defining image of *Le Jour se lève* is Jean Gabin's François barricaded alone at the top of his apartment block, with nothing left to live for. Pacing round his dark, cramped room, its space fractured by the bullet-scarred mirror, highlights from the shattered window playing on his face and eyes in close-up with drifting cigarette smoke, François looks at himself in the mirror. Turning over in his mind the events which led up to his *crime passionel* and seeing no way out, he shoots himself as the police close in.

François is a classic doomed, alienated *noir* hero, and the film's multiple flashback structure – novel for its time – closes down any sense of future possibility. Its pessimism has been taken by many as a metaphor for an economically depressed France on the eve of war. Like other French poetic realist films – not least Marcel Carné and Jacques Prévert's *Le Quai des brumes* (1938) and Jean Renoir's *La Bête humaine* (1938)*, both also starring Gabin – the film's *feel* is very different from 1940s/ 1950s US *film noirs*. This is partly because of François's strongly defined working-class position, then a key element of Gabin's persona. Great emphasis is placed on the nondescript town on the Paris outskirts and François's dangerous, dirty job; he sets off for the factory through empty, early-morning streets on his bicycle. This aspect of the film is very different from later US *film noirs*, but this has less to do with period than with a different culture and sensibility. In this sense *Le Jour se lève* can be linked as much to 1940s Italian neo-realist films like *Bicycle Thieves* (1948) as to Hollywood cinema.

As so often, the *noir* hero's – or antihero's – problems stem from his love life, but in very different ways than in US films. François is 'in love' with the 'innocent' young orphan girl, Françoise (Jacqueline Laurent), but he has a friendly, explicitly sexual affair with the older, disillusioned Clara (played very sympathetically by Arletty), who's 'sick of men talking about love'. François's idealistic love for Françoise dooms him but neither woman is remotely a *femme fatale*. Both are exploited in different ways, linked – fatally for François – by their relationships with the predatory, duplicitous Valentin (Jules Berry, in almost a reprise of his role in Renoir's *Le Crime de M. Lange* [1936]).

The 1947 US remake, *The Long Night*, directed by Anatole Litvak, retained much from the original, whose *mise en scène* in the opening

Le Jour se lève: imprisoned, trapped in his room, François (Jean Gabin) gazes at his reflection in the bullet-scarred mirror

scene is shamelessly copied, though the scenes inside Joe's room are more *chiaroscuro noir* in style than the original. However, it radically changes the original's bleak conclusion: Joe (Henry Fonda) surrenders, saved by the good girl (Barbara Bel Geddes), and in a conventional happy ending, Joe realises that with friends and love, he can 'make it'. Typically, the ex-serviceman angle is played up – 'a lot of vets go crazy' – softening the story's motivations and sympathies. The bitter irony of the French title, as well as the film's sexual and class charge and, oddly, its fatalism, get lost.

In *Sight and Sound*'s 1952 poll *Le Jour se lève* (best film at the 1939 Venice Film Festival) was the most highly rated French film, ahead of Renoir's *La Règle du jeu* (1939). That very high status was doubtless misplaced, but Carné and Prévert's fine film now looks significantly undervalued. ᴊʜ

Dir: Marcel Carné; **Prod**: Paul Madeux; **Scr**: Jacques Viot, Jacques Prévert; **DOP**: André Bac, Philippe Agostini, Albert Viguier (b&w); **Ed**: René Le Hénaff; **Score**: Maurice Jaubert; **Main Cast**: Jean Gabin, Jules Berry, Arletty, Jacqueline Laurent, Mady Berry, René Génin; **Prod Co**: Productions Sigma, Vauban Productions.

Journey into Fear
US, 1942 – 69mins
Norman Foster, Orson Welles

Most *film noirs* are, in Graham Greene's terms, 'entertainments', and a film like the determinedly tongue-in-cheek *Journey into Fear* (based on Eric Ambler's excellent spy thriller), thus fits the model perfectly. As cast and credits testify, this was a Mercury Theatre production, the third film in Welles's RKO deal, made in the aftermath of the *Citizen Kane* (1941) and *The Magnificent Ambersons* (1942) débâcles. Somewhat tossed off perhaps, it is hugely enjoyable and very *noir* in style despite its early place in the cycle – but then *Citizen Kane* was a crucial forerunner of the visual and narrative style of *noir*.

Very quickly, via a crane shot into a hotel bedroom where an obese, bespectacled assassin checks his weapon while playing a cracked recording of a French popular song, the film draws us into a nightmarish world in which everyone knows more than the American 'innocent abroad', arms engineer Howard Graham (Joseph Cotten), who is wanted by the Nazis. Here, everyone's motives, loyalty and identity are suspect. 'Abroad' is war-torn, wily Europe, or rather Turkey, where Europe meets the even more wily Orient and secret service chief Colonel Haki – Orson Welles clearly relishing the role, dressed and moustached to look like a jovial Stalin – controls events. The film-makers have fun with the silent assassin, Banat (played by Jack Moss, Welles's agent and accountant and a producer of the film) dressed in raincoat and fedora. The same goes for the crazy Italian ship's captain (Richard Bennett – last seen as Colonel Amberson), uproariously amused by Graham's account of the danger he is in.

Welles's love of magic must have motivated the extraordinary sequence in which Graham – drawn ever deeper into corruption, double-dealing and violence – is made to participate in a nightclub stunt in which he is tethered to a cross, while the magician takes refuge in a coffin. In the ensuing darkness, a shot rings out – but not from the magician's assistant. When the lights come on and Graham, full of admiration for the trick, clambers out of the coffin, the magician is now tethered to the cross, shot dead by a bullet meant for Graham. At one point, Graham's distraught wife (Ruth Warrick – Kane's wife) asks, 'What is to become of me?' To which Haki replies with a dark smile, 'We'll think of something.' At the end, somehow now remarkably contented, she welcomes Graham back only to lose him again in a remarkably well-orchestrated shoot-out on the hotel parapet in a rainstorm. Banat, blinded by the rain, falls to his death and 'innocent' Graham, resourceful American that he is, triumphs – at least until told by his wife, as if scolding an over-imaginative child, to 'stop all this nonsense'.

There is a barely a daylight scene in the film and Karl Struss's photography wonderfully renders the dark, confusing city and the claustrophobic setting of the boat – a world of shadows, constant menace and absurdity. The film's apparently truncated running time and its confused production – Welles recut the final reel, shot some additional scenes and, apparently, added a now lost voice-over for the beginning and end – only reinforce the overall atmosphere of chaos. David Thomson (2002) suggests that *Journey into Fear* was 'the Mercury film where Welles first essayed his magician's ploy of directing through another man'. Ambler's novel was remade in 1975 (directed by Daniel Mann, with Sam Waterston and Joseph Wiseman) to absolutely no acclaim. JH

Dir: Norman Foster, Orson Welles (uncredited); **Prod**: Jack Moss, George Schaefer, Orson Welles (all uncredited); **Scr**: Joseph Cotten, Richard Collins (uncredited), Ben Hecht (uncredited), Orson Welles (uncredited) from Eric Ambler's novel; **DOP**: Karl Struss (b&w); **Ed**: Mark Robson; **Score**: Roy Webb; **Main Cast**: Joseph Cotten, Orson Welles, Dolores del Rio, Ruth Warrick, Agnes Moorehead, Everett Sloane, Jack Moss, Richard Bennett; **Prod Co**: Mercury Productions, RKO Pictures.

The Killers
US, 1946 – 105 mins
Robert Siodmak

With its highly wrought *noir* visual style, complex flashback narrative and definitive alienated male hero and glamorously destructive *femme fatale*, *The Killers* is one of the most accomplished and quintessential 1940s *film noirs*. Former journalist and Universal producer Mark Hellinger, specialist in hard-hitting action films, assembled the various components: Ernest Hemingway's 1927 short story, the starting point for writers Anthony Veiller's and John Huston's heist-centred story; director Robert Siodmak, who brought his background in German and French cinema to dark Hollywood material like *Phantom Lady* (1944)* and *The Spiral Staircase* (1945); and debutant stars Burt Lancaster, in his first film, and Ava Gardner, in her first major role. Underused by MGM, Hellinger, by contrast, saw Gardner as perfect *femme fatale* material, believing, as Lee Server (2006) suggests, that she 'could convince audiences a man would steal, go to prison, die for her'.

The film's prologue, more or less faithful to Hemingway, infuses the story with *noir* iconography and bravura low-key photography: car headlights slice through the darkness and two tough-talking hit men in fedoras and raincoats (Charles McGraw and William Conrad) make their way to the sleepy small town's diner. Threateningly, they question the owner and young customer Nick about the whereabouts of ex-boxer Swede Andersen (Lancaster) and tie them up. Managing to escape to warn Swede, Nick finds him waiting, passively, on his bed, his face in shadow: 'I'm through with all that running around. I did something wrong – once.' Swede raises his weary face as the killers approach, flashing gunfire shatters the darkness and Swede's hands slide down the wall.

(*Opposite page*) Burt Lancaster as Swede in *The Killers*: 'I'm through with all that running around. I did something wrong – once'

The rest of the narrative – the writers' invention – explains the background to this opening: a heist gone wrong, double-crosses, duplicitous sexual loyalties. Structured as an investigation by dogged insurance man Reardon (Edmond O'Brien), the story incorporates eleven flashback sequences, in a non-linear time frame, told by six different characters. Though Reardon's objective is the stolen money, the narrative centres on explaining the reason for Swede not running – Swede's infatuation with Kitty Collins (Gardner). Swede is completely taken with Kitty – not introduced until the fourth flashback – and the *mise en scène* emphasises why, as she sits at the piano, half in shadow, cigarette smoke drifting, singing huskily. Later, as the heist is planned, Kitty, sitting on the bed, comes on to Swede despite being heist boss Colfax's (Albert Dekker) mistress. Though her duplicitous desire drives the narrative, her underlying motivations – like those of many *femmes fatales* – remain shadowy. What are her *real* feelings about Swede? What does she *really* want – the respectable bourgeois life, or something more dangerous? How does she feel about her actions – does she really hate herself and consider herself, as she tells Swede, 'poison'? Siodmak returned to similarly bleak but visually rich material with *Criss Cross* (1949)*, again with Lancaster, but with different producer, writers and cinematographer.

Don Siegel's 1964 colour remake – curiously, Hellinger had originally wanted Siegel to direct the 1946 version – was made for television but considered too violent and instead released to cinemas. Hemingway was largely jettisoned but the passivity of the hit (John Cassavetes) sparks the curiosity of the business-suited hit men with their guns in briefcases (Lee Marvin and Clu Gulager), who track down those who masterminded the heist and double-cross (Angie Dickinson in the Kitty role and Ronald Reagan in the Colfax role). The flashback structure is retained but the moody *noir* look of the original is replaced by bright pastel Florida and Southern California colours. Marvin excels as the ageing hit man too tired to keep running. As he says, most memorably as he dies at the end, 'We don't have the time.' JH

Dir: Robert Siodmak; **Prod**: Mark Hellinger; **Scr**: Anthony Veiller, John Huston (uncredited) from Ernest Hemingway's short story; **DOP**: Woody Bredell (b&w); **Ed**: Arthur Hilton; **Score**: Miklós Rózsa; **Main Cast**: Burt Lancaster, Ava Gardner, Edmond O'Brien, Albert Dekker, Sam Levene, Vince Barnett, Virginia Christine, Jack Lambert, Jeff Corey, Charles McGraw, William Conrad; **Prod Co**: Mark Hellinger Productions, Universal.

The Killing
US, 1956 – 80 mins
Stanley Kubrick

The Killing is a cheaply made racetrack heist movie which in an earlier period would have been a B-movie. By the mid-1950s, however, B-movies were becoming rarer (despite the fact that double bills were still the norm), and *The Killing* has more in common with the new breed of 'independent' films then appearing in the US. Kubrick's film is certainly a genre movie, owing something to *The Killers* (1946)*, *Criss Cross* (1949)*, *Rififi* (1955)* and, particularly, *The Asphalt Jungle* (1950)*. However, it also manifests considerable self-conscious artiness, striving for inventiveness (though less so than Kubrick's previous – debut – feature, made almost single-handedly, *Killer's Kiss* [1955], also a *noir*ish thriller). Here, Kubrick benefits from good writers (its source material a novel by Lionel White, with additional dialogue by Jim Thompson), first-class cinematography (Lucien Ballard), especially effective in low-key interiors and naturalistic location exteriors, and a great cast, resulting in one of the director's best, leanest movies, before he began to take himself too seriously.

The film follows the meticulous planning and execution of a racetrack robbery which, inevitably, goes wrong, with tragic repercussions. The protagonist and heist leader is ex-con Johnny Clay (Sterling Hayden), whose team includes a corrupt cop, Randy (Ted de Corsia), track employees George (Elisha Cook, Jr) and others, former drunk and father-figure Marvin (Jay C. Flippen) and sniper Nikki (Timothy Carey), all sketched in very concisely. Hayden's Johnny Clay is a close cousin of his 'hooligan' Dix in *The Asphalt Jungle*, here a tough leader rather than the hired muscle, wearily fatalistic and stoical, consistently sympathetic despite his criminality.

The film's most striking feature – generally considered a powerful influence on Quentin Tarantino's *Reservoir Dogs* (1992) and *Pulp Fiction* (1994) – is its complex, nonlinear narrative, structured around crosscut flashbacks for the planning and execution of the heist to create a sense of the simultaneous flow of events. Following problematic test screenings, Kubrick was forced to re-edit the film in more linear fashion. However, when this resulted in an even more confusing film, it was released in its original form, though with a voice-over and as a second feature. This complex structure does not detract from the film's overall impression of lean economy but there is sometimes a sense of striving a little clumsily after effect and significance. Think, for example, of the way the film uses *femme fatale* Sherry (Marie Windsor), who humiliates and betrays George and brings the heist down: there is a self-consciousness about the conception of her role here wholly lacking in Windsor's performance in, say, *The Narrow Margin* (1952)*. Similarly, Nikki's racial insult to the black parking attendant – a ploy to escape – knowingly exploits audiences' liberal sensibilities. But such criticism can't be made of the wonderfully inventive final sequence in which the money from the robbery falls out of a suitcase as it is carried out to the plane and is scattered by the wind from its propellers. Resigned to his fate, Johnny refuses his girlfriend's (Coleen Gray) urging to run away from re-arrest – 'What's the difference?' he wearily exclaims. JH

Dir: Stanley Kubrick; **Prod**: James B. Harris, Alexander Singer; **Scr**: Stanley Kubrick, Jim Thompson from Lionel White's novel *Clean Break*; **DOP**: Lucien Ballard (b&w); **Ed**: Betty Steinberg; **Score**: Gerald Fried; **Main Cast**: Sterling Hayden, Coleen Gray, Vince Edwards, Jay C. Flippen, Elisha Cook, Jr, Marie Windsor, Ted de Corsia, Joe Sawyer, Timothy Carey; **Prod Co**: Harris–Kubrick Productions.

Kiss Me Deadly
US, 1955 – 106 mins
Robert Aldrich

A rural Californian road at night and out of the Stygian shadows appears a distressed young woman dressed only in a pale raincoat. She hails a smart sportscar driven by the handsome but conceited private detective, Mike Hammer (Ralph Meeker), and together they set off for Los Angeles. Shortly afterwards, this archetypal *noir* pair are run off the road and held captive by a gang of anonymous thugs who torture and kill the woman and leave Hammer for dead. When Hammer comes to, he attempts to solve the mystery of his companion's death and swiftly becomes implicated in a labyrinthine underworld plot to seize a hidden case of Cold War era radioactive materials.

Adapted from one of Mickey Spillane's phenomenally successful series of New York crime novels by the pulp novelist turned screenwriter, A. I. Bezzerides (*On Dangerous Ground* [1952]*), *Kiss Me Deadly* is now seen by many as a scathing swansong to the noble tradition of the American private detective *film noir*. The savage portrayal of the virtual disintegration of the disreputable male protagonist situates the politics of Aldrich's film a generation away from the more idealistic, if no less convoluted, scenarios of *Murder, My Sweet* (1944)* and *The Big Sleep* (1946)*.

This trajectory from the past to the present is signalled within a number of the film's most interesting stylistic patterns. In particular, as Edward Dimendberg (2004) has observed, the film is remarkably prescient about the changing nature of Los Angeles's material infrastructure. Hammer's soulless West Side modernist bachelor apartment – replete with telephone answering machine embedded on the wall – overlooks a busy road intersection. It is specifically contrasted with the burrow-like decaying mansions of the streets of Bunker Hill, both in terms of spatial architecture and an attention to sound. We hear only the roar of traffic and a series of recorded voices in the former whereas the latter is quiet enough to make out the sound of footsteps on the pavement and a moving opera aria heard on a neighbourhood radio. Hammer's car is the bridge between these two worlds and, in apt reflection of Bezzerides's background in the Californian haulage business, the detective's only apparent friend in the whole city is an immigrant garage mechanic.

Sound also matters to the general atmospherics of the film, which contrasts a more sedate world of literature and private culture with a growing sense of paranoiac public unease. The film begins with a woman sobbing on an empty road and ends with a woman screaming by an empty beach. Throughout the densely structured threads of the investigation that take up the heart of its narrative, there is a mounting sonic portrayal of a world out of kilter in the new dispensation of Cold War panic and nuclear secrets. This is echoed by Ernest Laszlo's extraordinary camerawork, which assembles a virtual directory of *film noir* tropes in order to depict a dynamic screen space in which every shot resists stability and internal coherence.

It was this powerfully visceral uncoupling of America's modernity from a progressive future that appealed to contemporary French critics such as Borde and Chaumeton (authors of the now canonical *A Panorama of American Film Noir*, first published in 1953) and Jean-Luc Godard (who borrowed elements of Aldrich's oneiric dystopian vision for his 1965 film, *Alphaville*). For them, *Kiss Me Deadly* literally signalled the end of the road for the moral securities of the authentic American film detective. He would only resurface again in the context of the different political climate of the 1970s when the freeways mentioned in Bezzerides's dialogue have finally been constructed and when, in films like *The Long Goodbye* (1973)*, there were different, even less heroic, battles to be fought. AP

Dir, Prod: Robert Aldrich; **Scr**: A. I. Bezzerides from Mickey Spillane's novel; **DOP**: Ernest Laszlo (b&w); **Ed**: Michael Luciano; **Score**: Frank De Vol; **Main Cast**: Ralph Meeker, Maxine Cooper, Wesley Addy, Cloris Leachman, Albert Dekker, Nick Dennis, Gaby Rodgers, Paul Stewart; **Prod Co**: Parklane Pictures Inc.

Kiss of Death
US, 1947 – 95 mins
Henry Hathaway

Kiss of Death is a study in violent, failed masculinity and the pressures of social responsibility. Best remembered today for Richard Widmark's pitch-perfect debut as the unnerving, psychopathic gangster, Tommy Udo, the film also marks the development of Fox's integration of conventional *film noir* aesthetics with a predilection for location shooting and semi-documentary elements, including, in this instance, a close attention to the processes of the American legal system.

Christmas Eve in New York and an unsuccessful jewellery heist puts Nick Bianco (Victor Mature) behind bars for twenty years. Bianco, a devoted husband and father, refuses help from Assistant District Attorney, Louis D'Angelo (Brian Donlevy), preferring to rely on his crooked attorney, Earl Howser (Taylor Holmes), but when he learns of his wife's suicide and an earlier attack on her by Pete Rizzo, an old accomplice, he decides to turn informer. Bianco initially contrives to finger Rizzo and Tommy Udo is contracted to carry out his murder. Rizzo survives and later, with Bianco now released and living with his daughters and former babysitter Nettie (Coleen Gray), the police oblige the reluctant witness to pin Udo in connection with another case. Udo's trial ends with his unexpected acquittal and the ex-con's family, faced with inadequate police protection, are suddenly placed in mortal danger. Bianco is forced to take desperate measures to rid himself, once and for all, of the poisonous legacy of his criminal past.

Henry Hathaway's *Kiss of Death* was a commercial success for Fox and owes much to its director's taut and economical direction and the innovative pairing of its male protagonists. Mature (*I Wake Up Screaming* [1942]*, *Cry of the City* [1948]*) and Widmark (*Night and the City* [1950]*, *Pickup on South Street* [1953]*) bring a disturbing psychological edge to their characters that is conveyed largely through a combination of physique, costume, dialogue and body language. Mature's Bianco is

roughly hewn and spends most of the film in a broad, double-breasted
suit and fedora. His gait is anxious but purposeful and his recourse to
verbal self-expression sparing. The film is peppered with troubling close-
ups showing him responding to a constantly receding list of options.
Widmark's Udo is leaner and more quick-witted. Equally dapper, his suit
is tighter-fitting and his body language more agile and menacing. He
constantly dissolves into a snickering, utterly immoral, glee. The tensions
(and sometimes similarities) between the two are underscored by the
ambiguities of the parallel relationship between D'Angelo and Howser.
The more the film progresses, the more difficult it becomes to observe
the clear moral ground that separates the two attorneys in their
respective Machiavellian legal operations.

Fox based *Kiss of Death* on a short story by former Manhattan
Assistant District Attorney Eleazar Lipsky. Lipsky's interest in real-life
experience chimed with the direction in which the studio was taking *film
noir* and it subsequently employed the veteran screenwriter Ben Hecht

(who also co-wrote Robert Montgomery's *Ride the Pink Horse* the same year) to tighten the property's inherent dramatic potential. Fox's contract cinematographer, the talented Norbert Brodine (*Boomerang!* [Elia Kazan, 1947], *Thieves' Highway* [Jules Dassin, 1949]) combined various recognisable New York locations such as Sing Sing Prison with sensational set-piece sequences such as Udo's tense reunion with Bianco. Here, we slowly glimpse the thug's neurotic features come closer and closer to a single rectangular slit in the fabric of a nightclub curtain, his insistent, cold-blooded gaze momentarily meeting that of the spectator. In this fashion, Widmark's character brought a new element of psychosis to American *film noir* that, along with the film's unfurling portrait of compromised legal mores, helped disrupt the liberal certainties of the framing narrative detailing Bianco's moral redemption. Recounted, most unusually, by a female voice (that of Nettie), this element of the film now seems unnecessarily trite.

Victor Mature's persona in *Kiss of Death* owed something to the qualities he brought to his earlier portrayal of 'Doc' Holliday in John Ford's *My Darling Clementine* (1946). It is thus fitting that the film's plot was adapted for a Western a decade later: *The Fiend Who Walked the West* (Gordon Douglas, 1958). Barbet Schroeder remade *Kiss of Death* in 1995 with Nicolas Cage as Richard Widmark's character. There was no comparison. AP

Dir: Henry Hathaway; **Prod**: Fred Kohlmar; **Scr**: Ben Hecht, Charles Lederer from Eleazar Lipsky's short story *Stoolpigeon*; **DOP**: Norbert Brodine (b&w); **Ed**: J. Watson Webb, Jr; **Score**: David Buttolph; **Main Cast**: Victor Mature, Brian Donlevy, Coleen Gray, Richard Widmark, Karl Malden, Taylor Holmes; **Prod Co**: Twentieth Century-Fox.

L.A. Confidential
US, 1997 – 138 mins
Curtis Hanson

Curtis Hanson's appealing, award-winning screen adaptation of James Ellroy's source novel begins with a carefully managed montage of period archive footage, photography and publicity posters and more recent imagery designed to recreate the culture of Los Angeles in the early 1950s. As we move from glossy brochures advertising the allure of a new life in the Southern Californian sunshine to glimpses of the city's sordid criminal underworld, the opening of *L.A. Confidential* thus establishes a duality that will permeate the rest of the film. First, in its calibrated awareness of the shadows lurking underneath the palm trees and manicured lawns of Los Angeles, the montage anticipates the traditional narrative pleasures of the classic American *film noir*. Second, it explores the boundaries between artifice and the real, especially in the context of a Hollywood industry that explicitly services the dreams, myths and illusions of celebrity. Then third, it suggests a knowing recreation of a bygone era that like other revisionist *film noirs* such as *Devil in a Blue Dress* (1995)* will both venerate and destabilise the form. By going back to the heyday of *film noir* from the perspective of the 1990s, *L.A. Confidential*, as the title suggests, will be more intimate and truthful than any actual film from a time when popular crime cinema was still obliged to leave things unsaid.

How does Curtis Hanson's film therefore manage to both seduce and critique? In part, it is through recourse to intertextual storytelling techniques such as the inclusion of a television crime series, *Badge of Honour*, that one of the film's main cops, Jack Vincennes (Kevin Spacey), feeds with exciting 'real-life' narrative ideas. Then there's the sensational tabloid, *Hush-Hush*, whose sleazy editor, Sid Hudgens (Danny de Vito), is another of Vincennes's disreputable associates. Hudgens provides a light-hearted and sarcastic voice-over commentary to the first part of the film before the more 'modern-day' high-calibre action and suspense is cranked up to first gear. Taken together, these elements allow *L.A. Confidential* to project a witty kind of moral disapproval, as if both period print and small-screen titles rely on mere hollow heroics or tittle-tattle, while the more shocking and ethically ambivalent realities of the time can only be tackled by the greater truth of the surrounding fiction of the contemporary feature film.

The actual story concerns an overlapping series of investigations into a violent armed robbery at the Sleepy Owl café and the subsequent uncovering of a web of police corruption, racist brutality and sexual violence. As well as Vincennes, two other officers, the ambitious college-educated 'Ed' Exley (Guy Pearce) and the aggressive hothead Bud White (Russell Crowe), are involved and the friction between these three helps fuel the intrigue as the trail leads in unexpected directions. The character-based nature of the drama is the second way Hanson maintains the film's overall tension. Our degree of alignment with Vincennes, Exley and White – determined partly by multiple shallow-focus one-shots of the men – shifts constantly as the narrative progresses, with not one of the detectives being left unscathed by the film's relentlessly sardonic script.

Hanson's film is ingrained with the patina of *film noir*. One strand involves a call-girl ring employing women who look like prominent Hollywood film stars. Kim Basinger's underwritten female lead, Lynn Bracken, is a dead ringer for Veronica Lake, for example, and, just to underline the point, we see a projected extract from Lake's appearance in *This Gun for Hire* (Frank Tuttle, 1942). Dante Spinotti's unobtrusive cinematography generally avoids stylistic *noir* clichés but gets the timbre of the era just right. All in all, along with Jerry Goldsmith's music, which reprises the same melancholy of his score for *Chinatown* (1974)*, *L.A. Confidential* projects an assured updating of *film noir* conventions that stays on the right side of postmodern cynicism. AP

Dir: Curtis Hanson; **Prod**: Curtis Hanson, Arnon Milchan, Michael G. Nathanson; **Scr**: Brian Helgeland, Curtis Hanson from James Ellroy's novel; **DOP**: Dante Spinotti (colour); **Ed**: Peter Honess; **Score**: Jerry Goldsmith; **Main Cast**: Kevin Spacey, Russell Crowe, Guy Pearce, Kim Basinger, James Cromwell, Danny de Vito; **Prod Co**: Warner Bros., Monarchy Enterprises B.V., Regency Enterprises, The Wolper Organization.

The Lady from Shanghai
US, 1947 – 86 mins
Orson Welles

As in many of the best *film noirs*, such as *The Big Sleep* (1946)* and *Out of the Past* (1947)* the finer plot details of *The Lady from Shanghai* are pretty impenetrable, but the outline remains clear: Michael O'Hara (Orson Welles) saves Elsa (Rita Hayworth) from 'ruffians' in Central Park and is seduced into signing up to skipper Elsa and her husband, Bannister's (Everett Sloane) yacht from New York to Acapulco and Sausalito/San Francisco. En route, Michael becomes increasingly unsure about what he has got himself into, not least his romantic involvement with Elsa. A murky triple-cross finds him being defended in a murder trial by Bannister, who is determined, for once, to lose his case. Escaping into Chinatown, Michael is abducted to a deserted amusement park, where Bannister and Elsa destroy each other and Michael walks free.

Femme fatale Elsa – with a dark, never-revealed past in Macao ('The wickedest city in the world') and Shanghai ('You need more than luck in Shanghai') – is at the centre of the film's enigmas. Elsa's beautiful but unreadably masklike face complements her mystery. *Gilda* (1946)*, made a year earlier, finally established Hayworth as a glowing, soft, curvaceous pin-up. Here, her red hair dyed blonde and cut short, she looks quite different. Welles styles and photographs her almost as a parody of the Hollywood sex goddess. Juxtaposing her moonlit siren song with the next morning's vulgar hair-product radio commercial, his misogynistic portrayal perhaps reflects his feelings about Hayworth and their on-off marriage. Certainly, Elsa remains unredeemed, despite her final, romantic 'Give my love to the sunrise' and her desperate fear of death.

The story is told in typically *noir* retrospective style by Michael (who, it is hinted, may be a writer), his subjective voice-over attempting to make sense of the jumbled tale. Michael – like Jeff in *Out of the Past* – senses he is being framed but can't see the frame, though Michael is a good deal more naive. As he concedes in his final voice-over, walking

"I told you . . .
you know
nothing
about
wickedness"
COLUMBIA PICTURES presents
Rita HAYWORTH · Orson WELLES
in
The LADY from SHANGHAI
with EVERETT SLOANE and GLENN ANDERS · Screenplay and Production by ORSON WELLES

away from the crazed, self-destructive world of Elsa and Bannister (strikingly evoked earlier in the parable about the sharks tearing at each other's flesh), he is 'innocent officially, but that's a big word "innocent". Stupid's more like it. Well, everybody is somebody's fool … . Maybe I'll live so long I'll forget her. Maybe I'll die, trying.'

Citizen Kane (1941) – with its voice-overs and deep focus and *chiaroscuro* visual style – was a vital influence on *film noir*, and much of Welles's work (not least *Journey into Fear* [1942]* and *Touch of Evil* [1958]*) embodies a *noir* aesthetic. Unsettlingly, *The Lady from Shanghai* juxtaposes big close-ups with long shots, non-naturalistic night-time scenes with relatively naturalistic daytime sequences, location with studio shots. The Fun House sequence at the end, with its myriad reflecting mirrors shattering – consciously modelled on the expressionist *The Cabinet of Dr Caligari* (Robert Wiene, 1919) – gives way to the extended crane shot of Michael walking away across the deserted Play Land at dawn. The film builds up a dreamlike or nightmarish effect, its deliberate excesses threatening to push it towards a parody of the *noir* formula.

Welles's original cut ran almost twice as long as the release version. Columbia boss Harry Cohn found it incomprehensible and insisted on reshot close-ups and a song by his star and protégée Hayworth. The picture was savagely cut and held back from cinemas for almost a year, though this is not to suggest that much of Welles's baroque conception of the *noir* style is not up there on the screen. JH

Dir: Orson Welles; **Prod**: Orson Welles, Richard Wilson, William Castle; **Scr**: Orson Welles from Sherwood King's novel *Before I Die*; **DOP**: Charles Lawton, Jr (b&w); **Ed**: Viola Lawrence; **Score**: Heinz Roemheld; **Main Cast**: Rita Hayworth, Orson Welles, Everett Sloane, Glenn Anders, Ted de Corsia, Erskine Sanford, Gus Schilling; **Prod Co**: Columbia.

Lady in the Lake
US, 1946 – 105 mins
Robert Montgomery

Christmas in Los Angeles and private detective Philip Marlowe (Robert Montgomery) drops by the office of a prominent crime-fiction magazine to discuss the submission of a story he has written. He meets the company's editor-in chief, the self-assured and forceful Adrienne Fromsett (Audrey Totter), who discloses that she wishes to hire Marlowe to track down Chrystal Kingsby, her boss's missing wife. What then unfurls in this renowned Raymond Chandler adaptation is a typically labyrinthine investigation involving switched identities, violent police officers and duplicitous romantic intrigue set amid the vanity and corruption of the Californian upper-middle classes. What is different about actor Robert Montgomery's directorial debut is that *Lady in the Lake* has a purportedly sensational new angle: with the exception of a retrospective framing narrative in which Marlowe directly addresses the audience from his office, the entire film is shot from the central protagonist's point of view.

Film historians have largely considered Montgomery's inventive take on Philip Marlowe's screen persona to be nothing more than an interesting failure. It is certainly true that Montgomery's own rather leaden and brutal physical performance – at least what we actually see of it – has nothing on the wit and guile of Dick Powell's and Humphrey Bogart's seminal portrayals of Chandler's antihero in *Murder, My Sweet* (1944)* and *The Big Sleep* (1946)*. It is nonetheless worth reconsidering how the decision to prevent the audience actually seeing the detective directly affects our reading of *Lady in the Lake* as a *film noir*. Importantly, the rather mannered attention paid to only what Marlowe effectively notices forces the audience to continually evaluate the proceedings in a more pronounced visceral sense. This matters to the success of a number of mirror shots that determine vital narrative information not available to all of those within the frame. The most significant of these is the final shoot-out in a room with rear windows through which, unlike the gunman, we can make out the police detectives coming to Marlowe's rescue. When Marlowe also comes to blows earlier in the film, or when he is involved in a powerful car crash at night, there is a vivid sensation of a genuine physical reality to the drama that compensates for the more pedestrian elements of the film's direction. Above all, through this process, we are invited to define our allegiance in relation to the private eye's scrutiny of the evidence in front of him. Appearance, glances and body language are all read more carefully. In short, as a *film noir*, *Lady in the Lake* invites its audience to play detective.

Two other aspects of the film's style work in counterpoint to each other. First, because of a dependence on the detective's point of view, much of the narrative action functions as a kind of reiteration of the first-person narrative previously established at the beginning of the film. We only see what we are directed to see. There is thus an unusual materiality to the *mise en scène* in that doorways, furnishings and objects (especially guns) all have a sense of being overtly described in a more intensive fashion than one would normally encounter in other *film noirs* in which different aspects of the *mise en scène*, especially lighting, would conspire to evoke the requisite degree of menace and threat. Second, in a fashion that ironically has more of a correlation to the experience of reading Chandler than seeing a film based on Chandler, we digest all the proceedings through the determining first-person language of the main protagonist. Arguably, this produces an epistemological sensation much closer to the original mechanics of the literary private-eye genre than any Marlowe film before or since. It is tempting to conclude that this is not an accident. After all, *Lady in the Lake* begins with a supposedly real, but in fact fictional, private detective recounting how he went to a detective-story publisher to sell a made-up story that meanwhile got forgotten as another 'true-life' drama apparently took over. In this sense, *Lady in the Lake* appears a minor metaphysical puzzle. What *is* its genuine story? Robert Montgomery's undervalued film now seems more a precursor to contemporary *film noir* riddles such as David Lynch's *Mulholland Dr.*

(2001)* than a diminished partner to the more conventional Philip Marlowe *film noirs* of the 1940s. AP

Dir: Robert Montgomery; **Prod**: George Haight; **Scr**: Steve Fisher from Raymond Chandler's novel; **DOP**: Paul Vogel (b&w); **Ed**: Gene Ruggiero; **Score**: David Snell; **Main Cast**: Robert Montgomery, Audrey Totter, Lloyd Nolan, Tom Tully, Leon Ames; **Prod Co**: MGM.

Laura
US, 1944 – 88 mins
Otto Preminger

Halfway through *Laura* is one of the finest sequences in all *film noir*. Police Lieutenant McPherson (Dana Andrews), investigating the death of beautiful career woman Laura Hunt (Gene Tierney), has become intrigued by her life and enchanted by the painting of her that dominates her apartment. Following him as he roams through the half-lit apartment, looking through her clothes, toiletries and papers, the camera then tracks into close-up as, in an alcohol-fuelled reverie, he falls asleep below the painting. Fading in from black, the camera tracks back from the sleeping McPherson and the painting and we hear Laura returning. McPherson wakes, framed midway between Laura and the painting, and rubs his eyes, twitching in disbelief. Rarely have movies better exploited the oneiric potential of cinema to catch the hazy borderline between dream and reality, here centred on McPherson's disturbingly obsessive desire for a fantasy woman he thought was dead.

Reviewers at the time were sometimes surprised and disappointed that the living Laura didn't or couldn't live up to both McPherson's and spectators' expectations and imagination. But that is precisely the film's point: such women only exist in (mostly heterosexual men's) fantasies. In reality, they are, like us, merely human, ordinary. Laura is perfectly groomed and pretty, but there is nothing very deep or, finally, enigmatic about her. She certainly lacks the tough unknowability and unreliability of, say, Elsa in *The Lady from Shanghai* (1947)* or Kathy in *Out of the Past* (1947)*. McPherson is a good match for her: despite some smart one-liners, he is some distance from the witty, hard-boiled, knowing tradition of Sam Spade or Philip Marlowe as incarnated by Humphrey Bogart or Dick Powell in *The Maltese Falcon* (1941)*, *Murder, My Sweet* (1944)*, *The Big Sleep* (1946)*. Otto Preminger uses Dana Andrews to create an ordinary, slightly dull, wary, thin-lipped character with the permanent suggestion of a scowl. Nevertheless, we are clearly intended

to feel that Laura will be better off going to wholesomely American baseball games with McPherson than remaining in the empty social world and *objets d'art* of witty newspaper and radio columnist Waldo Lydecker (Clifton Webb), Laura's neurotically jealous mentor and protector, or Shelby Carpenter (Vincent Price), her morally flabby playboy fiancé.

Despite the presence of an enigmatic female protagonist and a hard-bitten investigator who falls under her spell, and despite its quota of scenes set in night streets and darkened apartments and its recourse to voice-over flashbacks to sketch in Laura's past, *Laura* is not a particularly typical *film noir*. Preminger's later *Fallen Angel* (1945)* and *Where the Sidewalk Ends* (1950)* (both also starring Andrews) are much more typically *noir* in look and theme. *Laura* had been prepared and begun by Rouben Mamoulian but Preminger, the film's producer, took over direction and no doubt gave the film a darker tone. His tracking camera and elaborate *mise en scène* probe the tastefully decorated surfaces of a morally corrupt, literally murderous society world rife with egotism, jealousy and greed.

Laura was remade as a '20th Century-Fox Hour' TV drama in 1955, with Robert Stack, George Sanders and Dana Wynter in the McPherson, Lydecker and Laura roles, and again as a US/UK television movie in 1968, with Stack and Sanders reprising their 1955 roles and Lee Bouvier as Laura. A 1962 German television movie version starred Helmut Lange, Anton Walbrook and Hildegard Knef. JH

Dir, Prod: Otto Preminger; **Scr**: Jay Dratler, Samuel Hoffenstein, Betty Reinhardt from Vera Caspary's novel; **DOP**: Joseph LaShelle (b&w); **Ed**: Louis Loeffler; **Score**: David Raksin; **Main Cast**: Dana Andrews, Gene Tierney, Clifton Webb, Vincent Price, Judith Anderson; **Prod Co**: Twentieth Century-Fox.

Lift to the Scaffold (Ascenseur pour l'échafaud)
France, 1958 – 88mins
Louis Malle

Louis Malle's mesmeric *Lift to the Scaffold* initially appears to be a *noir*ish tale of two doomed lovers, Florence (Jeanne Moreau) and Julien (Maurice Ronet), who plot to murder Florence's husband – a wealthy arms dealer – in what seems to be the perfect crime. Funded by the CNC's groundbreaking *prime à la qualité* scheme and loosely based on Nöel Calef's pulp crime novel, the film famously begins with a claustrophobic telephone exchange that anxiously blends sexual tension with criminal desire. The fly in the ointment though is that even the cunning Bressonian exactitude of the murder plot fails to ensure that the lovers are ever physically united again. On his way out of the office building where he has killed his boss, Julien becomes trapped in an elevator shaft for the duration of a fateful weekend. It is only in the very final images of the film, when the police reveal some accidentally exposed photographs depicting Florence and Julien earlier together in the country, that the now doomed (and now visibly guilty) couple are actually pictured together within the same frame. In the words of the police detective, played by French *film noir* stalwart, Lino Ventura (Angelo in *Touchez pas au grisbi* [1953]*), 'there are always various photos in a camera'.

Malle's preoccupation with this tension between desire and reality is exemplified in the justly celebrated sequence when Moreau sets off alone to walk the streets of night-time Paris in search of her missing lover. Florence's inner state of mind is plaintively evoked by the soulful, improvised jazz score of Miles Davis, almost to the extent that one feels that real narrative time has been temporarily suspended within the *mise en scène*. When we do hear Florence's voice break into the soundtrack, it is only to convey an internalised yearning for what is so vividly absent on the streets and in the cafés and bars around her. But what makes the sequence so particularly hallucinatory is the way in which the cinematography by Henri Decaë (favoured collaborator also of Jean-Pierre Melville) creates a stylised combination of subjective feeling and documentary statement in his powerfully atmospheric depiction of this nocturnal urban reverie. Taken together, these cinematic elements express a powerful reversal of the conventional male *noir* protagonist's prerogative to search the city at night for a woman.

Lift to the Scaffold develops by turning to some of the conventions of the police procedural and the tension slackens somewhat when a parallel, younger couple become central to the process of uncovering the guilty partners. Having said this, Malle's comparative strategy also allows him to portray a postwar French consumer culture in which new technologies of leisure and mobility figure prominently. The modernity of this world is seemingly implicated in the narrative of crime, especially when one remembers that both Julien and his boss are also bound up in the bloody weapons trade surrounding the decolonisation of French territories. In this sense, although the film evokes a sense of stasis by virtue of its title and key narrative conceit, it also tacitly suggests that there is something wrong with a society changing so rapidly that all we actually see of true love lies in an old photograph mistakenly processed with the aid of an automatic machine in an anonymous motorway motel. AP

Dir: Louis Malle; **Prod**: Jean Thuillier; **Scr**: Louis Malle, Roger Nimier from Noël Calef's novel; **DOP**: Henri Decaë (b&w); **Ed**: Léonide Azar; **Score**: Miles Davis; **Main Cast**: Jeanne Moreau, Maurice Ronet, Georges Poujouly, Yori Bertin, Jean Wall, Lino Ventura; **Prod Co**: Nouvelles Éditions de Films.

The Long Goodbye
US, 1973 – 113 mins
Robert Altman

Raymond Chandler's *The Long Goodbye* was published in 1954. The
taste for Chandler movie adaptations had ebbed and the novel was not
adapted for film until Robert Altman's iconoclastic film (though Dick
Powell played Marlowe in a 1954 live television version). By 1973, films
like *Point Blank* (1967)* had established a fashion for revisionist versions
of *noir*, and Altman's film was soon followed by films like *Chinatown*
(1974)* and *Night Moves* (1975)*. Altman, fresh from demythologising
the Western in *McCabe and Mrs Miller* (1971), and Leigh Brackett, who
had co-scripted *The Big Sleep* (1946)*, were well placed to offer a
different take on Chandler and Marlowe. Just as the novel was a kind of
epitaph for Marlowe, the movie too works as an ironic epitaph for the
1940s *noir* hero Marlowe embodied.

In a deliberately complicated plot, Marlowe (Elliott Gould) loyally
helps his best friend Terry Lennox (Jim Bouton) to escape from the police
into Mexico, but discovers later that Lennox is suspected of killing his
wife. Meanwhile, Eileen Wade (Nina Van Pallandt) engages Marlowe to
find her missing husband, alcoholic novelist Roger (Sterling Hayden).
Marlowe is interrogated by the police and threatened by gangsters
looking for missing money somehow connected to Lennox. The Lennox
and Wade strands come together when Eileen is revealed as Lennox's
lover and accomplice in his wife's death. Marlowe finds Lennox in Mexico
and, feeling betrayed, shoots him.

Sunny Los Angeles looks resolutely unlike the 1940s *film noir* city,
and we are invited to compare Gould's mumbling, shuffling character
with the 1940s Marlowes in *The Big Sleep*, *Murder, My Sweet* (1944)*
and *The Lady in the Lake* (1946)*. Gould's Marlowe, always unkempt,
wears a dark suit, but it's crumpled and messy. No-one else wears suits
or drives a black, old-fashioned sedan. He is an anachronism: Altman
referred to him as 'Rip Van Marlowe' – a 1940s private eye waking up in

a sun-drenched 1970s Los Angeles, bewildered by its laidback, hedonistic counter-cultural lifestyle.

Marlowe appears to passively accept this morally lax society: his response to everything is 'It's OK with me.' But though Marlowe may appear incompetent and impotent, Altman has his cake and eats it: Marlowe proves that he *does* have values and *is* in control. He pieces together what Lennox has been up to and, in a sharp divergence from Chandler's ending, tracks down the now officially dead Lennox in his Mexican hideaway. When Lennox insists that 'Nobody cares,' Marlowe replies, as he shoots him dead, 'Nobody but me.' In an overly cute final sequence, as Marlowe walks jauntily away, Altman overlays a tinny soundtrack 'Hooray for Hollywood' – one of many movie references in a film which is in many ways *about* Hollywood. David Thomson (2002) may be right that the film is all surface and no soul, but this seems to be Altman's point.

As well as re-imagining the private-eye hero, Altman plays radically with narrative conventions: the first ten minutes follow Marlowe's (failed) attempt to feed his cat. Indeed, Altman insisted that the film's greatest mystery was what happened to Marlowe's cat. Explanations for Lennox's disappearance come in confusing voices off, and the constant widescreen panning and zooming happily digresses from what would conventionally constitute the narrative focus. When *The Long Goodbye* did poor business, Elliott Gould, whose complex performance is central to the film, argued that it was an art movie which should have opened in New York, not Los Angeles. JH

Dir: Robert Altman; **Prod**: Jerry Bick; **Scr**: Leigh Brackett from Raymond Chandler's novel; **DOP**: Vilmos Zsigmond (colour); **Ed**: Lou Lombardo; **Score**: John Williams; **Main Cast**: Elliott Gould, Nina Van Pallandt, Sterling Hayden, Mark Rydell, Henry Gibson, Jim Bouton; **Prod Co**: E-K-Corporation, Lions Gate Films.

The Lost One (Der Verlorene)
Germany, 1951 – 98 mins
Peter Lorre

Peter Lorre, one of international *film noir*'s most compelling and recognisable faces, is best remembered for his landmark role as the psychopathic child-killer in Fritz Lang's *M* (1931)* and his successful line in wheedling, saturnine minor villains in Hollywood *film noirs* such as *The Maltese Falcon* (1941)*, *Black Angel* (Roy William Neill, 1946) and *The Chase* (1946)*. *The Lost One*, written and directed by Lorre, marked the actor's return to Germany after sixteen years of exile and, as many critics have noted, its title, as well as its narrative concerns, have as much to say about the autobiographical plight of the individual émigré actor's re-entry into European cinema as the politics of postwar German guilt. As Jennifer Kapczynski (2003) has argued,

> the actor and his character form a curious double [in the film]: Lorre plays out his return from exile through a character who, like him, has been shunted to the outskirts of society. … [As such, he thus] enacts his own personal displacement as well as the fictional lostness of his character.

Once again, Lorre plays a pathological serial killer, although the film contrasts with the conventions of Hollywood crime cinema. As Tim Bergfelder (2007) also notes, whereas in American *film noirs* of the 1940s such as Robert Siodmak's *Phantom Lady* (1944)*, 'the serial killer frequently stood for the dangers and inherent psychosis of antidemocratic elitism and fascist ideology', here Lorre specifically uses 'the story of a serial killer to comment allegorically on the war, on Nazi rule, and on questions of individual versus collective guilt'.

Karl Rothe (Peter Lorre) is a lonely, softly spoken scientist now working as a doctor in a displaced persons' camp in northern Germany some time after the end of World War II. A chance encounter with his former assistant, Hoesch (Karl John), activates a series of disturbing flashbacks that recount Rothe's experimental work for the Nazis and the cover-up initiated by Hoesch and a Gestapo agent after Rothe is found to have murdered his fiancée, Inge (Renate Mannhardt). Weaving backwards and forwards in time, but in a far more morally charged fashion than the conventional *film noir* flashback, the film reveals the chilling details of Rothe's further killings as the tormented psychopath is now denied access to the retribution of the law. The analogies between Rothe's own individual pathology and the wider murderous criminality of the Nazi regime are marked. In the film's closing scenes, Rothe finally confronts his demons and kills Hoesch before committing suicide in front of a passing train.

The *mise en scène* of the film is striking with its recurring motifs of troubled mirror reflections, shadowy streetscapes and atmospheric apartment rooms. Partly due to the pervasive tone of detachment taken towards the central protagonist, there is also a baleful sense of loneliness to the way that Rothe's fragmented subjectivity is never fully realised on screen. This may well be due to the deliberate emphasis placed on both an internal sense of synchronicity and dislocation to the film's construction of place and character. On the one hand, Lorre interweaves the past and present so as to allow the temporal elements of the film to comment on each other. This is especially noticeable with the overlapping components of the complex soundtrack. On the other hand, the film's spatial dynamics operate on the basis of an unsettling combination of alternating shallow horizontal planes (relating to the present) and more charged and insecure deep-space compositions full of psychological menace (relating to the past). It is as if the world of today is but a thin veneer only just about sheltering the trauma of history.

The Lost One, perhaps unsurprisingly, was not a box-office success. Today, it can be usefully compared to other postwar German serial-killer films such as *The Devil Strikes at Night* (*Nachts, wenn der Teufel kam*, 1957) directed by Robert Siodmak, another returning exile. As such, both films thus serve as the tail end of one of the most significant narrative elements in the long, and often oversimplified, history of the intercultural formation of *film noir*. AP

Dir: Peter Lorre; **Prod**: Arnold Pressburger; **Scr**: Peter Lorre, Axel Eggebrecht, Benno Vigny, Helmut Käutner (uncredited) from Peter Lorre's novel; **DOP**: Václav Vich (b&w); **Ed**: Carl Otto Bartning; **Score**: Willy Schmidt-Gentner; **Main Cast**: Peter Lorre, Karl John, Helmuth Rudolph, Johanna Hofer, Renate Mannhardt; **Prod Co**: Arnold Pressburger Filmproduktion.

M

Germany, 1931 – 117 mins

Fritz Lang

A serial child-killer is loose on the streets of Berlin. We do not see his body, merely an indication of a shadowy presence and the menacing sound of someone whistling the tune of 'In the Hall of the Mountain King' from Edvard Grieg's *Peer Gynt*. A man buys a balloon from a blind street-vendor and gives it to a young girl. A worried mother starts searching for her daughter. We then cut to the first of numerous startling images that pepper this still astonishingly modern film: a dark round balloon caught amid a set of taut, linear telegraph wires.

Fritz Lang's celebrated debut sound film begins with this simple conjugation of fear, innocence, threat and technology before opening

Haunted reflections and dynamic visual surfaces: the terrified killer Hans Beckert (Peter Lorre) in *M*

out to chart a broader social canvas in which the city itself becomes as much the subject of investigation as the isolated and terrified killer, Hans Beckert (Peter Lorre). Lang's relentlessly mobile camera charts the varied social spaces of Berlin from the crowded intimacy of its tenement rooms and staircases to the commercial modernity of its shops and offices. His architectural eye pauses now and then, usually from a fixed vantage point high above the streets, to pin the characters down in dynamic conflict with each other as the police, public and denizens of the city's underworld seek to find the murderer before he strikes again. There is barely a glimmer of daylight throughout.

Central to the film's method is its treatment of dynamic visual surfaces. The glass of shop windows is used to add density to key compositions such as when Beckert glimpses the reflection of a new victim in the centre of a pane. The manner of the design allows the girl to disappear from view and be replaced with Beckert's own haunted reflection. In another celebrated image we see him, alone at home, distorting his own face in childlike disgust at his appearance in the mirror. Elsewhere, we see, in a fashion anticipating many American procedural *film noirs* of the 1940s, an expanding series of concentric circles superimposed over a police map of the city. In a later echo of this, a shopfront is dominated by the edgy rotation of a circular optical toy, its suggestion of psychological disorientation providing an unsettling *mise en abîme* of the wider perceptual crisis that permeates the film as a whole.

M (short for *mörder*, 'murderer') was the result of careful preparation by Lang and his production team. Von Harbou and Lang researched accounts of a number of serial killings in late 1920s Germany, especially the infamous case of Peter Kürten in Dusseldorf; they also interviewed psychologists and familiarised themselves with contemporary police methods. This degree of verisimilitude is matched by an expressive attention to sound, lighting and set design. Future émigré *film noir* director, Edgar G. Ulmer (*Detour* [1945]*) prepared the latter. At the heart of the film is Peter Lorre's extraordinary, vivid portrayal of Beckert.

His bulging, anxious eyes and contorted, fearful, self-absorbed body language create a unique impression of existential terror. It was a role that was to haunt his career right up to his final return to the psychopathology of the serial killer in his postwar directorial effort, *The Lost One* (1951)*.

Joseph Losey remade *M* in 1951, under the guidance of Seymour Nebenzal, the film's original producer. Losey's undervalued, but hard-to-see, *film noir* filmography also includes *The Prowler* and *The Big Night* – all made the same year – and certainly merits greater attention. AP

Dir: Fritz Lang; **Prod**: Seymour Nebenzal (uncredited); **Scr**: Thea von Harbou, Fritz Lang from Egon Jacobson's article (uncredited); **DOP**: Fritz Arno Wagner (b&w); **Ed**: Paul Falkenberg; **Main Cast**: Peter Lorre, Ellen Widmann, Inge Landgut, Otto Wernicke, Theodor Loos, Gustaf Gründgens; **Prod Co**: Nero-Film AG.

The Maltese Falcon
US, 1941 – 100 mins
John Huston

Two versions of Dashiell Hammett's 1930 novel had been made before
John Huston's definitive 1941 film: *The Maltese Falcon* (Roy Del Ruth
[1931], with Bebe Daniels and Ricardo Cortez) and *Satan Met a Lady*
(William Dieterle [1936], with Warren William and Bette Davis). Both the
early sound 1931 version and the 1941 version stick closely to Hammett's
plot and dialogue and are also reasonably similar in iconography and
look. The 1936 film is more comic in tone, with a sophisticated, pipe-
smoking Spade, doubtless influenced by the commercial success of *The
Thin Man* (W. S. Van Dyke, 1934) (also adapted from Hammett) which,
despite some *noir* iconography, plays as much like screwball comedy as
crime thriller. Both earlier adaptations are slower paced than the 1941
version and look much more old-fashioned than the relatively few years
between them might suggest.

Huston's film thrusts us into recognisably modern urban spaces –
offices, apartments, streets – and contemporary rhythms of speech and
morality. The film's influence derives more from these factors than from
its visual style, which generally resembles the 1930s Warner Bros. high-
key look. Its modernity has also to do with Humphrey Bogart (though
George Raft was first choice for the role): after ten years in the movies
Bogart was only just establishing his lasting persona, in films like *They
Drive by Night* (Raoul Walsh, 1940) *High Sierra* (Walsh, 1941) and *The
Big Shot* (Lewis Seiler, 1941). Bogart's Spade is low key, professional, a
little weary but quick-thinking, morally ambivalent, suspicious about
women, averse to guns but not the odd punch, with a wry sense of
humour and a refusal to be bested. Trying to manipulate him is Mary
Astor – just a few years before playing the imposing matriarch of *Meet
Me in St Louis* (1944) – as *femme fatale* Brigid O'Shaughnessy, no Rita
Hayworth or Ava Gardner, but dangerous and duplicitous, constantly
pretending to be something and someone she isn't.

Also modern, and integral to *film noir*, is a darker moral universe in which loyalties mean little and no-one can be trusted. All the characters – Spade and Brigid, Cairo (Peter Lorre), Gutman (Sydney Greenstreet) and his gunsel Wilmer (Elisha Cook, Jr) – struggle to navigate this universe, all focused on finding the ancient falcon statuette that would bring them untold wealth – 'the stuff that dreams are made of', as Sam says – all doomed to fail. The only trusting relationship is between Spade and his secretary Effie (Lee Patrick) who adore and trust each other; she tells him – rightly – that he's too slick for his own good. Spade is, after all, having a casual affair, which he tries to pretend doesn't exist, with his partner's wife, Iva (Gladys George). Interestingly, the 1931 version retains Hammett's final scene, in which Effie ushers Iva into Sam's office, confronting him with the results of his womanising. Huston's ending, in which Spade insists that Brigid 'takes the fall' and 'sends her down', is more ambiguous: it is never really clear what Spade feels about Brigid – or what she feels about him – and the scene plays as if he needs to inject a moral dimension into an essentially amoral world and talk up both his professional obligation to do something about his partner's death and the love for Brigid which he is sacrificing.

As genres evolved in the post-classical period, many were subjected to parody: in the generally dire *The Black Bird* (David Giler, 1975), George Segal plays Sam Spade, Jr and roles are found for supporting actors from the 1941 version Lee Patrick and Elisha Cook, Jr. JH

Dir: John Huston; **Prod**: Hal B. Wallis; **Scr**: John Huston from Dashiell Hammett's novel; **DOP**: Arthur Edeson (b&w); **Ed**: Thomas Richards; **Score**: Adolph Deutsch; **Main Cast**: Humphrey Bogart, Mary Astor, Gladys George, Peter Lorre, Barton MacLane, Sydney Greenstreet, Ward Bond, Elisha Cook, Jr, Lee Patrick; **Prod Co**: Warner Bros.

Memories of Murder (Sarinui Chueok)
South Korea, 2003 – 130 mins
Bong Joon-ho

Like other international serial-killer films such as *Vengeance Is Mine* (Imamura Shohei, 1979) and *Zodiac* (David Fincher, 2007), Bong Joon-ho's award-winning *Memories of Murder* returns to the recent past in order to correlate the detailed investigation of a series of true-life murderous crimes with a vivid and unsettling portrait of a nation undergoing the convulsions of social change. The film takes place in a village community in South Korea's Gyeonggi province where, between 1986 and 1991, a series of young women are found murdered in the neighbouring woods and paddy fields. The local police detectives, with a reputation for brutal violence and corruption, fail to make headway in their chaotic search for the killer until the arrival of a university-educated officer from the capital, Seoul. Despite the arrest of a number of key suspects and intensive media scrutiny, the killer still remains elusive and the film concludes with the case unsolved.

Memories of Murder's riveting narrative unravels against the backdrop of wider unease in South Korean society. The village is regularly subject to civil-defence drills and blackouts that instil a permanent sense of instability and paranoia. Hints of the authoritarian nature of state politics emerge when at a crucial moment in the hunt for the killer – necessitating military support – all the local soldiers are unavailable as they are suppressing a civil-rights demonstration nearby. The local sources of employment – a factory and a quarry – indicate the progress of rapid industrialisation in the rural economy, but they also suggest the agency of a mysteriously menacing, dominating force through the way that they are visualised within the film's *mise en scène*.

Memories of Murder owes much of its force to a forensic sense of visual detail on the part of Bong Joon-ho and its cinematographer, Kim Hyeong-gu. Based, in part, on a stage play from the 1990s, the film makes provocative use of additional historical documentation uncovered by the production team. Aspects of the period's culture surface continuously in references to certain clothing, television programmes, popular films – Lawrence Kasdan's *film noir*, *Body Heat* (1981), is mentioned – and, most importantly, popular music. The main suspect becomes a man found to be responsible for requesting a melancholy pop song played by a local radio station on the night of every murder. His instructions: 'Please play this on a rainy night.'

These elements are embedded within a broader use of the surrounding landscape. The film begins with wide-angle views of the picturesque local farmland where the first body is discovered. As Detective Park Doo-man (Song Kang-ho) fails to prevent the local children from disturbing the evidence, Bong Joon-ho evokes an explicit and disquieting awareness of the contamination of nature. The film progresses, late summer turns to autumn and winter, and the sunlit fields have become darkened waterlogged mortuaries. Space becomes increasingly hard to define and much of the film's suspenseful action now occurs at night or in the claustrophobic interrogation chambers of the police station. When a sensationally filmed police chase through the village concludes at the nearby quarry, its cavernous floodlit character turns a site of ordinary human activity into a dystopian amphitheatre. The film ends with the suspect running into the forlorn darkness of a railway tunnel – his DNA results (sent from the US) having proved inconclusive.

In a short coda, years later, Park returns to the village fields, once again bathed in sunshine. South Korean society has now visibly advanced on a material level, but he remains confounded by the case. In one final disconcerting twist, he starts talking to a local girl. She reveals that there has been another recent visitor to the site: a man who told her he did something wrong there a long time ago. AP

Dir: Bong Joon-ho; **Prod**: Cha Seoung-jae, Kim Moo-ryung, No Jong-yun; **Scr**: Bong Joon-ho, Kim Kwang-rim, Shim Sung-bo from Kim Kwang-rim's play; **DOP**: Kim Hyeong-gu (colour); **Ed**: Kim Sun-min; **Score**: Iwashiro Taro; **Main Cast**: Song Kang-ho, Kim Sang-kyung, Kim Roe-ha, Song Jae-ho, Byeon Hui-bong; **Prod Co**: CJ Entertainment, Sidus Pictures.

Mildred Pierce
US, 1945 – 113 mins
Michael Curtiz

Mildred Pierce, like *The Reckless Moment* (1949)*, combines the psychological violence of the woman's picture with the physical violence of *film noir*. The film starts in high *noir* style, plunging the spectator into an incomprehensible sequence of events. It is night-time, and at an isolated beach house we hear the sudden sound of gunshots. Inside, amid confusing spaces, reflections and camera angles, a man falls down dead, muttering the name 'Mildred ...', but we are denied the crucial reverse angle that would reveal the actual identity of his murderer. The film then dissolves to a desperate-looking woman – Joan Crawford at her most statuesque and stoically tragic – dressed in furs, contemplating suicide on a dark, lonely pier. She lures an admirer, Wally (Jack Carson) back to the beach house and leaves him to discover the body. This opening action occurs with Mildred under police interrogation – in a rare example of a woman's voice-over flashback – recounting the events which led up to it. As Mildred tells her story – marriage, children, separation from discontented, unemployed husband Bert (Bruce Bennett), creating a restaurant business – the *noir* style of the opening (returned to later) gives way to a more classical, high-key, daytime look.

As in many women's pictures, Mildred's choices cast long shadows. Her one moment of 'selfish' attention to her own needs – the romantic interlude with playboy business partner Monte Beragon (Zachary Scott) – is 'punished' when her youngest daughter falls ill during her absence and dies. This loss encourages Mildred's ever-greater indulgence towards her monstrous older daughter Veda (Ann Blyth), who gradually displaces Mildred as *femme fatale*. The good-natured practicality of Mildred's business success – personified by career-woman manager Ida (Eve Arden) – becomes infiltrated by the dark passions and betrayals of a more *noir* world.

Mildred Pierce doubtless owes its *noir* elements to its period, but several commentators have noted that the film's production (1944–5) coincided with the later stages of World War II and government propaganda efforts to persuade the millions of women who had been encouraged into war work to return to family life (though the film does not refer directly to either the war or the Depression). Mildred, called upon to play many different roles – wife, businesswoman, possible *femme fatale* and murderer – is found wanting as a mother. As Jeanine Basinger (1993) puts it, 'To convince women that marriage and motherhood were the right path, movies had to show women making the mistake of doing something else.' Mildred's police interrogator usurps her control of the narrative, tricking her and Veda into revealing the murderer. The *noir* nocturnal interrogation over, Mildred's loyal ex-husband Bert is there to lead her into a new dawn of restored gender roles: as they leave, two women workers, on their knees, are scrubbing the floor of the Halls of Justice.

Like *Casablanca* (1942), another Michael Curtiz-directed Warners film, *Mildred Pierce* is the product of multiple talents – producer Jerry Wald, cinematographer Ernest Haller, composer Max Steiner and its writers. The critique of class and money in James M. Cain's source novel is toned down but survives. Although only Ranald MacDougal is credited, many different writers (including William Faulkner) worked on the script. Catherine Turney wrote two melodrama-accented versions, which seem to have been reworked as *noir* with the addition of the flashback structure and the murder (neither present in Cain). Joan Crawford's first film at Warners, following eighteen years under contract to MGM, won her an Academy Award and relaunched her then languishing career. JH

Dir: Michael Curtiz; **Prod**: Jerry Wald; **Scr**: Ranald MacDougal, Catherine Turney (uncredited) from James M. Cain's novel; **DOP**: Ernest Haller (b&w); **Ed**: David Weisbart; **Score**: Max Steiner; **Main Cast**: Joan Crawford, Jack Carson, Zachary Scott, Eve Arden, Ann Blyth, Bruce Bennett; **Prod Co**: Warner Bros.

Mulholland Dr.
US, 2001 – 145 mins
David Lynch

Accompanied by the dread-inducing synthesizer stirrings of his regular musical collaborator Angelo Badalamenti, David Lynch charts a nocturnal car journey high above Los Angeles along the sinister, meandering curves of Mulholland Drive. Two hoods threaten a beautiful unnamed woman (Laura Harring) and, after being injured in a sudden crash, she seeks refuge in an empty apartment nearby. When the bright-faced aspiring Hollywood actress Betty (Naomi Watts) arrives to stay in her aunt's beautiful period home, she finds this same woman shivering in the corner of the shower. The stranger, now named 'Rita' after a wall poster of Rita Hayworth in *Gilda* (1946)*, confides that she has no memory of who she is and the pair thus begin a tortured investigation into her true identity and the enigma of the bundled banknotes found inside her purse.

To describe David Lynch's elaborate and disturbing take on Hollywood myth and desire in this fashion is to reduce the film's core elements to a relatively stable tale of unfolding *film noir* intrigue. But as the film progresses, and new characters are introduced, an unsettling pattern emerges that destabilises any notional hold on diegetic reality. There appears to be an ominous overlap between the world of the gangsters glimpsed in the film's opening scenes and a film production directed by the self-regarding Adam Kesher (Justin Theroux) being cast in a nearby Hollywood studio. When 'Rita' begins to remember the name 'Diana Selwyn' things veer further out of kilter until, two-thirds of the way into the film, the spectator is forced to confront a new sequential logic and come to terms with the likelihood that all we have seen so far may be just a feverish dream in the tortured mind of one very different female protagonist.

Mulholland Dr.'s production history is equally complicated. Lynch originally shot the first section of the film as part of a planned ABC television series (in the vein of *Twin Peaks*), but after the project was abruptly cancelled, he decided to import additional new material that could begin (at least provisionally) to tie things together and provide an explanation for the mysteries we have witnessed. How successful this is depends on one's willingness to accept that the initial part of the film should now be seen as the sole product of one character's shifting subjectivity and multiple projected wishes and fears. It is certainly the case that the film one watches a second time is a radically altered one.

What gives this reading of *Mulholland Dr.* added impetus is the nature of the film's setting and its predominant concern with fictional fantasy. Like preceding oneiric *film noirs* such as *Detour* (1945)*, *Fear in the Night* (1947)* and *The Chase* (1946)*, Lynch's film is explicitly concerned with the dangerous borderlines between film and reality and between conscious ambition and unconscious anxiety. The difference here, though, is that by locating the narrative within the culture of Hollywood storytelling, these boundaries therefore become particularly contorted. At times, it becomes difficult to tell which film (or dream) one is actually in. Lynch adds to this confusion by citing other movies, most notably the similarly named *Sunset Boulevard* (1950)*; a shot of the Bronson Gate at Paramount, for example, is a direct quotation from Billy Wilder' s classic *noir*. Hollywood veteran, Ann Miller, also has an important character role as the all too knowing concierge, Coco Lenoix. With its combination of destabilising sound design (devised by Lynch), extensive ghostlike tracking shots and riveting air of menace and threat, *Mulholland Dr.* is surely one of the most unnerving *film noirs* ever made. Quite simply, it demands to be seen again and again. AP

Dir, Scr: David Lynch; **Prod**: Neal Edelstein, Tony Krantz, Michael Polaire, Alain Sarde, Mary Sweeney; **DOP**: Peter Deming (colour); **Ed**: Mary Sweeney; **Score**: Angelo Badalamenti; **Main Cast**: Naomi Watts, Laura Harring, Ann Miller, Dan Hedaya, Justin Theroux, Brent Briscoe; **Prod Co**: Les Films Alain Sarde, Asymmetrical Productions, Babbo Inc., Canal+, The Picture Factory.

Murder, My Sweet
US, 1944 – 95 mins
Edward Dmytryk

After Bogart's Sam Spade in *The Maltese Falcon* (1941)* and before
Bogart's Philip Marlowe in *The Big Sleep* (1946)*, there was Dick Powell's
Marlowe in *Murder, My Sweet*, one of the most accomplished *film noirs*.
The film was originally released in December 1944 as *Farewell, My Lovely*
(the title retained for its UK release) but re-released in March 1945 as
Murder, My Sweet, Raymond Chandler's original title. Its trailer promised
Dick Powell 'in an amazing new type of role', both a new persona for
Powell, who in the 1930s specialised in light musical-comedy youthful
crooner roles, and a new kind of hard-boiled, cynical detective hero type
– already well established in novels but still relatively new to movies
(despite Bogart's Sam Spade). Chandler felt that Powell's Marlowe came
closest to his own conception, and Powell's new persona was carried
forward in subsequent *film noirs* like *Cornered* (1945)* and *Pitfall* (1948)*.

Murder, My Sweet was particularly influential in establishing a *noir*
visual style and mode of narration, picturing the tough *noir* hero type up
against a fundamentally corrupt world. These elements are strikingly
announced from the start: we are plunged via a disorienting overhead
shot into a shadowy space, where a blindfolded Marlowe is being
interrogated by cops under a harsh spotlight and beginning to tell his
story in flashback. The high-contrast visual style, largely absent from *The
Maltese Falcon*, becomes positively expressionist in the subjective
dream/hallucination sequences during which Marlowe is knocked out or
drugged, while the voice-over flashback narration, smart and tough but
frank and wryly funny about his vulnerability and competence, defines
Marlowe's ironic distance on the people and events around him.

The flashback begins with images of night-time city streets and
Marlowe alone in his office, when the flashing neon light outside lights
up the 'not quite real' reflection of gigantic ex-wrestler Moose Malloy
(Mike Mazurki), back from a long stint in jail and seeking Marlowe's help

to find his former dancer girlfriend, Velma. This sets off a complicated plot in which an apparently entirely separate assignment to help someone pay a ransom for a stolen jade necklace ends in murder in a remote canyon – the first of several scenes in which Marlowe is knocked out or drugged. Marlowe's investigation leads him through the corrupt, duplicitous social strata of Los Angeles, from the low dives of Moose's and Velma's earlier lives to the mansions and beach houses of the seriously wealthy. The trail leads to the old-money Grayle (Miles Mander), his *femme fatale* younger wife, Helen (Claire Trevor) and enigmatically ingénue daughter Ann (Anne Shirley). As ever, the *femme fatale* here is a fascinating figure: humble origins, showgirl, wealthy wife, stepmother, overtly sexual, she plays many roles, though it is never quite clear who she is or what she really wants. Unlike some later *film noirs* where the hero ends up disenchanted or dead, Marlowe and good girl Ann end up together (though the ending avoids being too conventional with a smart joke).

Almost dreamlike, Moose Malloy (Mike Mazurki) materialises in the office of Philip Marlowe (Dick Powell) near the start of *Murder, My Sweet*

Chandler's 1940 novel was adapted for *The Falcon Takes Over* (Irving Reis, 1942), in RKO's B-movie private-detective Falcon series, but Dmytryk's 1944 movie was the first proper Chandler adaptation and the first Marlowe. The chief asset of the 1940s-set 1975 remake, *Farewell, My Lovely* (Dick Richards) is sixty-year-old Robert Mitchum as Marlowe. As the film begins, Marlowe/Mitchum (in fedora and what looks every bit like the raincoat he wears in *Out of the Past*, 1947*) looks down into the street intoning in voice-over, 'This past spring was the first I felt tired and realised I was growing old.' Though an eminently watchable movie, it nevertheless falls into the category of redundant remakes. JH

Dir: Edward Dmytryk; **Prod**: Adrian Scott; **Scr**: John Paxton from Raymond Chandler's novel *Farewell, My Lovely*; **DOP**: Harry J. Wild (b&w); **Ed**: Joseph Noriega; **Score**: Roy Webb; **Main Cast**: Dick Powell, Claire Trevor, Anne Shirley, Otto Kruger, Mike Mazurki, Miles Mander; **Prod Co**: RKO.

The Narrow Margin
US, 1952 – 71 mins
Richard Fleischer

Ever since the early days of cinema, film-makers have examined the intrinsic connections that can be drawn between one's perceptual experience of the moving image and the sensation of the train journey. In numerous thrillers such as *The Lady Vanishes* (1938) and *Strangers on a Train* (1951), Alfred Hitchcock, in particular, explored the expressive potential for tension and suspense in the confined but mobile narrative space offered by the synergy between celluloid and the railway track. The train carriage or train engine are key sites of action in *film noirs* such as *La Bête humaine* (1938)* and *Double Indemnity* (1944)*. In Richard Fleischer's critically undervalued B-movie, *The Narrow Margin*, the bulk of the film takes place on board a Chicago locomotive bound for Los Angeles in which police detective Walter Brown (Charles McGraw) is charged with the protection of a key witness in a planned anti-mob suit in the Californian courts. The former wife of gangster Frankie Neall –'the kind of dame who's poison under the gravy'– has to spend the journey in hiding while Neall's henchmen try to uncover her identity and prevent her from spilling the beans.

Despite its low-budget status, *The Narrow Margin* comes with a fine pedigree. It was based on a story written by Martin Goldsmith, the scriptwriter on *Detour* (1945)*. Charles McGraw, who plays his scenes with great panache and aggression, also starred in *The Killers* (1946)*, *Side Street* (1950)* and *His Kind of Woman* (John Farrow, 1951). Its atmospheric visual style, especially its suggestive use of the reflective surfaces of the train windows in the key dramatic scenes towards the end of the film, owes much to the cinematography of George E. Diskant, who shot *On Dangerous Ground** (1952). Finally, it is also worth noting the work of Clem Portman (*They Live by Night* [1948]*) and Francis M. Sarver (*Out of the Past* [1947]*), who controlled the production sound. Unusually, there is no non-diegetic music in the film though great use is made of a portable jazz record player in one of the hidden train compartments. The result is that there are long sections of the film with little dialogue and certainly little verbal exposition. Instead, we hear the constant rattling of the tracks that are at times aligned with other sounds such as the angry filing of nails, the suspenseful turning of door handles or the hasty sliding of doors.

The Narrow Margin: police detective Walter Brown (Charles McGraw) is charged with the protection of gangster Frankie Neall's wife (Marie Windsor) – 'the kind of dame who's poison under the gravy'

In order to make the most of the claustrophobic nature of the train as it moves through the Southern Californian towns and countryside, Fleischer sets much of the action in an elaborate series of corridors and private compartments. These are framed to maximise the narrative tension and induce a sense of desperation as Brown's enemies close in on him and his mystery charge. There is a constant play on how much the individual protagonists – and indeed the spectator – all know in relation to each other. As on any train, we learn to distinguish individual characters through one or two simple defining characteristics but, as the journey progresses, we gradually realise that not all is what it seems. Indeed, one of the most interesting things about the film is the way that it ends by reversing all our expectations regarding certain conventions of *film noir* femininity.

Peter Hyams remade *The Narrow Margin* in 1990, with Gene Hackman in the starring role, but the film – relocated to Canada – lacks the distinctive vernacular appeal of this tightly woven pulp *film noir* from the heyday of both black-and-white cinematography and pre-electric train travel. AP

Dir: Richard Fleischer; **Prod**: Stanley Rubin; **Scr**: Earl Felton from Martin Goldsmith and Jack Leonard's unpublished story; **DOP**: George E. Diskant (b&w); **Ed**: Robert Swink; **Main Cast**: Charles McGraw, Marie Windsor, Jacqueline White, Gordon Gebert; **Prod Co**: RKO.

Night and the City
UK/US, 1950 – 95 mins
Jules Dassin

Jules Dassin's captivating *film noir* begins with a leisurely title sequence
detailing scenic nocturnal views of the River Thames and Piccadilly Circus.
A sonorous off-screen voice introduces the title of the film, telling us 'the
night is tonight, tomorrow night or any night. The city is London.'
Suddenly, we cut to a dramatic chase sequence as a man in sharp hat
and suit flees a shadowy, unidentified threat across the steps of St Paul's
Cathedral and its nearby bombsites and alleyways. The sense of menace,
the low-key lighting and the vivid claustrophobic compositions transform
the vernacular surfaces of the city into the visual landscape of *film noir*.
And then, in one of many ensuing shots of the man, Harry Fabian
(Richard Widmark), running up the stairs, the film shifts gear again.
Dusting himself down and pinning a carnation in his lapel, he enters a
comfortably furnished London flat with tea on the table. We are now in
the mundane surroundings of a British realist drama from the 1940s.

Night and the City is a hybrid production in a number of ways. In
terms of visual and narrative style it marries the traditional conventions of
American *film noir* with a particularly British sensibility concerning the
representation of character and social space. Directed by the American
Jules Dassin, whose previous *noir* credits included *The Naked City* (1948)
and *Thieves' Highway* (1949), it brings two leading American *noir* actors,
Gene Tierney (*Laura* [1944]* and *Whirlpool* [Otto Preminger, 1949]) and
Richard Widmark (*Kiss of Death* [1947]* and *The Street with No Name*
[William Keighley, 1948]), into play with some of Britain's leading acting
talents from the period. At times, it feels as if the sardonic menace of
New York *noir* has been crossed with the satirical social observation of
Dickensian, or even Hogarthian, London. The film's transnational status is
not only signalled by the variety of international and local accents, but by
the prominent night-time location signage. In one telling transition,
Dassin cuts from a view of the illuminated front of the 'American Bar' to

the entrance of the 'Café de l'Europe'. *Night and the City* itself was similarly divided into two, in that separate versions were cut (with different musical scores) for British and American audiences. Years later (1992), the film was actually reshot in the US by Irwin Winkler, with Robert de Niro in the leading role.

Based on Gerald Kersh's eponymous novel, *Night and the City* recounts the rise and downfall of a scheming clubland tout and his illicit attempt to seize control of the capital's lucrative underworld wrestling scene. The property was developed by Fox to deal with two related priorities. First, under the terms of postwar regulations, designed to keep a portion of American film-company profits in the country, the studio was obliged to reinvest in local film production under the name Twentieth Century-Fox Productions. Then second, Dassin was brought over from the US to stave off the threat of being formally named in the HUAC hearings. He was even advised by Darryl F. Zanuck to shoot the most expensive scenes first, just in case he was fired after being denounced, like Edward Dmytryk (*Murder My Sweet* [1944]*, *Cornered* [1945]*, *Crossfire* [1947]*) as a left-winger. In the event, Dassin never did work in Hollywood again. His next film, a long five years later, was the influential French *film noir*, *Rififi* (1955)*.

Given these circumstances, *Night and the City* is therefore perhaps unsurprisingly replete with all kinds of references to betrayal and duplicity. Its central fated protagonist thrives only in a milieu of false promises and fake allegiances. As we have seen, the film begins with the general, but soon turns to the local. Like *The Naked City* then, it is a thrilling portrait of one particular place at one particular time, but as with its predecessor, in its very typicality, it also proposes a rich and disturbing territory of potentially endless loss, desire and personal corruption. AP

Dir: Jules Dassin; **Prod**: Samuel G. Engel; **Scr**: Jo Eisinger from Gerald Kersh's novel; **DOP**: Mutz Greenbaum (b&w); **Ed**: Nick DeMaggio, Sidney Stone; **Score**: Benjamin Frankel, Franz Waxman; **Main Cast**: Richard Widmark, Gene Tierney, Googie Withers, Francis L. Sullivan, Herbert Lom, Stanislaus Zbyszko, Mike Mazurki; **Prod Co**: Twentieth Century-Fox Productions.

Night Moves
US, 1975 – 99 mins
Arthur Penn

Arthur Penn's still underrated revisionist take on the private-detective *film noir*, like its preceding counterparts *The Long Goodbye* (1973)* and *Chinatown* (1974)*, is a compelling portrait of the loss of one man's professional and emotional bearings. Trading the ethical securities of the conventional gumshoe film for a more unsettling vision of moral displacement and investigative failure, *Night Moves* seems to ask unanswered questions not just about the role of the private eye, but about the wider political and social morass that mid-1970s America had found itself in. As Peter C. Knowles (1990) tellingly puts it, *Night Moves* is about 'the failure of both man and reason – in effect the analytical method – to penetrate the levels of ambiguity that define the contemporary experience'.

Night Moves begins, at least, like an old-style genre film with Harry Moseby (Gene Hackman) visiting a new client: a washed-up minor Hollywood actress living high in the hills above Los Angeles. Arlene Iverson (Janet Ward) employs Moseby to look for her missing teenage daughter who, as it later turns out, has absconded to the Florida Keys to stay with her stepfather Tom (John Crawford) and his lover, Paula (Jennifer Warren). Meanwhile, Moseby's own private life comes under scrutiny as he discovers that his wife, Ellen (Susan Clark), has been having an affair. As the hermeneutic element of the film's narrative proceeds to a violent and unresolved climax, Moseby's character gradually becomes as much the subject of investigation as the mysterious contents of a crashed plane found on the bottom of the Florida ocean floor.

Arthur Penn belongs to that generation of American film-makers influenced by European art cinema of the 1960s and this legacy permeates the visual and narrative style of the film. *Night Moves*, for example, explicitly withholds significant information from the spectator thus rendering the plot of the film as opaque and multifaceted as the circular concave mirrors embedded in the glass doors of two of its main protagonists. Its allegiance to Gene Hackman's typically languid but troubled character is slender. Characters regularly taunt him for being unable to live up to the heroic legacy of his *film noir* predecessors: 'take a swing for me, like Sam Spade would' and 'isn't that what you do – look for clues?' they say. Even the boat in which Moseby is finally left stranded is named ironically 'Point of View'.

Night Moves is replete with references to its time and a generation that in Penn's words 'knows there are no solutions'. Its close-ups of audio-tape recorders and air of political uncertainty and betrayal recall the Watergate scandal, while Paula's car runs on olive oil in apparent response to the country's recent oil shock. Also interesting is the film's ambivalent attitude towards the sexual revolution of the 1960s. Moseby is disgusted by the drug-addled 'freaks' in his midst, but the centre beneath his feet is also clearly shifting with the impact of second-wave feminism. The main female figures in Penn's film, played with great empathy and assurance by both Jennifer Warren and Susan Clark, are more than adequate foils for Moseby and his apparent psychological inadequacies; they are strong and rounded characters in their own right. *Night Moves* is unusual in this respect. Harry Moseby, heir to Sam Spade and Philip Marlowe, famously refuses to see *My Night at Maud's* (1969) at the local arthouse cinema, saying it would be 'like watching paint dry', but in its own way, Arthur Penn's sceptical and questioning *film noir* is as sly, observant, and ultimately sympathetic, as any drama directed by the likes of Eric Rohmer. AP

Dir: Arthur Penn; **Prod**: Robert M. Sherman; **Scr**: Alan Sharp; **DOP**: Bruce Surtees (colour); **Ed**: Dede Allen, Stephen A. Rotter; **Score**: Michael Small; **Main Cast**: Gene Hackman, Jennifer Warren, Susan Clark, Ed Binns, Harris Yulin, Melanie Griffith, Janet Ward, John Crawford; **Prod Co**: Warner Bros.

Nightmare Alley
US, 1947 – 110 mins
Edmund Goulding

Nightmare Alley is reminiscent of a number of Hollywood films such as
The Lusty Men (Nicholas Ray, 1952) and *Ace in the Hole* (Billy Wilder,
1951) that use the insecurities and duplicities of the world of itinerant
entertainment to comment on the price of personal and social fulfillment
when it comes to the workings of American capitalism. In its focus on
the mysteries of psychological trickery and theatrical illusion, it also
reaches back to *The Cabinet of Dr Caligari* (Robert Wiene, 1919), a film
commonly cited as one of the major progenitors of certain aspects of the
visual and narrative style of *film noir*.

Partly set against the atmospheric backdrop of the American
travelling carnival scene, Edmund Goulding's film tells the tale of the
dramatic rise and fall of Stanton Carlisle (Tyrone Power), a self-confident
huckster who tricks a fellow sideshow performer, Zeena (Joan Blondell),
into giving him the secret to her and her alcoholic husband's successful
mind-reading act. Stanton soon dispenses with Zeena and sets off with
Molly (Coleen Gray) to make his fortune seducing wealthy patrons in
theatre shows across the American Midwest. There, Stanton meets the
mysterious psychoanalyst, Lilith Ritter (Helen Walker), and the pair
concoct a phony 'religious' scam that proves his undoing. Stanton
eventually returns to the carnival a drunken wreck, the mirror image of
the man he once despised.

Based on William Lindsay Gresham's best-selling novel, *Nightmare
Alley* was originally designed by Fox to showcase the wider talents of
its leading actor. Tyrone Power certainly gives a thoroughly absorbing
portrayal of moral bankruptcy and naked ambition, on a par with any
conventional *film noir* villain, but what also distinguishes the film is its
director's characteristically supple and revealing handling of the three
main female characters. Joan Blondell's brassy, warm-hearted Zeena is
the perfect foil to the more ambiguous character of Molly, who marries

a girl-next-door innocence – seen also in *Kiss of Death** the same year – with her own determined take on personal desire. At the apex of this triangle is the extraordinary character of Lilith Ritter who would in any normal circumstances be called upon to play the *femme fatale* were it not for her apparent lack of any sexual interest in men. Lilith's ethical flaws, according to the film's quite starkly cynical schema, may be best explained it seems by her professed faith in psychoanalysis, though even that is called into question by her snappy retort to Stanton and his fraudulent showbusiness act: 'It takes one to know one.'

At times, *Nightmare Alley* feels more like a B-feature than an A-feature production. It has a curious elliptical narrative style that seems more reminiscent of an Edgar G. Ulmer *film noir* such as *Detour* (1945)* than a large-budget Fox feature of the late 1940s. Woody Haut (2005) has attributed this to the troubled relations between the film's producers and the Production Code Administration. Nonetheless, Lee Garmes's cinematography excels in portraying the darker contours of the various milieux Stanton inhabits. The night-time carnival scenes – all shot, of course, in the studio – are meticulously lit and compelling for their depiction of the sadness underlying the surface vivacity of carnival life. What really distinguishes the film for modern-day audiences though is its acerbic portrait of almost every social institution of the time, whether it be the family, religion, industrial capitalism or psychotherapeutic medicine. In this sense, the world of the carnival assumes a more metaphorical dimension. American society itself is the true subject of this film's typically bleak *noir* title. AP

Dir: Edmund Goulding; **Prod**: George Jessel; **Scr**: Jules Furthman from William Lindsay Gresham's novel; **DOP**: Lee Garmes (b&w); **Ed**: Barbara McLean; **Score**: Cyril Mockridge; **Main Cast**: Tyrone Power, Joan Blondell, Coleen Gray, Helen Walker, Taylor Holmes; **Prod Co**: Twentieth Century-Fox.

Odd Man Out
UK – 1947, 116 mins
Carol Reed

A gang plans a heist, but things go wrong during the robbery when the
gang leader/hero and innocent bystanders get shot and the leader falls
from the escape car and is left behind. Badly wounded and alone in the
city at night, in rain and snow, he tries to hide and make his way back,
while both police and gang search for him. Found and cared for by the
young woman who loves him, and whom he may love, he dies trying
to make the escape that she has arranged for him. This could be a
quintessential US *noir* narrative, but *Odd Man Out* is a British film –
though the postwar mood of moral ambiguity and urban alienation
works as well here as it does in its American counterparts. Moreover, the
gang are political activists carrying out the robbery not for personal gain
but to finance their organisation (though neither the IRA nor the
city – Belfast – are specifically named). The film's preface refers to 'a
background of political unrest' and 'the struggle between the law and
an illegal organisation', but shies away – unsurprisingly – from political
issues, claiming concern 'only with the conflict in the hearts of the
people'.

    Odd Man Out's evocation of the night-time city as hostile territory
(with policemen on every corner) is powerful, fully exploiting Robert
Krasker's images of dark, wet streets and tenements. James Mason's
gang leader, Johnny McQueen, a sympathetic portrait of an essentially
gentle IRA man who finds himself brought down by violence, remained
the actor's favourite role. Director Carol Reed is as good at handling
action – the gang's hold-up of the mill and its chaotic aftermath – as at
evoking atmosphere and place, and makes a good stab at simulating
Johnny's subjective disequilibrium when faced with the unfamiliar pace
of street life after lengthy imprisonment. There is no room here for a
femme fatale but vulnerable yet tough Kathleen (Kathleen Ryan) recalls
characters like Shelley Winters's Peg in *He Ran All the Way* (1951)*.

Despite its qualities, *Odd Man Out* is dogged by a certain stylistic academicism and the tendency to take itself too seriously. In the 1940s – before André Bazin revolutionised thinking about film language – Reed's restrained expressionist style was seen as the epitome of 'film art' (provided it was at the service of 'serious' subject matter). Though less self-consciously arty than John Ford's IRA story *The Informer* (1935), *Odd Man Out* is not content – as so many US *film noirs* are – to be a thriller whose deeper meanings remain implied. Instead, Reed keeps reaching for religious symbolism and significance, particularly in the theatrically 'Oirish' sequences involving the priest, the ratlike would-be informer and the – narratively largely redundant – sequences with the artist, Lukey (Robert Newton) (who wants to paint the dying Johnny to capture 'the truth of life and death'). As Bosley Crowther commented in the *New York Times*, 'the author and … the director go searching for a philosophy of life … for some vague illumination of the meaning of charity and faith' (24 April 1947).

When it appeared, *Odd Man Out* was considered by many one of the greatest British films ever made. Its reputation remains high, although its status as a British *film noir* was overtaken by Reed's more international *The Third Man* (1949). Along with his more domestic *noir The Fallen Idol* (1948), these films constitute a period of enormous critical and commercial success for Reed. Greene's novel was remade as *The Lost Man* (Robert Alan Arthur, 1969), its Irish nationalists replaced by black militants, with Sidney Poitier in the James Mason role. JH

Dir, Prod: Carol Reed; **Scr**: F. L. Green, R. C. Sherriff from Graham Greene's novel; **DOP**: Robert Krasker (b&w); **Ed**: Fergus McDonell; **Score**: William Alwyn; **Main Cast**: James Mason, Robert Newton, Cyril Cusack, Kathleen Ryan, F. J. McCormick, Fay Compton, Denis O'Dea, W. G. Fay, Robert Beatty, Dan O'Herlihy; **Prod Co**: Two Cities Films.

Odds against Tomorrow
US, 1959 – 96 mins
Robert Wise

This innovative and critically undervalued heist film was one of Jean-Pierre Melville's favourite American crime movies, along with *The Asphalt Jungle* (1950)*. Like *The Asphalt Jungle*, it predominately concerns the unravelling of a painstakingly planned robbery, but here the tensions within the conventional male criminal group are explicitly played out in racial terms, with the black musician Harry Belafonte taking a leading role as the film's ostensible moral voice, Johnny Ingram, opposite Robert Ryan who, as Earle Slater, reprises the virulent racist type he played in *Crossfire* (1947)*.

The film brilliantly captures the moment just before the onset of the civil-rights campaigns of the 1960s when a black American citizen in a suburban small town north of New York is still so sufficiently differentiated from white mainstream America that he may unwittingly become the lynchpin in the planning of a bank robbery. This sense of a nation on the cusp of social and cultural change pervades the film as a whole with its recourse to television sets and expressways within the *mise en scène*, references to satellites and Sputnik within the carefully delivered script and depiction of the clapped-out, angry last gasps of a relationship conducted by those earlier *noir* stalwarts of the previous decade, Robert Ryan and Gloria Grahame. In fact, as the title suggests, *Odds against Tomorrow* feels like *noir* at the end of the road. Its final words are 'Stop. Dead End' which, in addition to signifying the outcome of the heist and the futility of differentiating between white and black, also point to the sense of drift in the film in relation to its expressive use of *film noir* conventions.

Odds against Tomorrow was originally devised by Belafonte for his newly established black-interest production company HarBel and was based on the novel by the American crime novelist and screenwriter, William P. McGivern, whose previous work adapted into *film noir* included Fritz Lang's *The Big Heat* (1953)*. McGivern's source novel was reworked substantially by the blacklisted director and screenwriter, Abraham Polonsky, who was, in turn, fronted by the black writer John O. Killens on the production because of political restrictions. The book's original upbeat ending, for example, was changed to the more pessimistic conclusion showing the police unable to identify the similarly charred remains of Ingram and Slater.

The film mainly dwells on the tripartite relationship between Ingram, a stylish jazz singer and gambler; Slater, a vicious-tongued hardened criminal and Burke (Ed Begley), an ageing convicted former police officer who mediates between the two leads. It also evokes the tensions in the characters' respective private lives, thus unusually opening up a space in mainstream American cinema for the depiction of the familial and social lives of ordinary urban black Americans.

Unlike many American *film noirs* which use jazz to signify exotically charged difference and sexual energy, jazz music is woven more seamlessly into the threads of the film's narration so that the timbre and patina of *noir*'s conventional – and thus white – generic spaces such as the sidewalk, the boarding-room and the warehouse seem more tired and faded than ever. In the atmospheric transition from New York to Melton, Joseph C. Brun's evocative cinematography captures this sense of unease as if the pastoral of the American small town seen in earlier generations of *film noir* to suggest a counterpoint to the city's inequities has now utterly vanished. Instead, it has been replaced by an uncomfortable late autumnal industrial melancholy reminiscent of Robert Frank's then contemporaneous photographic portrayal in *The Americans* (1959) of an America tragically lost in its quest for the elusive American Dream. AP

Dir: Robert Wise; **Prod**: Robert Wise, Harry Belafonte; **Scr**: Abraham Polonsky, John O. Killens, Nelson Gidding from William P. McGivern's novel; **DOP**: Joseph C. Brun (b&w); **Ed**: Dede Allen; **Score**: John Lewis; **Main Cast**: Harry Belafonte, Robert Ryan, Gloria Grahame, Shelley Winters, Ed Begley; **Prod Co**: HarBel Productions.

On Dangerous Ground
US, 1952 – 82 mins
Nicholas Ray

On Dangerous Ground is loosely based on a British hard-boiled novel by
Gerald Butler, but Nicholas Ray was also inspired by a Boston cop he had
accompanied on assignments. Ray shows again his abiding interest in
the nature of violence, here the inner turmoil and outer violence of Jim
Wilson (Robert Ryan, superb as usual as an embittered character of great
physical power). Wilson, once a prime athlete, now a lonely cop, is
constantly on the edge of, and tipping over into, violence (like Humphrey
Bogart's character in *In a Lonely Place*, 1950* – another highly expressive
Ray title). Wilson is partnered by, and contrasted with, two married cops
who are able to leave their jobs behind when they return to wives and
family. The city sequences, all shot at night – dark streets, alleyways, bars
and cheap walk-up apartments – paint one of the bleakest *noir* pictures
of city life. Everything is refracted through Wilson's bitterness, and some
hand-held shooting – unusual for the time – implicates the audience in
his violent point of view. When Wilson oversteps the mark yet again and
beats up a suspect, he is 'exiled' to a snowy upstate rural community
both to help find the murderer of a young girl and to cool off.

Some critics have found the film 'broken-backed', its episodic first
thirty minutes sitting uncomfortably with the powerful linear narrative of
the second part. But that first part establishes very effectively Wilson's
intense loneliness, his sense of going nowhere, his alienation from his
work and colleagues and his disgust at the urban environment, as well
as the violence which he is unable to keep in check and whose moral
dimension he is unable to see. Almost the only hint of a Wilson for
whom there might be some hope comes in the early-morning street
encounter with the young paperboy with whom he plays football and
who asks, solicitously, if Wilson is OK.

As he travels north, the city gives way to snowbound countryside
and darkness to light, seen from Wilson's point of view through the car

windscreen; the style and pace of the film change and we enter a quite different world. That new world is far from 'innocent', however. Wilson recognises his own violence in Brent, the murdered girl's father (Ward Bond), hot for violent revenge, as they hunt down the killer together. The 'killer' turns out to be a disturbed adolescent – perhaps a reminder of the city paperboy – and young brother of blind Mary Malden (Ida Lupino), with whom Wilson becomes involved and who helps him to 'see' and feel.

On Dangerous Ground is a favourite of Martin Scorsese and a key influence on *Taxi Driver* (1976)*. Both were scored by Bernard Herrmann, whose score for Ray's film is one of its major assets – especially in the evocative transition from city to countryside. Shooting completed in May 1950 but the film was not released until February 1952, and is not quite the way Ray wanted it. Rather than the effectively two-part structure of the finished film, Ray had envisaged a three-part structure of city/countryside/city, incorporating the bleakest of endings with Wilson returning to the city and his old life for good, rather than returning to Mary. Doubtless this contributed to Ray's own sense of the film as a failure. Ida Lupino may have shot some scenes in Ray's absence, but there seems no hard evidence for this. JH

Dir: Nicholas Ray; **Prod**: John Houseman; **Scr**: A. I. Bezzerides, Nicholas Ray from Gerald Butler's *Mad with Much Heart*; **DOP**: George E. Diskant (b&w); **Ed**: Roland Gross; **Score**: Bernard Herrmann; **Main Cast**: Robert Ryan, Ida Lupino, Ward Bond, Charles Kemper, Anthony Ross, Ed Begley, Sumner Williams; **Prod Co**: RKO.

Out of the Past
US, 1947 – 96 mins
Jacques Tourneur

Not much remarked on at its initial release, though it did well commercially, *Out of the Past* is now firmly established as an archetypal, indeed quintessential, *film noir*. Consider the ingredients: smart but weary male private detective, in thrall to the *femme fatale* and compromised by his past; beautiful but untrustworthy *femme fatale*, opportunistically changing sexual partners; domesticated 'good girl' as a counter for the *femme fatale*; voice-over flashback narration and complex temporal structure and plotting – even after several viewings some plot points remain obscure; striking use of *chiaroscuro* black-and-white cinematography, particularly in the night-time city sequences.

The male protagonist here is former private detective Jeff Bailey (Robert Mitchum), now trying to live quietly – in a sense in hiding – running a small-town gas station, but pulled back into a final job for gambler Whit Sterling (Kirk Douglas). Years before – as Jeff tells current girlfriend Ann (Virginia Huston), in voice-over flashback – Sterling hired him to find his absconded girlfriend Kathie Moffatt (Jane Greer). Jeff found her in Acapulco, but fell hopelessly for her and the pair ran away and lived together, until their secret was found out. Back in the present, Jeff finds Kathie back with Sterling and soon figures out that his assignment in San Francisco is in fact designed to frame him for murder. Jeff outwits Sterling and the denouement finds Sterling, Kathie and Jeff all together; Kathie murders Sterling and insists Jeff leaves with her; Jeff warns the police and in the ensuing ambush, Kathie is killed, but not before killing Jeff.

Director Jacques Tourneur and cinematographer Nicholas Musuraca, who had worked together on RKO's early 1940s low-budget fantasy-horror movies, including *Cat People* (1943), were, as James Naremore

(1998) says, 'especially good at creating a lyrical or sensuous play of shadow'. They strikingly evoke the romantic and erotic – but essentially illusory – attractions of Acapulco and *femme fatale* Kathie stage managing her own entrances to ensnare the willing hero, or the mountains, lakes and meadows of small-town rural California and the quiet, wistful but determined 'good girl' Ann – perhaps just as illusory – or the threatening, chaotic atmosphere of San Francisco and the renewed encounter with Kathie. We are encouraged to feel very powerfully both what Jeff would like to hang on to in the present, and the force of the past which threatens it.

Mitchum, by then one of RKO's major star assets, never inhabited his smart but weary and resigned 'tough guy' persona – wilder, tougher and more socially marginal than Humphrey Bogart's or Dick Powell's – better than here, or looked more archetypal in crumpled trench coat and fedora. Alongside him, newcomer Jane Greer excels as the alluring *femme fatale*, amoral, certainly, but her actions nevertheless comprehensible as those of a woman exploiting her only source of power – her sexual attraction – as best she can in a male-dominated world.

The film was adapted by screenwriter and novelist Daniel Mainwaring, under the pseudonym Geoffrey Homes, from his novel *Build My Gallows High* and was originally shown under that title. When a test audience showed some resistance to the title, it was changed to *Out of the Past*, but the original title was retained for the film's UK release. The film's opening announces its setting as 'Bridgeport, California'; curiously, Mitchum was born in Bridgeport, Connecticut. *Against All Odds* (Taylor Hackford, 1984) was a very dull remake, with Jeff Bridges and Rachel Ward in Mitchum's and Greer's roles. Among its very few compensations were a smart performance

(*Next page*) *Femme fatale* Kathie (Jane Greer) stage managing her first appearance for Jeff Bailey (Robert Mitchum) in *Out of the Past*

by James Woods in the Kirk Douglas part, and a cameo role for sixty-year-old Greer. JH

Dir: Jacques Tourneur; **Prod**: Warren Duff; **Scr**: Geoffrey Homes (Daniel Mainwaring), Frank Fenton (uncredited), James M. Cain (uncredited) from Homes's novel *Build My Gallows High*; **DOP**: Nicholas Musuraca (b&w); **Ed**: Samuel E. Beetley; **Score**: Roy Webb; **Main Cast**: Robert Mitchum, Jane Greer, Kirk Douglas, Rhonda Fleming, Richard Webb, Steve Brodie, Virginia Huston, Dickie Moore, Paul Valentine; **Prod Co**: RKO.

Phantom Lady
US, 1944 – 87 mins
Robert Siodmak

Like Alfred Hitchcock's *Rear Window* (1954), Robert Siodmak's *Phantom Lady* was adapted from a novel by the pulp crime novelist, Cornell Woolrich. The connections don't end there. The rights to the book had been obtained for Universal by Joan Harrison, a young, independent and intellectually minded producer, who had formerly been Hitchcock's private secretary. Furthermore, both films have similarly passive male leads and active female protagonists called upon to take a determining performative role in order to resolve the central narrative enigma.

Scott Henderson is a businessman arrested for the murder of his wife. His only alibi, a mysterious lady he had met in a bar the night of the death, has vanished. In order to clear his name, his admiring secretary, Kansas (Ella Raines), sets out into New York's lonely jazz-infested nightlife scene in disguise. Eventually, the real murderer is found: Scott's schizophrenic artist friend, Marlow (played dementedly to the hilt by Franchot Tone), whose unhealthy obsession with his hands (à la Conrad Veidt in *The Hands of Orlac* [1924]) nearly leads to the intrepid Kansas's demise.

Phantom Lady was Siodmak's first commercial Hollywood success and it has numerous fascinating parallels with both his previous European work such as *Pièges* (1939) (remade as *Lured* by Douglas Sirk in 1947) and later American films such as *Criss Cross* (1949)* and *The File on Thelma Jordon* (1949). The emphasis on certain objects within the *mise en scène* – especially the lady's hat – relates, for example, to a pervasive tone of detachment and scepticism about material surfaces. The lighting set-ups are also highly detailed and atmospheric. The American cinematographer, Woody Bredell, said, for instance, that after being coached by Siodmak he felt he could 'light a football pitch with a match'.

Perhaps because of Siodmak's émigré background, the film is also curiously ambivalent about the status of European-style private high culture in relation to its presumed opposite: the seedy public world of the American vaudeville circuit. The effete artist/killer has a Van Gogh print in his living quarters, whereas the musical cabaret scenes are represented in terms of almost manic, sexualised excess. It is as if a pathological Weimar-style murderer has landed up in the economic and physical consumerism of modern-day New York. 'I've never liked cities, noise confusion, dirt', Marlow admits at one point. To this extent, only one kindly (German) immigrant couple running a dime store late into the night seem to offer any moral compass in Siodmak's dark survey of urban anomie.

The key to the film's persistent sense of dislocation rests in the analogy it draws between Kansas's necessary impersonation of the *femme fatale* (in order to lure the killer) and wider patterns of masquerade accepted as commonplace on the part of women struggling to find a place within the metropolis. There are, in fact, several 'phantom ladies' uncovered throughout the course of the narration. Although the plot of the film bears resemblance to another Woolrich adaptation of the same era (Roy William Neill's *Black Angel* [1946]), in this sense its truer counterparts are other *noir* explorations of the insecurity of men's control over women in the American city such as Fritz Lang's seminal *The Woman in the Window* (1944) and Otto Preminger's later *Where the Sidewalk Ends* (1950)*. AP

Dir: Robert Siodmak; **Prod**: Joan Harrison; **Scr**: Bernard C. Schoenfeld from Cornell Woolrich's novel; **DOP**: Woody Bredell (b&w); **Ed**: Arthur Hilton; **Score**: Hans J. Salter; **Main Cast**: Franchot Tone, Ella Raines, Alan Curtis, Aurora, Thomas Gomez, Fay Helm, Elisha Cook, Jr; **Prod Co**: Universal.

Pickup on South Street
US, 1953 – 83 mins
Samuel Fuller

Pickup on South Street is one of several *film noirs* which incorporated
some of the anti-Communist hysteria rife in the early 1950s but – unlike
I Married a Communist (1949)* – it does not simply graft an anti-
Communist story onto a familiar *noir* thriller format. As in his other genre
films, Samuel Fuller offers an idiosyncratic take on the *noir* approach. The
film has hard-boiled and pulp elements but lacks any investigative hero,
femme fatale, voice-over narration or flashback structure. As Fuller says,
his protagonists – three-time loser pickpocket Skip (Richard Widmark),
sleazy prostitute Candy (Jean Peters) and ageing stool pigeon Moe
(Thelma Ritter) – are 'marginal people', already at some distance from
mainstream morality. These characters come together when, in an
extended, brilliantly orchestrated sequence without dialogue set on
the New York subway, Skip picks Candy's handbag. Candy is under FBI
surveillance because she is carrying, unknowingly, microfilm with atomic
secrets. Skip, confident in his pickpocketing skills and therefore suspicious
that he has been spotted, works out that he must have stolen something
important. Candy is intimidated by her 'Commie' boyfriend Joey to track
Skip down and get the microfilm back, in exchange for either sex or
money.

Remarkably, we warm to these characters much more than to the
cops or FBI agents, though only Moe is immediately sympathetic. As Skip,
Widmark only slightly moderates the insolent sneer and propensity for
violence manifest in *Kiss of Death* (1947)* and Peters (in her best role)
relishes her part as the coarsely erotic floozy Candy. As Fuller intends,
they take much longer to engage us. Their extraordinary scenes together,
mixing casually brutal violence and raw sexual attraction, mark their
progress to becoming a – hardly romantic – couple and a 'happy end'.
The national security/microfilm plot is not quite the MacGuffin some have
claimed: it allows Fuller to contrast the abstractions of patriotism and

Skip McCoy (Richard Widmark), insolent as ever, with police captain Dan Tiger (Murvyn Vye) in *Pickup on South Street*

flag-waving – Skip, Candy and Moe profess to know nothing about Commies – with the more concrete and immediate realities of personal loyalties and commitments. Skip's real moment of salvation, for example, comes when he reclaims Moe's coffin from the fate she most dreaded – an anonymous burial in Potters Field.

Pickup on South Street scores most powerfully as a *film noir* in its visual style. One of the best New York City films, it mixes location and studio shooting. Important scenes are played out at Skip's geographically marginal South Street shack, perched over the river, literally beyond the city, and in the subway. Much of the film is shot in high-contrast photography, with some scenes, like the 'love scenes', played out in strikingly large close-ups, and others, like Candy's discovery that she has lost the microfilm, Moe's death scene or Candy's brutal beating by Joey, in complex long takes that are far from stylistically 'invisible' in the usual classical way.

Disliking the film's explicit anti-Communism, but recognising that they had a terrific movie, the film's French distributors dubbed in a plot about drugs rather than military secrets and retitled the film *Le Port de la drogue* (which remains the film's official French title). It seems to work quite well that way, demonstrating how unideological the film's villains are – they're simply gangsters. Fuller's script was reworked for a – by all accounts unwatchable – 1967 US/South African remake, *The Cape Town Affair* (Richard D. Webb). JH

Dir: Samuel Fuller; **Prod**: Jules Schermer; **Scr**: Samuel Fuller, from Dwight Taylor's (unpublished) story; **DOP**: Joe Macdonald (b&w); **Ed**: Nick De Maggio; **Score**: Leigh Harline; **Main Cast**: Richard Widmark, Jean Peters, Thelma Ritter, Murvyn Vye, Richard Kiley; **Prod Co**: Jules Schermer Productions, Twentieth Century-Fox.

Pitfall
US, 1948 – 86 mins
André de Toth

While many *film noirs* privilege the city as the site of entrapment,
temptation and alienation, several American *film noirs* – particularly those
with links to the woman's film, such as *The Reckless Moment* (1949)* –
also make dramatic use of the incursion of crime and disorder into the
supposedly safe, respectable suburbs, which expanded rapidly in the
postwar period. *Pitfall*, set in Los Angeles, a sharp critique of US consumer
society and 'the organisation man', is a notable example. Insurance man
John Forbes (Dick Powell) and his wife Sue (Jane Wyatt) – the high-school
boy and girl most likely to succeed – are typical suburban 'successes' in
terms of work, family and home. Forbes doesn't want to be the average
American even though here – true to Powell's star persona of the period,
in films like *Murder, My Sweet* (1944)* and *Cornered* (1945)* – he is both
a wisecracking smart guy and a dissatisfied, troubled company man. In
many *film noirs* alienation and restlessness are linked to traumatic war
service. Forbes, however, as he says, spent most of the war in Denver
'doing what he was told'; clearly, his deep dissatisfaction owes something
to the conformist 'normality' of the postwar world.

Forbes's investigator, Mac (Raymond Burr), a menacing borderline
psychopath, has located, and become obsessively attracted, to Mona
Stevens (Lizabeth Scott), the beneficiary of some funds embezzled by her
former lover Smiley (Byron Barr), presently in jail. When Forbes takes over
the case and goes to see her she reacts spiritedly, telling him what he
fears he already knows, that he's 'a little man with a briefcase and you
do what you're told'. Forbes, enacting a more 'normal' version of Mac's
behaviour, is attracted to Mona, and she to him; they spend the day and
then, observed by Mac, the evening together. Forbes, in many ways
rejuvenated, neglects to tell Mona that he is married.

From this moment of 'temporary insanity' on, Forbes is caught in a
trap of his own making and the film becomes noticeably darker in both

mood and look. Mona discovers that Forbes is married and, in a very fine sequence, asks him difficult questions, not least why he was ready to risk all those things that she would like to have but hasn't. Initially confident in his ability to control events, things now spiral out of his control. Forbes kills Smiley when Mac sets up a night-time assault on his home and Mona has to shoot Mac when he tries to force her to go away with him. Warned by his wife not to drag his family through the dirt, Forbes spends the night with his conscience – a ghostly, dreamlike sequence of rear-projected night streets – before deciding to confess all.

The film is tough on Forbes and offers no easy solutions. Mona, a feisty, attractive figure who through no fault of her own is a victim of male fantasy and weakness, certainly no *femme fatale*, will be tried and convicted for the shooting of Mac. Forbes himself will go free for shooting Smiley but, heavily burdened with guilt, will be forced back into his routine life. Though his wife, who has her own dissatisfactions, picks him up from the police station, the best they can agree is 'to try to live with it'. Earlier, Forbes tells his disturbed son, though not very convincingly, 'Contentment – that's the secret of happiness.' JH

Dir: André de Toth; **Prod**: Samuel Bischoff; **Scr**: Karl Kamb, from Jay Dratler's novel; **DOP**: Harry Wild (b&w); **Ed**: Walter Thompson; **Score**: uncredited (music director: Louis Forbes); **Main Cast**: Dick Powell, Lizabeth Scott, Jane Wyatt, Raymond Burr, John Litel, Byron Barr, Ann Doran; **Prod Co**: Regal Films.

Point Blank
US, 1967 – 92 mins
John Boorman

Point Blank is a key film in the evolution of *film noir* from classical genre cinema to New Hollywood art cinema and neo-*noir*, at both the visual level – widescreen and colour, with studied composition and extensive use of the zoom – and the narrative level – in its employment of repetition, flashbacks and flashes forward, asynchronous sound, and fractured chronology. Excited by developments in European cinema in the late 1950s and early 1960s, John Boorman, like Alain Resnais in *Hiroshima mon amour* (1959), mixes up the past, present and imagined, with memories triggered by gestures or images. Like Michelangelo Antonioni, Boorman places characters in alien or inimical landscapes, here the Los Angeles built environment, with its faceless office blocks, neon-lit boulevards and the concrete expanses of the Los Angeles River storm drains.

Nevertheless, these formal strategies serve what is, essentially, a revenge crime story (based on Richard Stark's tough 1962 novel, *The Hunter* – since retitled *Point Blank*). Loner Walker (Lee Marvin), helping out in a heist on an abandoned Alcatraz, is double-crossed by his wife Lynne (Sharon Acker) and old friend Mal (John Vernon), shot point blank and left for dead. But he is 'left for dead' rather than actually seen to *be* dead, and this opens up different possibilities. Perhaps Walker survives, escapes from Alcatraz, then sets about retrieving the $93,000 he's due, presiding over the deaths of his wife, Mal and the increasingly senior executives of what appears an outwardly legitimate corporation. Alternatively, the film may be the hallucinatory projection of the dying Walker, imagining a scenario involving Lynne, her sister Chris (Angie Dickinson) and Mal. Certainly, the film is palpably dreamlike – one of the ways in which it relates most strongly to earlier *film noir*: Walker often seems to be sleepwalking or strangely immobile, and several exchanges suggest that Walker may be already dead and that the 'story' is taking place in his mind. The film's circularity and intentionally open ending – another money drop on Alcatraz, Walker failing to come forward to claim his money and disappearing into the shadows – could suggest that he had never really left.

Point Blank is a violent film and Walker a violent character – as befits Marvin's iconic status – but he never kills anyone: Lynne commits suicide, Mal's death appears accidental, and corporate bosses Carter (Lloyd

Figures in a cityscape: Walker (Lee Marvin) watching Stegman (Michael Strong) from the shadows in *Point Blank*

Bochner) and Brewster (Carroll O'Connor) are killed by the corporation's own hired sniper. Though Walker is a maverick on the wrong side of the law, his character here – suited, single-minded, introspective (owing something to Marvin's role in 1964's *The Killers*) – looks almost a principled, crusading figure compared with the corrupt bosses he confronts. Seeking, like Burt Lancaster in *I Walk Alone* (1948)*, to disrupt or destroy a new kind of organised crime, Walker is a *noir* hero trying to comprehend a world in which he no longer fits and which is intent on eliminating him.

For all its connections to *noir*, *Point Blank* looks very different to 1940s movies, with largely daytime settings, bright colours and hard surfaces. Like Jean-Pierre Melville's *Le Samouraï*, also 1967, it points to a more self-conscious form of *noir* and films like *The Long Goodbye* (1973)* and *Night Moves* (1975)*. Its more experimental approach to narration influenced neo-*noir* films like Steven Soderbergh's *The Underneath* (1995) (a remake of *Criss Cross* [1949]*) and *The Limey* (1999). Ringo Lam's Hong Kong *Full Contact* (1993) was an (unacknowledged) remake of *Point Blank*; *Payback* (Brian Helgeland, 1999) adapted the same novel (with Mel Gibson in the Marvin role).   JH

Dir: John Boorman; **Prod**: Judd Bernard, Robert Chartoff; **Scr**: Alexander Jacobs, David and Rafe Newhouse from Richard Stark's (Donald E. Westlake) novel *The Hunter*; **DOP**: Philip H. Lathrop (colour); **Ed**: Henry Berman; **Score**: Johnny Mandel; **Main Cast**: Lee Marvin, Angie Dickinson, Keenan Wynn, Carroll O'Connor, John Vernon, Sharon Acker, Lloyd Bochner; **Prod Co**: Judd Bernard–Robert Chartoff Productions, MGM.

The Postman Always Rings Twice
US, 1946 – 113 mins
Tay Garnett

The main characters of James M. Cain's powerful novel and Garnett's
fine movie, Frank Chambers (John Garfield) and Cora Smith (Lana
Turner), bring into conflict two central strands in American culture: Frank
is an optimistic young male with ideas and ideals, unconcerned about
wealth, but with 'itchy feet'; Cora is a young woman anxious for social
respectability and financial stability (much like another Cain creation,
Mildred Pierce [1945]*). The movie also unites two different stars and
modes of performance. Turner, 'sweater girl' and popular World War II
pin-up, plays and speaks in a rather mannered style, while Garfield,
schooled in 1930s theatre, works more naturalistically. Both stars draw
on their own backgrounds – Garfield on his tough, 'wrong-side-of-the-
tracks' childhood and period of drifting, Turner on her slightly cheap,
manufactured, highly stylised 'sexy' image (when Cora talks about
fighting off men since she was fourteen, Turner must surely be talking
about herself). Their characters are brought down by a combination of
powerful desire for each other and contradictory ambitions. Though they
try to deny and repress their emotions, passion draws them together and
pushes them apart almost against their wills. This is something close to
the surrealist idea of *amour fou* – the ending, after all, reunites them in
death.

The compelling first five minutes quickly establish Frank as a 'happy-
go-lucky' drifter, turning up at a roadside diner with a 'Man Wanted'
sign and wondering if this might be his future. The elderly owner has a
beautiful, young, blonde wife and Frank's – and our – first sight of Cora
is startling: her dropped lipstick – accidentally or on purpose – rolls to
Frank's feet and he (and we) look slowly upwards, taking in her white
heels, her bare legs, her white sun-suited body, her face, her hair in a
white turban. This recalls the introduction of Barbara Stanwyck's Phyllis in
Double Indemnity (1944)*, another Cain adaptation, whose story closely

resembles that of *The Postman Always Rings Twice*. Fate plays its hand
even before Frank's first sight of Cora: both the local DA who has given
Frank a lift and the passing highway motorcycle cop will be crucial to the
film's outcome. It is this sense of inexorable fate, and Frank's voice-over,
which makes the film seem so *noir*, despite its largely high-key lighting.
Late in the film, after the bewildering legal machinations which
exonerate them for murder, Frank and Cora take a moonlight swim and
re-establish their love and fidelity. Cora announces that she is pregnant,
but their demise – caused by 'kisses from life, not from death' – is only a
bend in the road ahead.

MGM bought the rights to Cain's novel in 1934, but the property
posed too many censorship problems. The postwar loosening of the Hays
Code made a Hollywood version possible, but meanwhile two good
European versions giving due weight to Cain's heady mix of sexual
passion and violence had been made. *Le Dernier tournant* (Pierre Chenal,
1939), was a legal French version, while Luchino Visconti's Italian version,
Ossessione (1943), set in the bleak Po delta and often considered a
precursor to Italian neo-realism, was made without copyright
acknowledgment. *The Postman Always Rings Twice* was remade in 1981
by Bob Rafelson, with Jack Nicholson and Jessica Lange. Although less
restrictive Hollywood censorship allowed considerably more explicit sex
scenes, there is something listless and redundant about it compared with
the 1946 version, whose very repression of explicit sexuality is precisely
what gives it its powerful charge.   JH

Dir: Tay Garnett; **Prod**: Carey Wilson; **Scr**: Harry Ruskin, Niven Busch, from James M. Cain's
novel; **DOP**: Sidney Wagner (b&w); **Ed**: George White; **Score**: George Bassman; **Main
Cast**: Lana Turner, John Garfield, Cecil Kellaway, Hume Cronyn, Leon Ames, Audrey Totter;
Prod Co: Loew's Incorporated/MGM.

Pursued
US, 1947 – 101 mins
Raoul Walsh

Generic boundaries are never very watertight, and *Pursued* could be validly discussed as Western, *film noir* or family melodrama. As family melodrama, it involves, in Laura Mulvey's (1987) phrase, sensitive areas of repression and conflict 'not between enemies, but between people tied by blood and love', but its setting and iconography belong clearly to the Western, and its visual and narrative style are typically *noir*. Niven Busch, the film's screenwriter, helped script *The Postman Always Rings Twice* (1946)*, but was best known for the novel on which King Vidor's spectacularly Freudian Western-cum-melodrama *Duel in the Sun* (1946) was based. *Pursued* was made in the same year as *Out of the Past**, Robert Mitchum starred in both films, and their titles could easily be switched. Our fascination with classical US *film noir* as emblematic of the 1940s *Zeitgeist* can obscure the fact that stars and directors we often associate with *film noir* – Mitchum, Dick Powell, Alan Ladd, Veronica Lake, Jane Greer, directors like Raoul Walsh, Robert Wise, André de Toth, Jacques Tourneur, Henry Hathaway – moved readily between *film noirs* and Westerns and other genres. Mitchum, for example, also starred in Robert Wise's *noir* Western *Blood on the Moon* (1948). The intensely psychological nature of many *film noirs* clearly derives from the growing interest in psychoanalysis in this period rather than being inherent in the 'genre'. And the heyday of the psychological Western was also beginning, not least in the hands of Anthony Mann who, with films like *T-Men* (1947)* and *Side Street* (1950)*, was a major director of 1940s *film noir*.

Jeb Rand (Mitchum) is a lone, alienated figure whose insecure identity relates to a childhood trauma which returns as a nightmare centred on flashing cowboy boots and silver spurs, seen from a low vantage point, in a burned-out ranch house. Jeb, raised by Ma Callum (Judith Anderson) alongside her own children, Thor (Teresa Wright) and

Adam (John Rodney), never quite belongs and is constantly menaced by the metaphorically and visually dark presence of Grant Callum (Dean Jagger). Callum's brother, Ma's husband, was killed by Jeb's father (who, we discover, was in an adulterous relationship with Ma Callum). Callum provokes Adam and Thor's suitor to try to murder Jeb, who kills them in self-defence, turning Thor against him. After a strange courtship – outwardly cool formality, inwardly seething passions – Jeb marries Thor and, on their wedding night, invites her to kill him. What may be Grant Callum's repressed desire for Ma, and the repressed desire between half-brother and sister which later becomes lust for revenge, make clear the plot's intensely Oedipal and incestuous dynamics. Jeb's nightmare is finally explained as the murder of his father and at the burned-out ranch Ma finally kills Jeb's nemesis, Callum. Jeb and Thor are now free to marry – a happy end which, given the intensity of the familial passions involved, remains less than convincing.

Oddly for a Western, but not for a *film noir*, almost all scenes take place at night or in dark interiors, and cinematographer James Wong Howe makes full use of low-key and *chiaroscuro* lighting, perhaps most notably in the gunfight in what could pass for a dark urban alleyway and the bitter fistfight between Jeb and Adam. The cycle of killing and revenge may be more familiar in the Western, but in typically *film noir* fashion, and appropriately for the film's overall fatalistic mood, the story is told in flashback, from Jeb's point of view. JH

Dir: Raoul Walsh; **Prod**: Milton Sperling; **Scr**: Niven Busch; **DOP**: James Wong Howe (b&w); **Ed**: Christian Nyby; **Score**: Max Steiner; **Main Cast**: Robert Mitchum, Teresa Wright, Judith Anderson, Dean Jagger, Alan Hale, John Rodney, Harry Carey, Jr; **Prod Co**: Warner Bros.

Quai des Orfèvres
France, 1947 – 106 mins
Henri-Georges Clouzot

Very loosely based on a book by the Belgian pulp novelist, Stanislas-André Steeman, like his debut feature, *L'Assassin habite ... au 21* (1942), Henri-Georges Clouzot's *Quai des Orfèvres* inhabits the milieu of what Ginette Vincendeau (1993) has termed 'social noir'. According to Vincendeau, French 'social noir' displayed 'a skilful integration of generic noir features with French quotidian realism' yet differed from its immediate counterpart of poetic realism (e.g. *La Bête humaine* [1938]*) in its emphasis on a harsher, more inherently cynical treatment of human psychology. For a crime film then (especially one named after the French equivalent of Britain's Scotland Yard), *Quai des Orfèvres* is remarkably disinterested in the process of police detection itself. Rather it embodies the virtues, as many have noticed, of great novelists such as Dickens and Balzac in its precise attention to the nuances of character detail and the textures of urban place.

The film is set in wintry postwar Paris and the characters spend most of the time in their overcoats amid the city's vividly rendered rundown music halls, backstreet bars and claustrophobic city courtyards. The outwardly gruff Detective Lieutenant Antoine, played with meticulous sensitivity by the great Louis Jouvet, is charged with the murder investigation of the sleazy theatrical roué, Brignon (Charles Dullin). The three main suspects form an interlinked triangle, with Jouvet's character called upon to penetrate and gauge their turbulent emotional allegiances and conflicts. Maurice Martineau (Bernard Blier) is a weak-willed variety musician married to the glamorous and ambitious singer, Jenny Lamour (Suzy Delair). The argumentative couple live across the way from Dora, a professional photographer who, after initially introducing Jenny to Brignon, is forced to realise that Martineau's scheming wife has naively seen the man as a means of attaining the true stardom she aspires to.

Clouzot's interest initially appears to lie in examining the differences between the social world of the police and that of the theatre. While the

Character nuance and the textures of urban place: Jenny Lamour (Suzy Delair) and
Maurice Martineau (Bernard Blier) in *Quai des Orfèvres*

first is marked especially by the codes of realism and moral authority, the
music-hall milieu seems an unstable location in which characters move
constantly between being on stage and off and a predominance
of reflective mirrors conveys an underlying sense of mutability and
masquerade. The latter is concerned with surfaces while the former
wants to uncover what lies beneath. Dora's profession as a showbusiness
photographer is to create a stylised mirage while Antoine's amateur
photographic interests lie, like his presumed counterpart the great urban
ethnographer Eugène Atget, in the visual mysteries of ordinary Parisian
streets.

Gradually, as the film progresses, Clouzot weaves these two concerns
together and an unlikely alliance is produced between the police
detective and the theatrical portraitist. In one key scene, for example, we

see Dora running into the courtyard clutching a newly minted publicity image of Jenny. She looks up at the couple's apartment window and turns away crestfallen as she sees Martineau's silhouette pulling the curtains to as he and Jenny embrace passionately. Inside, a *chanteuse réaliste* mournfully voices the words Dora can't yet articulate: that 'other girls get all the breaks'. This telling conjugation of aural and visual registers resonates in a subsequent private conversation between Dora and Antoine when the ageing detective discreetly remarks that what now uniquely links them is the fact that they will never get the women they desire.

Clouzot's interest in hidden feelings and complex psychologies informed many of his subsequent features, including other 'social noirs' such as *Les Diaboliques* (1955), but this intimate, intensely poignant portrait of the Parisian theatrical underworld nonetheless remains one of the most enduring and perceptive examples of an important, if still critically neglected, vein of European crime cinema from the classical period. AP

Dir: Henri-Georges Clouzot; **Prod**: Roger de Venloo; **Scr**: Henri-Georges Clouzot, Jean Ferry from Stanislas-André Steeman's novel *Légitime Défense*; **DOP**: Armand Thirard (b&w); **Ed**: Charles Bretoneiche; **Score**: Francis Lopez; **Main Cast**: Louis Jouvet, Suzy Delair, Bernard Blier, Simone Renant, Charles Dullin; **Prod Co**: Majestic Films.

The Reckless Moment
US, 1949 – 81 mins
Max Ophuls

The Reckless Moment is one of several films of the 1940s/1950s –
another is *Mildred Pierce* (1945)* – which plays in subtle ways on the
borderlines between the woman's picture or family melodrama and *film
noir* itself. As would be expected, the central character is a woman, Lucia
Harper (Joan Bennett), coping with two adolescent children and her
live-in father in the postwar absence in Europe of her husband. When
daughter Bea (Geraldine Brooks) becomes involved with an unsavoury
older man, Ted Darby (Shepperd Strudwick), Lucia travels to Los Angeles
from her suburban middle-class community to talk to him. Darby
demands money in return for stopping seeing Bea. When Lucia later
finds Darby dead in their boathouse, she assumes Bea is responsible and
secretly disposes of the body at sea. Murder and blackmail bring in their
train the outwardly polite but chillingly ruthless enforcer Donnelly (James
Mason). Donnelly's arrival in Lucia's community takes us to the dark heart
of the film: in a disturbing twist, Donnelly becomes attracted to and
protective towards Lucia and her respectable lifestyle, and Lucia, against
all her better instincts becomes attracted to Donnelly.

Director Max Ophuls deftly evokes the spaces of the two genres –
the woman's film's comfortable, sunny lifestyle of Balboa's island
community and the sleazy, threatening dark milieu of the *film noir*
city. When Lucia first crosses the bridge which physically as well as
metaphorically links and separates Balboa and the city she dons dark
glasses, signalling entry into the *noir* world, and she wears them, too,
when she finds and disposes of Darby's body. Gradually, as Donnelly and
the *noir* world increasingly threaten Lucia's everyday space and routine,
her domestic stability begins to collapse, and the *noir* visual style
increasingly predominates, as lonely, fraught, respectable bourgeois wife
and lonely underworld blackmailer and enforcer become attracted to one
another and to unfamiliar values and lifestyles.

Of course, it is a relationship that cannot be and Donnelly –
recognising the impossibility of his desires – finally sacrifices his own
life to protect Lucia's reputation. The end of the film finds Lucia on
the phone to her absent husband, assuring him that all is well. But,
as in all the best melodramas, we have seen how fragile the façade
of respectability can be, and in the apparently 'happy ending' Lucia
is framed behind the bars of the stairs, imprisoned again with her
family, and markedly failing to efface the memory of the dark, violent
forces unleashed in the course of the film. The performances by
Mason and Bennett, among their very best, are crucial to the film's
success. Mason manages to combine threat, diffidence and emotional
need, while Bennett – very different here than in her sexualised
femme fatale roles in Fritz Lang's *film noirs Scarlet Street* (1945)* and
The Woman in the Window (1944) – superbly evokes a basically

Lucia (Joan Bennett) discovers the body of blackmailer Ted Darby (Shepperd Strudwick) in
The Reckless Moment

ordinary, middle-class woman suddenly cut adrift from her social and emotional moorings.

Though it credits Elizabeth Sanxay Holding's source novel rather than the film, Scott McGehee and David Siegel's *The Deep End* (2001) is effectively a remake of *The Reckless Moment*, retaining the earlier film's focus on the mother (Tilda Swinton, almost as superbly caught between control and panic as Joan Bennett in the original). *The Deep End* shifts its setting to an upper-middle-class Lake Tahoe community and is given a contemporary twist by centering the blackmail on the son's gay indiscretions rather than the daughter's heterosexual ones. JH

Dir: Max Ophuls; **Prod**: Walter Wanger; **Scr**: Robert W. Soderberg, Henry Garson, Robert E. Kent, Mel Dinelli from Elizabeth Sanxay Holding's novel *The Blank Wall*; **DOP**: Burnett Guffey (b&w); **Ed**: Gene Havlick; **Score**: Hans Salter; **Main Cast**: Joan Bennett, James Mason, Geraldine Brooks, Henry O'Neill, Shepperd Strudwick; **Prod Co**: Columbia.

Rififi (*Du rififi chez les hommes*)
France, 1955 – 122 mins
Jules Dassin

Du rififi chez les hommes, directed by the blacklisted Hollywood exile
Jules Dassin, was both a landmark in the history of French crime film and
a key instance of the fertile interrelationship between American and
French popular culture in the postwar period. François Truffaut (1986)
called it 'the best Film Noir I have ever seen' while one French film critic
memorably called it 'a Greek tragedy in Pigalle'. It is best remembered
today for its influential wordless robbery sequence, played in 'real time',
its powerful evocation of a Parisian criminal milieu in transition and the
insinuating song 'Rififi' performed by Magali Noël that attempts to
explain the meaning of the title word – 'trouble' – despite the fact that it
is never actually uttered by the film's cast of treacherous French gangsters
and nightclub habitués.

    Rififi (as it was known in English and internationally) was based on
the eponymous popular Série Noire thriller by Auguste le Breton whose
firsthand knowledge of the Parisian underworld lent the source material
authenticity, especially in its inclusion of the impenetrable idiomatic
criminal slang of the time. Dassin found the novel problematic in other
respects and chose to dilute the novel's explicit racism in favour of a
complex narrative structure that concerned the conflicted loyalties of a
set of criminals as they plan and execute a daring raid on a Parisian
jewellery shop. The film's central character, amid a cast that included
Dassin himself, is Tony le Stéphenois (played with weary candour by Jean
Servais) whose days in the milieu are coming to an end. The heist is his
valedictory crime.

    Dassin's film, unsurprisingly for someone with his pedigree in
American *film noirs* such as *The Naked City* (1948) and *Thieves' Highway*
(1949), incorporates many of the conventions of the genre. There is an
atmospheric cityscape evoked by key sites such as the street (shot on
location by Philippe Agostini) and the nightclub (designed by fellow

émigré, Alexandre Trauner). The film focuses tightly on dysfunctional male relations, especially in terms of its depiction of the interrelationship between violence, sexuality and betrayal. In *Rififi* though, the aggression hinted at in the title is actually sublimated, in part, in favour of the detailed examination of the mechanics of criminal activity. This deliberate foregrounding of co-operative homosociality in the famous extended all-male heist sequence is underscored by the lack of dialogue and an attentiveness paid by the camera to gesture, process and the mediation of space in terms of what can be seen/heard and what remains invisible/unnoticed. It can thus be argued that the presentation of the robbery becomes a reiteration of the collaborative nature of the film-making process itself.

This point is important for, given the fact that the film was a cinematic adaptation of an American-influenced French crime novel which was then shot in France by an émigré American director, it is a useful text from which to observe the tensions felt by a domestic European film industry simultaneously threatened by the cultural and economic hegemony of American popular culture and attracted by the creative possibility of refracting this 'American-ness' through a distinctively national lens. *Rififi* was a key instance of the rising popularity of French *film noir* (see also Jacques Becker's *Touchez pas au grisbi** of 1954), but as an ostensibly 'French' film it also remains of historical interest because it so clearly raises the possibility of a challenge to normative fixed definitions of cultural identity and national cinema at a time when both film critics and political and cultural analysts actively sought to repress such concerns. AP

Dir: Jules Dassin; **Prod**: René Gaston Vuattoux; **Scr**: Jules Dassin, René Wheeler from Auguste le Breton's novel; **DOP**: Philippe Agostini (b&w); **Ed**: Roger Dwyre; **Score**: Georges Auric (song by Michel Philippe-Gérard); **Main Cast**: Jean Servais, Carl Möhner, Jules Dassin, Robert Manuel, Marie Sabouret, Robert Hossein; **Prod Co**: IndusFilms, Société Nouvelle Pathé Cinéma, Prima Film.

Le Samouraï
France/Italy, 1967 – 105 mins
Jean-Pierre Melville

France has its own tradition of crime fiction but independent director and producer Jean-Pierre Melville developed a French take on the US crime thriller's treacherous world of guns, heists and double-crosses during the 1950s and 1960s. Ginette Vincendeau (2003), for example, describes films such as *Bob le Flambeur* (1956), *Le Doulos* (1962) and *Le Deuxième souffle* (1966) as distinctively *reworking* rather than copying American models. Like *Bob le Flambeur*, *Le Samouraï* foregrounds its Paris settings; like *Bob* and *Le Deuxième soufflé*, its plot ties cops and criminals closely together. Melville's earlier thrillers focused on the male criminal group – just as *Touchez pas au grisbi* (1954)*, *Rififi* (1955)* and one of Melville's favourite *noirs*, *The Asphalt Jungle* (1950)* do – but *Le Samouraï* favours one central character (though considerable screentime is devoted to police procedures, as if it was not quite sure what kind of film it wanted to be).

Le Samouraï represents a distillation of ritualised generic dress and gesture. When he checks his 'look' in the mirror, obsessively repeating gestures to adjust his trench coat collar or align his fedora, he seems to assume a role entirely defined by his iconographic appearance. Dialogue is minimal, and there is no dialogue at all during the first ten minutes. Jef (Alain Delon) is a cold-blooded, meticulous hit man apparently unconcerned about what he does or its consequences. The film gives us no sense of Jef's motivation or, for example, his relationship with his 'girlfriend' Jane (Nathalie Delon). Except for the company of his caged bird, he lives a solitary life based on some honour code – suggested by the (invented) samurai quote that begins the film. Jef seems uninterested in money or power and lives in an almost impossibly drab room. His routine is disturbed by the black jazz pianist Caty (Cathy Rosier), whose refusal to identify him to the police prompts his desire to know why. Though no typical *femme fatale*, Caty throws Jef off his accustomed

Iconic hit man Jef Costello (Alain Delon) in *Le Samouraï*

track and sets in train the events which lead him, pursued by both police
and mob, to his inevitable, violent – and for Melville, tragic – death.

Much of *Le Samouraï* was shot on real Paris streets and picturesquely
distressed metro stations, but Melville has limited interest in 'realism'. *Le
Samouraï* – shot by Henri Decaë, whose other credits include *Lift to the
Scaffold* (1958)* – is more *gris* than *noir* in look, with a restricted palette
of grey-blues for both interiors and exteriors, highlighted by intermittent
notes of the vivid blue, red or orange of incidental Evian bottles, Gitanes
packets or Orangina posters. Melville has said that he wanted to 'make
black and white films in colour'. Together with the film's pared-down
visual style – reminiscent of Robert Bresson's style in films like *Pickpocket*

(1959) – the mix of realism and abstraction gives the film a dreamlike quality similar to many other *noir* films. Perhaps this is why it requires only a slight shift of perspective to see the film as comic or absurd, with Jef as a romanticised, schoolboy image of the gangster as existential loner.

Though itself the product of different influences – perhaps 'Jef', for example, derives from Jeff in *Out of the Past* (1947)* – *Le Samouraï* has been influential in its turn. Walter Hill claims he had not seen it, but *The Driver* (1978)* is so close in plotline (apart from its ending) that this seems barely credible. John Woo thinks of his Hong Kong thriller *The Killer* (1989) as a homage to Melville in general and *Le Samouraï* in particular, thus further extending the text's transnational undercurrents. JH

Dir: Jean-Pierre Melville; **Prod**: Raymond Borderie, Eugène Lépicier; **Scr**: Jean-Pierre Melville, Georges Pellegrin from Joan McLeod's novel *The Ronin* (uncredited); **DOP**: Henri Decaë (colour); **Ed**: Monique Bonnot, Yo Maurette; **Score**: François de Roubaix; **Main Cast**: Alain Delon, François Perrier, Nathalie Delon, Cathy Rosier, Jacques Leroy, Michel Boisrond; **Prod Co**: Compagnie Industrielle et Commerciale Cinématographique (CICC), Fida Cinematografica, Filmel, TC Productions.

Scarlet Street
US, 1945 – 103 mins
Fritz Lang

Fritz Lang's American adaptation of Jean Renoir's *La Chienne* (1931),
itself a version of a play by Georges de la Fouchardière, remains a
fascinating location from which to observe the intercultural history of *film
noir*. As critics such as Janice Morgan (1996) have observed, *Scarlet
Street*'s narrative of the moral, emotional and financial downfall of a
respectable urban bourgeois male – here, the New York company cashier,
Christopher Cross (Edward G. Robinson) – first reminds one of influential
Weimar Germany's 'street films' of the 1920s such as *Die Strasse* (Karl
Grüne, 1923) or *Asphalt* (Joe May, 1929). Like a number of other
classical Hollywood *film noirs* such as *The Long Night* (Anatole Litvak,
1947), *Human Desire* (Fritz Lang, 1954) and *Lured* (Douglas Sirk, 1947),
it also reworks an established tradition of French urban crime cinema
from the 1930s – in this case, *Le Jour se lève* (1939)*, *La Bête humaine*
(1938)* and *Pièges* (Robert Siodmak, 1939) respectively. Then finally, as
an American *film noir* directed by a prominent European exile, like
Double Indemnity (1944)*, it brings a sceptical and satirical eye to the
foibles of a central protagonist at sea in the serial modernity of America's
advanced urban capitalism.

The film opens with Christopher Cross receiving an award from his
male office colleagues for twenty-five years of service. Leaving the party
early, the mild-mannered cashier foils what seems to be a violent attack
on a woman in the street. Cross later befriends this character, an out-of-
work 'actress' named Kitty March (Joan Bennett), and she is foolishly
encouraged to mistakenly assume he's a famous and wealthy local artist.
Cross, in reality a frustrated Sunday painter living unhappily with his
nagging wife, Adèle (Rosalind Ivan), sets Kitty up in a Greenwich Village
studio where the couple continue to meet illicitly. Meanwhile, Kitty and
her violent 'fiancé', Johnny (Dan Duryea), scheme to defraud Cross by
convincing a prominent gallery owner that Kitty is in fact the mysterious

artist behind the canvases suddenly considered to be of masterpiece quality. Both Kitty and Cross's intertwined dreams end in tragedy and the film ends with Cross, now a lonely, broken man, wandering the city streets unrecognised as one of the art scene's most celebrated talents.

Scarlet Street was the first film produced by Diana Productions, the independent production company co-founded by Lang with Joan Bennett and her husband, Walter Wanger. For their debut feature they turned to a property that had initially been optioned by Ernst Lubitsch for Paramount in the 1930s. The company also made Lang's subsequent *film noir* with Bennett, *The Secret beyond the Door* (1948). Central to the project's success was the pairing of Bennett with Edward G. Robinson. Bennett gives Kitty a wily but brittle vulnerability that deepens the ambiguities of the film's shifting subjectivities while Robinson, as in Lang's *The Woman in the Window* (1944), is deliberately cast against type from his 1930s street-gangster persona and seems to spend the film slumped in a haze of unfulfilled desire. Called upon by Adèle to don a frilly apron and do the dishes while she listens to the highly ironic 'Happy Household Hour' on her neighbour's radio, Cross needs little incentive to heed the siren call of one of classical American *film noir*'s most troubling *femme fatales*.

Kitty undoubtedly fits Mary-Ann Doane's (1991) template of the highly exaggerated figure of the *femme fatale* who emerged in the late nineteenth century as a form of imaginary sensory compensation for the loss of autonomy experienced by men working in the factories and offices of the west's newly industrialised economies. Surely for censorship reasons alone, she and Johnny are never explicitly defined as prostitute and pimp. What makes her so interesting though is how she evolves as the key site from which the film explores the broader illusions, deceptions, betrayals and desires underlying human relationships in general. Crucial to this purpose is the way that she becomes both subject and agent in the subsidiary economy of the art world. In this sense, she becomes an intriguing counterpart to characters in other female portrait *film noirs* of the time such as the aforementioned *The Woman in the Window* and, most especially, Otto Preminger's equally despairing *Laura* (1944)*. AP

Dir, Prod: Fritz Lang; **Prod**: Aubrey Schenck; **Scr**: Dudley Nichols from Georges de la Fouchardière's novel and play *La Chienne*; **DOP**: Milton R. Krasner (b&w); **Ed**: Arthur Hilton; **Score**: Hans J. Salter; **Main Cast**: Edward G. Robinson, Joan Bennett, Dan Duryea, Margaret Lindsay, Rosalind Ivan; **Prod Co**: Diana Productions.

Shoot the Pianist (*Tirez sur le pianiste*)
France, 1960 – 82 mins
François Truffaut

The city at night. Out of the darkness, a mysterious man comes running, pursued by some external threat. The low-key lighting, canted angles, empty urban streets and shadows all suggest that we are in the midst of a classic American *film noir* and then … the man runs into a lamppost and meets a complete stranger – who we never see again – and the pair start digressing about the secrets of a happy marriage. The beginning of François Truffaut's inventive second feature, *Shoot the Pianist*, thus immediately establishes the playful integration of *film noir* and *nouvelle vague* aesthetics that will predominate for the rest of the film. The man turns out to be Chico Saroyon (Albert Rémy), a small-time crook wanted by two hoods, Momo (Claude Mansard) and Ernest (Daniel Boulanger). Seeking refuge with his brother, Edouard (Charles Aznavour), a former classical concert pianist now lowlife piano-player known as Charlie Kohler, Chico sets in train a sequence of dramatic events that will have significant repercussions for the shy and melancholic Edouard and the rest of his chaotic family.

Shoot the Pianist, like other important French *nouvelle vague* films such as Jean-Luc Godard's *Breathless* (1960), relates to the earlier extensive cross-fertilisation of French and American *film noir* traditions that included the Lemmy Caution comic-thriller series starring the American émigré actor Eddie Constantine (e.g. *La Môme vert-de-gris* [1953] and *Ça va barder* [1954]) and Jean-Pierre Melville's gangster and crime films *Bob le Flambeur* (1956) and *Deux hommes dans Manhattan* (1959). The script for Truffaut's film was based, in part, on David Goodis's novel *Down There*, one of a tranche of American pulp crime novels originally translated into French for Marcel Duhamel's influential Série Noire series in the 1940s and 1950s. Goodis's work had previously been adapted for the screen by Hollywood: *Dark Passage* (1947)* and the vastly underrated late classical *film noir*, *Nightfall* (Jacques Tourneur,

1957). These films, along with other American *film noirs* such as *On Dangerous Ground* (1952)* – a direct influence on *Shoot the Pianist* – were admired by Truffaut in his days as a fledgling film critic in France.

Shoot the Pianist also owes much to the rapid-fire, innovative style of Raoul Coutard's cinematography that, along with various jump cuts and flashbacks, gives the film an elusive modernist quality. As Truffaut's musical collaborator, Georges Delerue, said of the film, evoking the twin elements of music and crime indicated by its title, *Shoot the Pianist* was 'a *noir* thriller treated in the style of Raymond Queneau and [Charles] Trenet'. Like all of Truffaut's films though, including other *noir*-related features such as *La Mariée était en noir* (1968) and *Vivement Dimanche!* (1983), *Shoot the Pianist* generally engages its genre elements to accommodate what is essentially an intensive scrutiny of human character. Truffaut himself argued that 'the idea was to make a film without a subject, to express all I wanted to say about glory, success, downfall, failure, women and love by means of a detective story'. At the core of the film, then, is an almost tactile portrait of the anxious, introspective, but fundamentally likeable, figure of Edouard: undoubtedly one of the most recognisable, but at the same time least likely, *film noir* protagonists featured in this book. AP

Dir: François Truffaut; **Prod**: Pierre Braunberger; **Scr**: François Truffaut, Marcel Moussy from David Goodis's novel *Down There*; **DOP**: Raoul Coutard (b&w); **Ed**: Claudine Bouché, Cécile Decugis; **Score**: Georges Delerue; **Main Cast**: Charles Aznavour, Marie Dubois, Nicole Berger, Michèle Mercier, Serge Davri, Claude Mansard, Richard Kanayan, Albert Rémy, Jacques Aslanian, Daniel Boulanger; **Prod Co**: Les Films de la Pléiade.

Side Street
US, 1950 – 83 mins
Anthony Mann

After a run of now classic independent *film noirs* such as *Railroaded!* (1947), *T-Men* (1947)* and *Raw Deal* (1948), Anthony Mann's move to MGM in the late 1940s secured the director access to the studio's enhanced production budgets and technical resources. The results are clearly visible in this underrated but compelling *film noir*, which reunited Farley Granger and Cathy O'Donnell after their leading roles together in Nicholas Ray's *They Live by Night* (1948)*. The film benefits from Joseph Ruttenberg's outstanding location cinematography (recalling the vivid New York street photography of his contemporary, Louis Faurer), the striking art direction by MGM regular, Cedric Gibbons, and a cast of regular supporting actors that lend vigour and clarity to the intricately realised social detail of the narrative.

Like many *film noirs* of the period, *Side Street* recounts the momentary downfall of an impoverished 'regular guy' who finds himself outwitted by the lowlife denizens of the city's criminal underworld before a final act of moral redemption. Joe Norson (Farley Granger), a working-class New Yorker, is married to Ellen (Cathy O'Donnell). One day on his postal round, he succumbs to temptation and steals some money from a crooked attorney's filing cabinet. He thus becomes embroiled in a network of society blackmailers and, when he confesses his crime to Ellen, just after the birth of their baby, he is forced on the run as the prime suspect in a related murder case.

Mann utilises elements of the documentary *noir* tradition – already seen in *T-Men* – as a framing device for the film. *Side Street* begins and ends with some spectacular aerial footage of Manhattan accompanied by the guiding voice-over of the main detective on the case. Its moral core, featured in the film's opening and closing sections, is a real-life location: Federal Hall with its prominent statue of George Washington on the steps outside. Nonetheless, the film also deploys more conventional melodramatic elements. Ruttenberg's cinematography combines naturalistic imagery with intensely focused shots that recall the expressionistic camera angles and lighting set-ups of Mann's previous *noir* collaborator, John Alton. Granger's subtle performance is crucial here. His mobile face, especially his eyes, reveals a combination of tender purity and deep-seated anxiety that comes to the fore in the dramatically lit interior close-ups that punctuate the more mundane scenes of outdoor daily city life.

It can, in fact, be argued that New York is the most significant character of the entire film. From the views suggesting the then evolving 'architectural jungle' of its skyline, to the lengthy takes evoking the ordinary daytime and night-time sights and sounds of late 1940s Lower Manhattan, *Side Street* now partly seems a paean to a place long since vanished. Two elements stand out in particular. First, there is the recurring use of the city's vernacular style of windows and doorways within the *mise en scène*. Joe's descent to crime, for example, is motivated by his desire for Ellen to have the fur coat he sees in a store window display; the way this particular shot is composed suggests a tangible sense of distance and impenetrability as if Joe is explicitly locked out from the class above him. Later on, we see Joe looking through the glass of a café door; the shard-like motif etched into it neatly conveying the splintered existence he now faces as a fugitive. Second, the fabric of New York's architecture also becomes embedded within the narrative in a more fluid way. In the film's finale chronicling a car chase through the city's labyrinthine streets, for example, we shift from high-angle bird's-eye view shots to sensational close-ups of the protagonists inside their speeding vehicles. As Jeanine Basinger (2007) has observed, the film's compositions continually 'stress the sense of space as divided, enclosed'. Indeed, the 'storyline itself is architectural, as it builds layer upon layer of incident upon incident, while still taking strange turns and angles'. *Side Street*'s increasing use of narrative ellipsis is certainly provocative. Although it ends with the restitution of moral order and the reunion of the married couple, Mann's cunning narrative style leaves one questioning, as in so many *film noirs*, whether things will ever return to where they were before the exposure of what lies beneath the supposedly secure monuments of urban American capitalism. AP

Dir: Anthony Mann; **Prod**: Sam Zimbalist; **Scr**: Sidney Boehm; **DOP**: Joseph Ruttenberg (b&w); **Ed**: Conrad A. Nervig; **Score**: Lennie Hayton; **Main Cast**: Farley Granger, Cathy O'Donnell, James Craig, Paul Kelly; **Prod Co**: MGM.

Sin City
US, 2005 – 124 mins
Robert Rodriguez, Frank Miller, Quentin Tarantino

Primarily an exercise in style, *Sin City*'s main debt is to the visual style of comic books and graphic novels in general and Frank Miller's source graphic novel in particular. Robert Rodriguez talks of his movie being a faithful 'translation' of Miller's work, making it very different from other blockbuster comic-book adaptations. Rodriguez argues that his *mise en scène* merely transposes Frank Miller's stories to film – the film was made digitally (almost all of it shot against green-screen backgrounds) and could only really exist in digital form. Hence Rodriguez's insistence that Miller be credited as co-director even though Miller did no actual 'directing' (and the film is also known as *Frank Miller's Sin City*).

Sin City deserves a place in a book about *film noir* because of its many filmic references, *noir* is the most obvious – in its highly stylised largely black-and-white *chiaroscuro* visual imagery and urban setting (Basin City), its complex narrative structure, its use of (multiple) voice-overs, its narrative focus on police, city and even church corruption. *Sin City* offers three relatively conventional heroic male protagonists: detective Hartigan (Bruce Willis), who tries to protect a young girl from harm, street thug Marv (Mickey Rourke), who wreaks havoc avenging the murder of his girlfriend and Dwight (Clive Owen), who tries to cover up a cop's death to protect the tough Old Towne hookers. But if the men remain essentially comic-book versions of *noir* action heroes, there are few, if any, proper duplicitous *femmes fatales* – the women here being typically wronged but strong.

The titles of Miller's stories – *The Hard Good-Bye*, *The Big Fat Kill* – tell their own story about his debt to Raymond Chandler. Of course, this influence has been updated with a harder, more ironic edge with dialogue which seeks to outdo – to the point of absurdity – the hard-boiled tradition of *film noir* dialogue ('The night's as hot as hell. It's a lousy room in a lousy part of a lousy town', and so on). However, *Sin City* borrows liberally from other genres – particularly post-1960s ones – primarily the extreme, visceral violence of the horror film. The grotesque figures of the villain, Kevin (Elijah Wood), and the superhuman half-man, half-beast 'hero' are worthy of films like *Last House on the Left* (1972), *The Texas Chainsaw Massacre* (1974) and *The Hills Have Eyes* (1977). There is also imagery associated with Hitchcock's seminal *Psycho* (1960). Another influence, strongly evoked in the central story of the city-controlling hookers led by Gail (Rosario Dawson), is Roger Corman's 1970s New World exploitation pictures which featured sexy, Amazonian, violent women resisting oppression (in films like *The Hot Box* [1972] or *Caged Heat* [1974]). The samurai sword-wielding Miho (Devon Aoki) also summons up martial-arts movies (or, at least, Tarantino's *Kill Bill* [2003–4]).

Popular comic books were influenced by the visual and narrative style of movies and, in turn, influenced movies: both influenced Miller's graphic-novel style. Though the freeing of action from the constraints of credibility belong very much to the comic book, the development of digital effects has made this more routinely possible in the movies too. Another highly self-conscious attempt to merge graphic novel with *film noir* via highly stylised extremes of *chiaroscuro* is the French film *Renaissance* (Christian Volckman, 2006), which used motion capture to computer-animate live action. Its multiethnic, dystopian 2054 Paris owes much to *Blade Runner* (1982) and *Minority Report* (2002). JH

Dir: Robert Rodriguez, Frank Miller, Quentin Tarantino; **Prod**: Elizabeth Avellán, Bob Weinstein, Harvey Weinstein; **Scr**: Frank Miller from his graphic-novel stories *Sin City/The Hard Good-Bye*, *The Big Fat Kill*, *That Yellow Bastard*, *The Customer Is Always Right*; **DOP, Ed**: Robert Rodriguez (b&w & colour); **Score**: John Debney, Graeme Revell, Robert Rodriguez; **Main Cast**: Jessica Alba, Powers Boothe, Rosario Dawson, Benicio Del Toro, Devon Aoki, Josh Hartnett, Rutger Hauer, Michael Madsen, Brittany Murphy, Clive Owen, Mickey Rourke; **Prod Co**: Dimension Film, Troublemaker Studios.

Story of a Love Affair (*Cronaca di un amore*)
Italy, 1950 – 98 mins
Michelangelo Antonioni

As Mary P. Wood (2007) has pointed out, the concept of Italian *film noir* is uniquely complicated by the prior existence of the term, *giallo*, that 'has come to be used both as a short-hand term [in Italian culture] for any type of detective fiction and, more widely, as a generic term for stories with any mystery element'. No other country uses another colour – yellow – to indicate many of the narrative and stylistic qualities associated with what is conventionally known elsewhere as *noir*. Having said this, a strong case can be made for considering Michelangelo Antonioni's debut feature, *Story of a Love Affair*, in the light of both its nationally specific origins and a broad awareness of trends in international narrative visual culture of the time. Its director, for example, had worked with Marcel Carné (*Le Jour se lève* [1939]*) in the 1940s and its assistant director, Francesco Maselli, has said in interview that both he and Antonioni were specifically conscious of such recent American *film noirs* as *Double Indemnity* (1944)* and *The Killers* (1946)* when planning the project.

Story of a Love Affair certainly begins like an American *film noir* such as Otto Preminger's *Laura* (1944)*, with the inception of an investigation into the figure of a wealthy society woman. In this case, a jealous Milan industrialist, Enrico Fontana (Ferdinando Sarmi), employs a private detective to delve into the past of his younger, glamorous wife, Paola (Lucía Bosé). In the course of the narrative, Fontana unwittingly draws Paola closer to her former lover, Guido (Massimo Girotti), and we learn more about the couple's possibly murderous past in relation to the unexplained death of another of Guido's previous girlfriends. As their affair develops, Paola and Guido begin to plot Enrico's death, but the film ends with unexpected results that have tragic repercussions for their fated, rekindled romance.

On the surface, especially in terms of lighting, iconography and costume, Paola is portrayed as a cold-hearted and scheming *femme*

Space, architecture, desire and constraint: Paola (Lucía Bosé) and Guido (Massimo Girotti) in *Story of a Love Affair*

fatale. Lucía Bosé's skilful performance, on a par with her work in Juan Antonio Bardem's equally interesting *Death of a Cyclist* (1955)*, nonetheless instils an element of tragedy within her character. The anomie of her chosen life in Milan, a world away from provincial Ferrara in the northeast, thus becomes part of a wider social tapestry picked at and then unravelled by Antonioni's sombre, restless and ambiguous camerawork. Like many of the director's subsequent films of the 1960s, *Story of a Love Affair* is as much about Italy's troubled postwar urban modernity as about the romantic sufferings of its protagonists.

Central to this conception of the film is its use of space and architecture. Key scenes are filmed against the changing social landscape of the country in ways to suggest that the characters are constrained or limited by their material circumstances. Guido and Paola, in *noir* fashion, are not free and active agents of their own destinies; rather they appear increasingly defined by a logic lying somewhere beyond their control.

The tradition of the cinematic *giallo* proper emerged later within the sphere of popular Italian culture with titles such as the Hitchcockian *The Girl Who Knew Too Much* (*La ragazza che sapeva troppo* [Mario Bava, 1963]) and other violent and sexually explicit films including *The House with Laughing Windows* (*La casa dalle finestre che ridono* [Pupi Avati, 1976]) and Dario Argento's *Tenebrae* (1982). Nonetheless as with Luchino Visconti's *Ossessione* (1943), based like *The Postman Always Rings Twice* (1946)* on James M. Cain's novel, *Story of a Love Affair* remains an intriguing fusion of high and low culture that explicitly engages a recognisably *noir* sensibility in the service of penetrating social analysis. AP

Dir: Michelangelo Antonioni; **Prod**: Stefano Caretta, Franco Villani; **Scr**: Michelangelo Antonioni, Daniele D'Anza, Silvio Giovannetti, Francesco Maselli, Piero Tellini; **DOP**: Enzo Serafin (b&w); **Ed**: Eraldo Da Roma, Michelangelo Antonioni; **Score**: Giovanni Fusco; **Main Cast**: Lucía Bosé, Massimo Girotti, Ferdinando Sarmi, Gino Rossi, Marika Rowsky; **Prod Co**: Villani Film.

Sunset Boulevard
US, 1950 – 110 mins
Billy Wilder

Reportedly David Lynch's favourite film, *Sunset Boulevard*'s fascination with the hidden memories, dreams and illusions behind the façade of Hollywood's system of industrialised glamour undoubtedly suggests interesting parallels with Lynch's own recent *noir*-related projects set in Los Angeles such as *Mulholland Dr.* (2001)* and *Inland Empire* (2006). Scripted with great wit and clarity by Billy Wilder and his colleagues and photographed like Wilder's seminal LA *noir*, *Double Indemnity* (1944)*, by John F. Seitz, *Sunset Boulevard* is today not only regarded as a major *film noir*, it is also justifiably seen by many as *the* canonical 'Hollywood on Hollywood' film.

   Sunset Boulevard begins with scenes of police cars arriving at a Hollywood mansion in the hills above the city off Sunset Boulevard. We see the police officers discover a corpse floating head down in the swimming pool. A disorienting shot from below the water looking up at the body provides the unsettling clue that the off-screen narrator recounting the tale is, in fact, the dead man. As the film progresses into flashback, we learn that the film is really the story of two corpses: Gillis (William Holden), a failing Hollywood scriptwriter, and Norma Desmond (Gloria Swanson), a faded silent-film star who, though physically still alive, has retreated into a kind of tomblike madness inside her decaying mansion. Gillis has encountered Norma while on the run from men seeking car repayments and she mistakenly assumes him to be the undertaker dealing with her pet chimpanzee's funeral. To remain in hiding, he stays in the house as the actress's new 'pet' and together the pair spend their time concocting a film script which will take Norma out of the shadows and back under the bright lights of the studio soundstage.

   The early scenes of *Sunset Boulevard* are partly played as gothic comedy drawing irony from the gaps in perception between the cynical, wisecracking scriptwriter and the clearly delusional former screen idol. But what makes the film so insightful is the way in which the couple are increasingly drawn together by their respective ambitions and desires to the extent that, as the film moves increasingly between the world of the mansion and the world of the studio system, it becomes more and more difficult to determine what is and what is not artifice. Wilder's film complicates this by bringing real Hollywood figures (e.g. Cecil B. DeMille) and locations (e.g. Paramount Studios) into the 'fictional' world of the film.

One of the *sine qua non* for *film noir* historians is that Wilder and his fellow émigrés such as Max Ophuls, Fritz Lang and Robert Siodmak were responsible for exporting the visual legacy of German expressionism to Hollywood. This is more or less a myth. As Thomas Elsaesser (2000) has persuasively argued, what these directors distilled instead into their many American *film noirs*, was a certain cynical middle-European fascination with the brittle and ambiguous surfaces of material life that immediately lent itself to *film noir*'s obsessive tonal register of disenchantment. Thus, like many other émigré *film noirs*, *Sunset Boulevard* uses unconventional narrative structure and cinematography in order to strategically reframe our understanding of conventional reality. What makes Wilder's film particularly fascinating is that, in having shown this reality to be permanently corrupted by fantasy and ambition, the film then turns in on itself, much like David Lynch's own fusion of *noir* and Hollywood myth, so that finally the only verifiable source of information remains the recollected imaginings of a dead man seen floating in an ageing film star's swimming pool.   AP

Dir: Billy Wilder; **Prod**: Charles Brackett; **Scr**: Charles Brackett, Billy Wilder, D. M. Marshman, Jr; **DOP**: John F. Seitz (b&w); **Ed**: Arthur P. Schmidt; **Score**: Franz Waxman; **Main Cast**: William Holden, Gloria Swanson, Erich von Stroheim, Nancy Olsen, Fred Clark; **Prod Co**: Paramount.

Taxi Driver
US, 1976 – 113 mins
Martin Scorsese

Taxi Driver famously opens with a portrait of a modern-day Hades seen through the shallow-focus windscreen of a New York cab. The blurred neon impressions of night-time New York, the angry palette of washed reds and oranges, the darting eyes of the driver, the rising steam from the asphalt and the unsettled anxiety of Bernard Herrmann's jazz-influenced score conspire to create the sensory impression of an urban dystopia that lies halfway between what's outside on the streets and what lies inside within the fevered imagination of Travis Bickle (Robert de Niro), the film's protagonist. From its very start, Scorsese's film thus appears to deploy conventional, expressive *film noir* aesthetics in order to define a troubled relationship between male identity and society. The difference with *Taxi Driver* is that, whereas in classical *film noir* narratives the male's unstable psychology was more commonly explained in terms of an overwhelming existential crisis or the repercussions of World War II, here in mid-1970s America it is as if it is the violence and chaos of society itself that defines the malaise inside Bickle's head. In this sense, as we watch Bickle act upon these impressions, arm himself with guns and ultimately turn into a dangerous vigilante, the film proposes a new and hugely influential level of material and psychological ambiguity that courses through its images like a cancerous faultline. Is Bickle hero or villain (for us as well as for the film's other characters)? How much of what he sees is really there? When Bickle, in the film's notorious mirror scene asks 'Are you talking to me?' *who* exactly is he looking at?

   Taxi Driver was scripted by Paul Schrader, who just a few years previously had authored the highly influential essay, 'Notes on Film Noir' (republished 1996), that sought to define some of *film noir*'s 'more subtle qualities of tone and mood'. In his writing, Schrader argued for the necessary periodisation of American *film noir* suggesting that by the mid-1950s it had 'come to a halt'. Part of the underlying tenor of his essay was therefore a call for contemporary film-makers to rediscover the virtues of a form that, uniquely, could integrate aesthetic purpose with social critique. In some ways though, despite its transparent overture to *film noir* traditions, it makes more sense to see *Taxi Driver* in terms of its ancillary debt to the Western. Bickle is an ironic 'cowboy' – he's referred to as such by Harvey Keitel's pimp, 'Sport' Matthew – who operates to salvage a delusional form of honour in the wilderness of New York's frontier. Like the film itself, Bickle is a volatile object, his mutability just one more aspect of an underlying loneliness and desperation.

Taxi Driver undoubtedly provides an extraordinary picture of 1970s New York – many daylight sequences directly recall, for example, contemporaneous street photographer Joel Meyerowitz's colours and compositions – but what also makes the film so interesting is the way it draws a specific analogy between Bickle's cab and cinema itself. As Amy Taubin (2000) has astutely observed, 'Scorsese frames [the world of the film] as if all of it is a movie. Inside his cab, Travis is as much a spectator as he is in the nearby empty porn theatre. The windows and mirrors of the cab turn the real world into a reflection that he observes without being observed. The cab is the best seat in the house, but it's also Travis's protection, his armour.' In this manner, Scorsese's dark *film noir* draws us in even further to ask not only who Travis is talking to, but what exactly *we* are doing when we are looking at him. AP

Dir: Martin Scorsese; **Prod**: Julia Phillips, Michael Phillips; **Scr**: Paul Schrader; **DOP**: Michael Chapman (colour); **Ed**: Tom Rolf, Melvin Shapiro; **Score**: Bernard Herrmann; **Main Cast**: Robert de Niro, Cybill Shepherd, Peter Boyle, Jodie Foster, Harvey Keitel; **Prod Co**: Bill/Phillips, Columbia, Italo/Judeo Productions.

They Live by Night
US, 1948 – 95 mins
Nicholas Ray

Although the familiar *noir* theme of characters trapped by their past is central to *They Live by Night*, and although it is shot in a distinctively *noir* style, Nicholas Ray's film is a somewhat curious example of the cycle. A couple-on-the-run narrative, it looks forward to *Gun Crazy* (1950)* without that film's obsession with guns, violence and sexuality. It shares its sense of fate hanging over the characters and its transcendence of the social-problem genre with Fritz Lang's proto-*noir You Only Live Once* (1937), though Ray apparently did not know the film.

Bowie (Farley Granger), wrongfully imprisoned at age sixteen, breaks out of prison hoping to prove his innocence but the men he escapes with suck him into a spiral of violent crime which closes down his options. The narrative holds together two trajectories on a collision course: Bowie's fleeting, vulnerable romance and marriage with feisty but innocent Keechie (Cathy O'Donnell) and the criminal life Bowie finds himself pulled into. The first images dramatise this tension, with close-ups of Bowie and Keechie's intimacy, in a world of their own outside time and space. This mood is quickly undercut by a caption announcing that 'This boy … and this girl … were never properly introduced to the world we live in,' and definitively broken when they appear startled by the dramatic music and images of the film's title, diverting their attention away from each other and towards the camera, as if they – like us – are looking at the film's credit sequence.

The opening establishes a pattern of more lyrical, softly lit, naturalistic sequences of the doomed lovers – as in the defensive 'courtship' in which they begin to express their feelings for each other – alternated with more quickly edited, often harshly lit scenes of violence. The fragility of their makeshift married life and 'home' is constantly threatened by Bowie's unwelcome criminal life, famously in the sequence in which the one-eyed, devilish Chicamaw (Howard Da Silva) visits

Keechie and Bowie's cabin and, while fondling the decorations on the Christmas tree, clumsily crushes one.

In the film's conclusion, Ray continues to combine the harsh working of fate with a kind of romantic escape. Bowie is betrayed by the desperate, bitter Mattie to secure her husband's release from jail (though the film intimates that the pair will be consumed by shame and guilt). Bowie is mercilessly gunned down but the film ends with Keechie reading the love letter Bowie has left for her. We see Keechie walk away from his body, turning to face the camera only at the last moment, as she reads 'I love you' and mouths her own response before being finally swallowed by darkness.

Ray's reputation as an *auteur maudit* was established with this first film. RKO's Dore Schary had encouraged adventurous low-budget productions – *Crossfire* (1947)* was another example – but after shooting was completed the studio did not know what to do with it. It was released in June 1948 as *The Twisted Road* but shelved when Howard Hughes took over the studio. Though it found enthusiastic supporters in Britain in 1948, it was only re-released, under its present title, in November 1949. Robert Altman's *Thieves Like Us* (1973), which retains the title of Edward Anderson's source novel, puts more emphasis on the Depression context, but its central couple (Keith Carradine as Bowie, Shelley Duvall as Keechie) remain vulnerable innocents. JH

Dir: Nicholas Ray; **Prod**: John Houseman; **Scr**: Charles Schnee, Nicholas Ray from Edward Anderson's novel *Thieves Like Us*; **DOP**: George E. Diskant (b&w); **Ed**: Sherman Todd; **Score**: Leigh Harline; **Main Cast**: Cathy O'Donnell, Farley Granger, Howard Da Silva, Jay C. Flippen, Helen Craig, Will Wright; **Prod Co**: RKO.

T-Men
US, 1947 – 92 mins
Anthony Mann

Anthony Mann and John Alton's first collaboration – a gripping account
of two undercover agents' investigation of a major counterfeit money
operation – superficially follows the template of other procedural semi-
documentary *film noirs* of the 1940s such as *The House on 92nd Street*
(Henry Hathaway, 1945) and *Boomerang!* (Elia Kazan, 1947). The film
begins with a genuine introduction by the Head of the US Treasury
Department's law enforcement agency, Elmer Lincoln Ray (responsible, we
are told, for bringing down Al Capone), it has an authoritative 'voice of
God' male narrative voice and it provides a detailed account of the devious
technical and psychological methods deployed by Washington's T-Men in
their day-to-day operations. What makes the film so distinctive and,
alongside Mann and Alton's subsequent *Raw Deal* (1948), so influential, is
the way that *T-Men* melds together these features with a dynamic *mise en
scène* that integrates the documentary aspects of the narrative action with a
sensational awareness of the full expressive potential of *film noir* aesthetics.

Dennis O'Brien (Dennis O'Keefe) and Tony Genaro (Alfred Ryder), two
experienced government agents, are given new criminal identities and
ordered to infiltrate a gangster ring in Detroit. Winning the trust of the
leader, they move on to Los Angeles, where they gradually insinuate
themselves in the operations of a cartel operating across town. The true
mastermind behind the scenes remains elusive though and it is only in the
film's dramatic concluding scenes that all the pieces come together, with
fatal consequences for one of the detectives. The co-ordination of the
film's visual style traces this descent into the moral and literal darkness of
the criminal milieu. It begins with stable, daylight compositions promising
to 'take [us] inside' the T-Men's departmental affairs in 'our nation's
capital'. When the agents begin their investigation, a series of
straightforward montage sequences delineates the mundane footwork
necessary for their long-term subterfuge to work. During this part of the

film, the lecturing voice-over reiterates what is already transparently obvious on the image track as if to reassure the spectator of the putative legitimacy of what we are witnessing. Slowly, though, this pattern changes. By the point when the agents' disguises seem to have finally worked and the pair have successfully entered the generic domain of cheap boarding-houses, nightclubs and gambling dens, Alton's fully fledged *noir* style has taken over, ensuring a new kind of visual authenticity. From here on in, the voice-over more or less disappears. For any one who had missed *T-Men*'s expository prelude, it would now be impossible to distinguish, either by manner or appearance, the agents from the gangsters.

The success of Alton's cinematography rests on a combination of factors. First, there is the fastidious co-ordination of light sources to underline the tone of menace, threat and incertitude. Characters literally reveal their contours from the darkness and shafts of penetratingly hard light determine the edges of key objects within the frame. This is not a subjective environment capable of any satisfactory assimilation. It is as if the *mise en scène* has a brutal life force of its own. Second, as Jeanine Basinger (2007) notes, key sequences are first composed to define the parameters of a narrative space then redefined for more dramatic ends, throwing the spectator's initial perceptions into subtle disarray. This is especially true when Alton shifts from extreme low-angle to high-angle shot or from one lens to another.

Dennis O'Keefe reappeared in a similar roughly hewn role in *Raw Deal* and with the success of both films, Mann moved to MGM where, with greater resources, he also directed *Side Street* (1950)*. *T-Men* was remade as *The File of The Golden Goose* (Sam Wanamaker, 1969) and the action transposed to London. Today, the original still captivates. In its own way, it is one of the most tightly woven and compelling *film noirs* of the 1940s. AP

Dir: Anthony Mann; **Prod**: Aubrey Schenck; **Scr**: John C. Higgins from Virginia Kellogg's story; **DOP**: John Alton (b&w); **Ed**: Fred Allen; **Score**: Paul Sawtell; **Main Cast**: Dennis O'Keefe, Mary Meade, Alfred Ryder, Wallace Ford, June Lockhart, Charles McGraw; **Prod Co**: Eagle-Lion Films.

Touch of Evil
US, 1958 – 95 mins
Orson Welles

In his formative 1972 essay charting the history of classical American *film noir*, Paul Schrader famously called Orson Welles's magisterial Mexican American border drama 'film noir's epitaph'. It is commonly acknowledged that, along with films such as *Kiss Me Deadly* (1955)*, *Touch of Evil* marked the end of Hollywood's fascination with *film noir* until the form's rediscovery and reevaluation during the early 1970s. Subject to much negative criticism at the time, *Touch of Evil* is now seen by many as not just a milestone in the tangled evolution of *film noir*, but one of the finest American films of the last century.

The version of the film most people see today is not the print that was originally distributed by Universal. After a typically protracted shoot, Welles submitted a rough cut of the film to the studio which, apprehensive about its box-office potential, ordered various significant changes: the addition of new footage by studio hack Harry Keller, a thorough re-edit by Aaron Stell, a remix of the soundtrack and the superimposition of a credit sequence over the now infamous long take that begins the film. Dismayed, Welles fired off a fifty-eight-page memo detailing further suggestions. Many of these went unheeded until a restored version – as close to Welles's wishes as possible – was released in the 1990s.

This meta-history is significant because it indicates the almost fetishistic esteem in which *Touch of Evil* is held by international cinephiles. Central to this engagement with Welles's densely structured, profoundly baroque *film noir* is the initial three-and-a-half-minute shot that introduces the story's main location – the provincial border town of Los Robles – and two of the central protagonists: the Mexican detective Ramon Miguel Vargas (Charlton Heston) and his new wife,

Susie (Janet Leigh). Subject of much critical discussion, including within Robert Altman's *The Player* (1992), the shot ends with the bomb seen in the very first frame exploding off screen as Vargas and Susie passionately embrace.

The disruptive quality of this image, as well as later scenes of torture, shocked André Bazin (1978), one of many French critics who recognised the film's narrative and stylistic virtues long before the majority of American audiences. Relating the film explicitly to the violence of *Kiss Me Deadly*, Bazin argued that the two films shared 'the same thriller ethos, pushed to an almost intolerable tension, as well as sexual sadism'. What distinguished *Touch of Evil* for Bazin, especially in its portrayal of the battle between Vargas and the monstrously corrupt local police chief, Hank Quinlan (Orson Welles), was the way in which 'its direction [seemed] to be conceived on the basis of two fundamental notions, plastic and rhythmic'. While the film profoundly distorted conventional cinematic space through its virtuoso deep-focus cinematography, its editing was 'truly vertiginous' he noted; 'the velocity of characters who are always in motion within the frame is superimposed on that of the editing'.

This combination of sexuality, speed and violence is certainly part of the film's suggestive modernity – as it is in *Kiss Me Deadly* – and one clue to why it is now seen as a turning point in *film noir* history. In terms of visual style and characterisation, *Touch of Evil* literally pits the old against the new. The steely world of Susie and Vargas is placed at odds with the older compromised charisma of Quinlan and his friend Tanya, the gypsy madam played by Marlene Dietrich. The drama of the local gang members with their rock music, drugs and motorbikes seems a world away from the older treacheries of the town's ageing citizenry. In this sense, the film looks both backwards and forwards. It anticipates the emergence of the new youth culture, but still reminds one of the virtues of classical Hollywood storytelling. Paul Schrader was right. The film's elegiac closing sequence, with Quinlan dead and Tanya disappearing into the darkness of the night, does indeed feel like the end of an era. AP

Dir: Orson Welles; **Prod**: Albert Zugsmith; **Scr**: Orson Welles, Paul Monash (uncredited), Franklin Coen (uncredited) from Whit Masterson's novel *Badge of Evil*; **DOP**: Russell Metty (b&w); **Ed**: Aaron Stell, Virgil W. Vogel, Edward Curtiss (uncredited); **Score**: Henry Mancini; **Main Cast**: Charlton Heston, Janet Leigh, Orson Welles, Joseph Calleia, Akim Tamiroff, Ray Collins, Marlene Dietrich, Dennis Weaver; **Prod Co**: Universal.

Touchez pas au grisbi
France, 1954 – 94 mins
Jacques Becker

Jacques Becker's elegant adaptation of Albert Simonin's best-selling Série
Noire novel marked a crucial turning point in the history of French *film
noir*, leading to a proliferation of related titles including *Razzia sur le
chnouf* (Henri Decoin, 1955) and *Rififi* (1955)*. The film represented a
more authentic version of the French crime thriller that both reworked
literary traditions going back to the nineteenth century and looked
forward to Jean-Pierre Melville's subsequent genre masterpieces such as
Bob le Flambeur (1956) and *Le Samouraï* (1967)*. Crucial to its success
was its combination of the stylistic attributes of the French 'tradition of
quality' and the central figure of Jean Gabin (*La Bête humaine* [1938]*
and *Le Jour se lève* [1939]*) who, as an enduring icon of French screen
masculinity, helped define the film's main theme of the poignant but
necessary passing of the generations in postwar French culture and
society.

Max (Jean Gabin) is an ageing patriarch in the Parisian underworld
with his own discreet network of local haunts and personal associates.
Having recently carried out his final crime – a bullion heist at Orly Airport
– he now expects to lead a peaceful retirement in the company of his
girlfriends, his close friend Riton (René Dary) and the habitués of his
favourite restaurant run by the protective Madame Bouche (Denise Clair).
Others have their eye on the loot as well though and, through a devious
set of betrayals, Max is reluctantly forced into a showdown with Angelo
(Lino Ventura), his younger and more unscrupulous gangland rival.

Becker's film is distinguished by its alert and sympathetic attention
to location and character detail. Its atmospheric location topography of
nocturnal city streets is matched by the detailed intimacy of the Parisian
nightclubs, bars and rooms designed by Jean d'Eaubonne. This network
of spaces accommodates a larger community that serves as a kind of
metonym for the smaller family-like structures of Max and Angelo's

An alert and sympathetic attention to location and character detail: Max (Jean Gabin) (left) and Riton (René Dary) (right) in *Touchez pas au grisbi*

individual gangs. The two are distinguished by their ethics and manners. Whereas Max and his accomplices dine handsomely listening to their mentor's favourite jukebox tune in Madame Bouche's convivial dining room, Angelo and his other foreign-looking cronies deal drugs in sleazy local nightclubs. At the film's core lies the implacable and laconic face of Jean Gabin. The camera lingers repeatedly on his mute and still reactions to events thus providing an emotional metronome for the broader, equally subtle, rhythms of the narration.

Touchez pas au grisbi's storytelling style was greatly admired by critics such as the future director François Truffaut (*Shoot the Pianist* [1960]*), who praised Becker and his editor Marguerite Renoir for their careful delineation of temporal relations. Truffaut (1986) noticed the articulate 'economy of the gestures' and the way that 'what happens to Becker's characters is of less importance than the way it happens to them'. The insightfully staged sequence in which Max and Riton retire to Max's quarters to share pâté and red wine is a fine example of this.

One of the most interesting things about *Touchez pas au grisbi* is indeed its projection of 'Frenchness'. During the 1950s, French *film noir* became one of the key cultural fields from which the shifting relations between French national identity and the influence of American culture in the postwar period could be distinguished. It is symptomatic, if also problematic, for example, that at the end of the film Max decides to relinquish his French Renault – whose 'F' for France has repeatedly been foregrounded within the film's *mise en scène* – for a smart new American car. In the film's coda, he visits Madame Bouche's restaurant in it, but he now sits apart from the others with his new American girlfriend, Betty (Marilyn Buferd). Only his 'air' – the insistent, wistful theme tune devised by Jean Wiener – marks the fact that, despite the violence and tragedy of the preceding drama, some things might just remain unchanged. AP

Dir: Jacques Becker; **Prod**: Robert Dorman; **Scr**: Albert Simonin, Jacques Becker, Maurice Griffe from Albert Simonin's novel; **DOP**: Pierre Montazel (b&w); **Ed**: Marguerite Renoir; **Score**: Jean Wiener; **Main Cast**: Jean Gabin, René Dary, Dora Doll, Vittorio Sanipoli, Lino Ventura, Jeanne Moreau, Michel Jourdan; **Prod Co**: Del Duca Films, Antares Produzione Cinematografica.

Where the Sidewalk Ends
US, 1950 – 95 mins
Otto Preminger

Where the Sidewalk Ends was the final film in the run of *film noirs* that Preminger shot for Fox in the 1940s and, as well as reuniting Dana Andrews and Gene Tierney from *Laura* (1944)*, it also brought the director back in contact with previous influential collaborators such as the cinematographer Joseph LaShelle, art director Lyle R. Wheeler and scriptwriter Ben Hecht. This adaptation of William L. Stuart's novel, *Night Cry*, feels a world away from the smart society interiors of Preminger's initial *noir* though. Here, Andrews plays a hard-bitten violent police detective, Mark Dixon, who accidentally kills the main suspect in a gangland murder and covers up his crime even while the police arrest an innocent man, the father of the dead man's girlfriend, Morgan (Gene Tierney). This is a film drenched in the permanent night and rain of New York. The only relief from the succession of downbeat boarding-houses, diners and gangster hideouts are either the streets themselves (especially the tinsel glamour of Times Square) or – a recurrent visual trope in the *mise en scène* – when characters pass an office or apartment window to briefly acknowledge the promise of an urban landscape beyond the claustrophobic intensity of the investigative narrative.

Hecht's typically tough-minded script emphasises the psychological dimensions of Dixon's plight when he acts to pin the rap on Scalise, a local mobster played with louche sarcasm by Gary Merrill. Like so many *noir* protagonists, Dixon is a man trapped by the ghosts of the past. In a key scene, we learn that Dixon's own father too had been a criminal and once gave Scalise a leg-up in the rackets. As Chris Fujiwara (2008) has suggested, Dixon's malaise is thus more than just an attempt to settle an ethical score; his attempt to frame his adversary may also be read as a symbolic desire for patricide. He wants to kill the thing he loathes and has always feared becoming.

Preminger's direction articulates this moral tension with superb fluidity. Each shot is managed with precise attention to not just Dixon's anguish, but also the play between the detective's private guilt and the public face he has to present to his unwitting colleagues and romantic partner. As Fujiwara also notes, this is a film of comings and goings. Dixon never seems to stand still and is constantly pictured moving through spaces and doorways having to adjust his demeanour to suit. Overall *Where the Sidewalk Ends* presents one of Dana Andrews's finest

Joseph LaShelle's low-key cinematography illuminates Mark Dixon's (Dana Andrews) chiselled, weary features in *Where the Sidewalk Ends*

screen performances with his chiselled, weary but hurt features lit disturbingly by the unsparing shards of LaShelle's low-key cinematography.

Several scenes of the film went through revisions on the order of Darryl Zanuck in order to clarify Dixon's motivations. But there is also evidence that Fox was aware of another competing property being developed by Paramount that bore some similarities to *Where the Sidewalk Ends*: William Wyler's *Detective Story* (1951). Preminger's film is undoubtedly the richer project. Its tightly coiled narrative structure, revealing mobile framings, keen character insight and above all its emphasis on an utterly pervasive sense of urban despair all mark it as a major film of the same year that saw such other important city *noirs* as John Huston's *The Asphalt Jungle* (1950)* and Anthony Mann's *Side Street* (1950)*. AP

Dir, Prod: Otto Preminger; **Scr**: Ben Hecht, Victor Trivas, Frank P. Rosenberg, Robert E. Kent from William L. Stuart's novel *Night Cry*; **DOP**: Joseph LaShelle (b&w); **Ed**: Louis Loeffler; **Score**: Cyril Mockridge; **Main Cast**: Dana Andrews, Gene Tierney, Gary Merrill, Karl Malden; **Prod Co**: Twentieth Century-Fox.

References

Alloway, Lawrence, *Violent America: The Movies 1946–1964* (New York: Museum of Modern Art, 1971).

Armstrong, Stephen B., '*Touch of Evil* (1958) and the End of the Noir Cycle', in Alain Silver and James Ursini (eds), *Film Noir Reader 4* (New York: Limelight Editions, 2004), pp. 133–43.

Arthur, Paul, 'Los Angeles as Scene of the Crime', *Film Comment*, July/August 1996, pp. 20–6.

Basinger, Jeanine, *A Woman's View: How Hollywood Spoke to Women, 1930–1960* (New York: Knopf/Random House, 1993).

Basinger, Jeanine, *Anthony Mann* (Middletown, CT: Wesleyan University Press, 2007).

Bazin, André, *Orson Welles: A Critical View* (London: Elm Tree Books, 1978).

Bergfelder, Tim, 'German Cinema and Film Noir', in Andrew Spicer (ed.), *European Film Noir* (Manchester: Manchester University Press, 2007), pp. 138–64.

Biesen, Sheri Chinen, *Blackout: World War II and the Origins of Film Noir* (Baltimore, MD: Johns Hopkins University Press, 2005).

Borde, Raymond and Chaumeton, Etienne, *A Panorama of American Film Noir 1941–1953* (San Francisco: City Lights, 2002). [First published 1953.]

Britton, Andrew, 'Detour', in Ian Cameron (ed.), *The Book of Film Noir* (New York: Continuum, 1993), pp. 174–83 [published as *The Movie Book of Film Noir* (London: Studio Vista, 1992)].

Buhle, Paul and Wagner, Dave, *A Very Dangerous Citizen: Abraham Lincoln Polonsky and the Hollywood Left* (Berkeley: University of California Press, 2001).

Chartier, Jean-Pierre, 'Americans Are Also Making *Noir* Films', in Alain Silver and James Ursini (eds), *Film Noir Reader 2* (New York: Limelight Editions, 1999), pp. 21–5. [First published 1946.]

Chibnall, Steve, *Get Carter* (London and New York: I. B. Tauris, 2003).

Cowie, Elizabeth, '*Film Noir* and Women', in Joan Copjec (ed.), *Shades of Noir*

(London and New York: Verso, 1993),
pp. 121–66.

Davis, Mike, *City of Quartz: Excavating the Future in Los Angeles* (London: Pimlico, 1998).

Diawara, Manthia, 'Noir by Noirs: Towards a New Realism in Black Cinema', in Joan Copjec (ed.), *Shades of Noir* (London and New York: Verso, 1993), pp. 261–78.

Dimendberg, Edward, *Film Noir and the Spaces of Modernity* (Cambridge, MA: Harvard University Press, 2004).

Doane, Mary-Ann, *Femmes Fatales* (London and New York: Routledge, 1991).

Dyer, Richard, *White* (London and New York: Routledge, 1997).

Dyer, Richard, 'Postscript: Queers and Women in Film Noir', in E. Ann Kaplan (ed.), *Women in Film Noir*, new edn (London: BFI, 1998), pp. 123–9.

Dyer, Richard, 'Resistance through Charisma: Rita Hayworth and *Gilda*', in E. Ann Kaplan (ed.), *Women in Film Noir*, new edn (London: BFI, 1998), pp. 115–22.

Elsaesser, Thomas, *Weimar Cinema and After: Germany's Historical Imaginary* (London and New York: Routledge, 2000).

Engelstad, Audun, *Losing Streak Stories: Mapping Norwegian Film Noir* (unpublished PhD thesis, University of Oslo: Faculty of Humanities, 2006).

Evans, Jo, 'Sex and the Censors: The *Femme Fatale* in Juan Antonio Bardem's *Muerte de un ciclista*', *Screen*, Autumn 2007, pp. 327–44.

Frank, Nino, 'A New Kind of Police Drama: The Criminal Adventure', in Alain Silver and James Ursini (eds), *Film Noir Reader 2* (New York: Limelight Editions, 1999), pp. 15–20. [First published 1946.]

Fujiwara, Chris, *The World and Its Double: The Life and Work of Otto Preminger* (New York: Faber & Faber Inc., 2008).

Grost, Michael, 'The Films of Robert Siodmak' <www.members.aol.com/MG4273/siodmak.htm> [accessed 27 March 2008].

Haut, Woody, '*Nightmare Alley: Geeks, Freaks and Rubes*', DVD booklet, Masters of Cinema, 2005.

Hugo, Chris, '*The Big Combo*: Production Conditions and the Film Text', in Ian Cameron (ed.), *The Book of Film Noir* (New York: Continuum, 1993), pp. 247–53 [published as *The Movie Book of Film Noir* (London: Studio Vista, 1992)].

Kapczynski, Jennifer M., 'Homeward Bound? Peter Lorre's "The Lost Man" and the End of Exile', *New German Critique*, Spring–Summer 2003, pp. 145–71.

Kinder, Marsha, *Blood Cinema: The Reconstruction of a National Identity in*

Spain (Berkeley: University of California Press, 1993).

Kitses, Jim, *Gun Crazy* (London: BFI, 1996).

Knowles, Peter C., 'Genre and Authorship: Two Films of Arthur Penn', *Cineaction!*, Summer/Fall 1990, pp. 76–83.

Krutnik, Frank, *In a Lonely Street: Film Noir, Genre, Masculinity* (London and New York: Routledge, 1991).

Lipkin, Steven J., 'Real Emotional Logic: Persuasive Strategies in Docudrama', *Cinema Journal*, Summer 1989, pp. 68–85.

Lott, Eric, 'The Whiteness of Film Noir', in Michael Hill (ed.), *Whiteness: A Critical Reader* (New York: New York University Press, 1997), pp. 81–101.

Morgan, Janice, 'Scarlet Streets: Noir Realism from Berlin to Paris to Hollywood', *Iris*, Spring 1996, pp. 31–53.

Mulvey, Laura, 'Notes on Sirk and Melodrama', in Christine Gledhill (ed.), *Home Is Where the Heart Is* (London: BFI, 1987), pp. 75–82.

Murphy, Robert, 'British Film Noir', in Andrew Spicer (ed.), *European Film Noir* (Manchester: Manchester University Press, 2007), pp. 84–111.

Naremore, James, *More than Night: Film Noir in Its Contexts* (Berkeley and Los Angeles: University of California Press, 1998).

O'Brien, Charles, 'Film Noir in France: Before the Liberation', *Iris*, Spring 1996, pp. 7–20.

Pechter, William, 'Abraham Polonsky and "Force of Evil" ', *Film Quarterly*, Spring 1962, pp. 47–54.

Perkins, V. F., 'In a Lonely Place', in Ian Cameron (ed.), *The Book of Film Noir* (New York: Continuum, 1993), pp. 222–31 [published as *The Movie Book of Film Noir* (London: Studio Vista, 1992)].

Place, Janey and Peterson, Lowell, 'Some Visual Motifs of *Film Noir*', in Alain Silver and James Ursini (eds), *Film Noir Reader* (New York: Limelight Editions, 1996), pp. 65–76. [First published 1974.]

Polan, Dana, *In a Lonely Place* (London: BFI, 1993).

Rabinovitz, Lauren, 'The Hitchhiker', in Annette Kuhn (ed.), *Queen of the 'B's: Ida Lupino behind the Camera* (Trowbridge: Flicks Books, 1995), pp. 90–102.

Schrader, Paul, 'Notes on Film Noir', in Alain Silver and James Ursini (eds), *Film Noir Reader* (New York: Limelight Editions, 1996), pp. 53–64. [First published 1972.]

Server, Lee, *Ava Gardner: Love Is Nothing* (New York: St Martins Press/London: Bloomsbury, 2006).

Sobchack, Vivian, ' "Lounge Time":
Post-War Crises and the Chronotope
of Film Noir', in Nick Browne (ed.),
*Refiguring American Film Genres:
History and Theory* (Berkeley:
University of California Press, 1998),
pp. 129–70.

Spicer, Andrew, *Film Noir* (Harlow:
Longman, 2002).

Stone, Rob, 'Spanish Film Noir', in Andrew
Spicer (ed.), *European Film Noir*
(Manchester: Manchester University
Press, 2007), pp. 185–209.

Taubin, Amy, *Taxi Driver* (London: BFI,
2000).

Telotte, J. P., *Voices in the Dark: The
Narrative Patterns of Film Noir* (Urbana
and Chicago: University of Illinois
Press, 1989).

Thomson, David, 'A Cottage at Palos
Verdes', *Film Comment*, May–June
1990, pp. 16–21.

Thomson, David, *The New Biographical
Dictionary of Film*, 4th edn (New York:
Alfred A. Knopf/London: Little, Brown,
2002).

Truffaut, François, 'The Rogues Are Weary',
in Jim Hillier (ed.), *Cahiers du Cinema:
The 1950s: Neo-Realism, Hollywood,
New Wave* (London: Routledge, 1986),
pp. 28–30.

Turim, Maureen, *Flashbacks in Film: Memory
and History* (London and New York:
Routledge, 1989).

Vernet, Marc, '*Film Noir* on the Edge of
Doom', in Joan Copjec (ed.), *Shades of
Noir* (London and New York: Verso,
1993), pp. 1–32.

Vincendeau, Ginette, 'Noir Is Also a French
Word: The French Antecedents of Film
Noir', in Ian Cameron (ed.), *The Book
of Film Noir* (New York: Continuum,
1993), pp. 49–58 [published as *The
Movie Book of Film Noir* (London:
Studio Vista, 1992)].

Vincendeau, Ginette, *Jean-Pierre Melville:
An American in Paris* (London: British
Film Institute, 2003).

Vincendeau, Ginette, 'French Film Noir', in
Andrew Spicer (ed.), *European Film Noir*
(Manchester: Manchester University
Press, 2007), pp. 23–54.

Walker, Michael, 'Film Noir: Introduction', in
Ian Cameron (ed.), *The Book of Film
Noir* (New York: Continuum, 1993),
pp. 8–38 [published as *The Movie Book
of Film Noir* (London: Studio Vista,
1992)].

Wood, Mary P., 'Italian Film Noir', in
Andrew Spicer (ed.), *European Film Noir*
(Manchester: Manchester University
Press, 2007), pp. 236–72.

Further Reading

Ballinger, Alexander and Graydon, Danny, *The Rough Guide to Film Noir* (London: Rough Guides Ltd, 2007).

Biesen, Sheri Chinen, *Blackout: World War II and the Origins of Film Noir* (Baltimore, MD: Johns Hopkins University Press, 2005).

Borde, Raymond and Chaumeton, Etienne, *A Panorama of American Film Noir 1941–1953* (San Francisco, CA: City Lights, 2002).

Bould, Mark, *Film Noir: From Berlin to Sin City* (London: Wallflower Press, 2005).

Buss, Robin, *French Film Noir* (London: Marion Boyars, 2001).

Cameron, Ian (ed.), *The Book of Film Noir* (New York: Continuum, 1993) [published as *The Movie Book of Film Noir* (London: Studio Vista, 1992)].

Chibnall, Steve and Murphy, Robert (eds), *British Crime Cinema* (London and New York: Routledge, 1999).

Christopher, Nicholas, *Somewhere in the Night* (New York: Free Press, 1997).

Conard, Mark T. (ed.), *The Philosophy of Film Noir* (Lexington: University Press of Kentucky, 2007).

Copjec, Joan (ed.), *Shades of Noir* (London and New York: Verso, 1993).

Crowther, Chris, *Film Noir: Reflections in a Dark Mirror* (London: Columbus Books, 1988).

Décharné, Max, *Hardboiled Hollywood* (London: No Exit Press, 2005).

Dickos, Andrew, *Streets with No Name: A History of the Classic American Film Noir* (Lexington: University Press of Kentucky, 2002).

Dimendberg, Edward, *Film Noir and the Spaces of Modernity* (Cambridge, MA: Harvard University Press, 2004).

Gifford, Barry, *Out of the Past: Adventures in Film Noir* (Jackson: University Press of Mississippi, 2001).

Hirsch, Foster, *Detours and Lost Highways: A Map of Neo-Noir* (New York: Limelight Press, 1999).

Hirsch, Foster, *The Dark Side of the Screen: Film Noir* (Cambridge, MA: Da Capo Press, 2008).

Kaplan, E. Ann (ed.), *Women in Film Noir*, 2nd edn (London: BFI, 1998).

Keaney, Michael, *Film Noir Guide: 745 Films of the Classic Era, 1940–1959* (Jefferson, NC: McFarland, 2003).

Krutnik, Frank, *In a Lonely Street: Film Noir, Genre, Masculinity* (London and New York: Routledge, 1991).

Lyons, Arthur, *Death on the Cheap: The Lost B Movies of Film Noir* (Cambridge, MA: Da Capo Press, 2000).

Muller, Eddie, *Dark City: The Lost World of Film Noir* (New York: St Martin's Griffin, 1998).

Naremore, James, *More than Night: Film Noir in Its Contexts*, 2nd edn (Berkeley and Los Angeles: University of California Press, 2008).

Neale, Stephen, *Genre and Hollywood* (London and New York: Routledge, 2000).

Neve, Brian, *Film and Politics in America: A Social Tradition* (London and New York: Routledge, 1992).

Oliver, Kelly and Trigo, Benigno, *Noir Anxiety* (Minneapolis: University of Minnesota Press, 2003).

Ottoson, Robert, *A Reference Guide to the American Film Noir* (Metuchen, NJ and London: Scarecrow Press, 1981).

Palmer, R. Barton, *Hollywood's Dark Cinema: The American Film Noir* (New York: Twayne, 1994).

Palmer, R. Barton (ed.), *Perspectives on Film Noir* (New York: G. K. Hall, 1996).

Porfirio, Robert, Silver, Alain and Ursini, James (eds), *Film Noir Reader 3* (New York: Limelight Editions, 2002).

Rabinowitz, Paula, *Black & White & Noir: America's Pulp Modernism* (New York: Columbia University Press, 2002).

Rich, Nathaniel, *San Francisco Noir: The City in Film Noir from 1940 to the Present* (New York: The Little Backroom, 2005).

Richardson, Carl, *Autopsy: An Element of Realism in Film Noir* (Metuchen, NJ and London: Scarecrow Press, 1992).

Robson, Eddie, *Film Noir* (London: Virgin Books, 2005).

Schwartz, Ronald, *Noir Now and Then: Film Noir Originals and Remakes (1944–1999)* (Westport, CT and London: Greenwood Press, 2001).

Schwartz, Ronald, *Neo Noir: The New Film Style from Psycho to Collateral* (Metuchen, NJ and London: Scarecrow Press, 2005).

Silver, Alain, *The Noir Style* (New York: Overlook Press, 1999).

Silver, Alain, *L.A. Noir: The City as Character* (Los Angeles, CA: Santa Monica Press, 2005).

Silver, Alain and Ursini, James (eds), *Film Noir Reader* (New York: Limelight Editions, 1996).

Silver, Alain and Ursini, James (eds), *Film Noir Reader 2* (New York: Limelight Editions, 1999).

Silver, Alain and Ursini, James (eds), *Film Noir Reader 4* (New York: Limelight Editions, 2004).

Silver, Alain and Ward, Elizabeth (eds), *Film Noir: An Encyclopedic Reference to the American Style*, 3rd edn (New York: Overlook Press, 1993).

Spicer, Andrew, *Film Noir* (Harlow: Longman, 2002).

Spicer, Andrew (ed.), *European Film Noir* (Manchester: Manchester University Press, 2007).

Stephens, Michael L., *Film Noir: A Comprehensive Illustrated Reference to Movies, Terms and Persons* (Jefferson, NC: McFarland, 1995).

Telotte, J. P., *Voices in the Dark: The Narrative Patterns of Film Noir* (Urbana and Chicago: University of Illinois Press, 1989).

Tuska, J., *Dark Cinema: American 'Film Noir' in a Cultural Perspective* (Westport, CT and London: Greenwood Press, 1984).

Another 100 Film Noirs

Act of Violence, Fred Zinnemann, US, 1948

The Aura, Fabiàn Bielinsky, Argentina/Spain/France, 2005

Beyond a Reasonable Doubt, Fritz Lang, US, 1956

Black Angel, Roy William Neill, US, 1946

The Black Book, Anthony Mann, US, 1949

Blade Runner, Ridley Scott, US, 1982

Blind Shaft, Li Yang, China, 2003

Blood Simple, Joel Coen, US, 1983

The Blue Gardenia, Fritz Lang, US, 1953

Bob le Flambeur, Jean-Pierre Melville, France, 1956

Body Heat, Lawrence Kasdan, US, 1981

Border Incident, Anthony Mann, US, 1949

Bound, Andy & Larry Wachowski, US, 1996

Branded to Kill, Suzuki Seijun, Japan, 1966

The Brasher Doubloon, John Brahm, US, 1946

Brick, Rian Johnson, US, 2004

Caught, Max Ophuls, US, 1949

Clash by Night, Fritz Lang, US, 1952

Classe tous risques, Claude Sautet, France, 1960

Coeur de Lilas, Anatole Litvak, France, 1932

Coup de torchon [Clean Slate], Bertrand Tavernier, France, 1981

Crack-Up, Irving Reis, US, 1946

Crime Wave, André de Toth, US, 1954

Croupier, Mike Hodges, UK, 1997

The Dark Mirror, Robert Siodmak, US, 1946

The Dark Past, Rudolph Maté, US, 1948

Dead Men Don't Wear Plaid, Carl Reiner, US, 1982

The Deep End, Scott McGehee & David Siegel, US, 2001

Le Dernier tournant, Pierre Chenal, France, 1939

Desperate, Anthony Mann, US, 1947

The Devil Thumbs a Ride, Felix E. Feist, US, 1947

The Element of Crime, Lars von Trier, Denmark, 1984

The Fallen Idol, Carol Reed, UK, 1948

The File on Thelma Jordon, Robert Siodmak, US, 1949

Gheisar, Masud Kimiai, Iran, 1969

Hard Eight, Paul Thomas Anderson, US, 1996

Harikomi, Nomura Yoshitaro, Japan, 1958

The High Wall, Curtis Bernhardt, US, 1947

His Kind of Woman, John Farrow, US, 1951

The Hot Spot, Dennis Hopper, US, 1990

The House on 92nd Street, Henry Hathaway, US, 1945

Human Desire, Fritz Lang, US, 1954

Infernal Affairs, Wai-keung Lau & Siu Fai Mak, Hong Kong, 2002

It Always Rains on Sunday, Robert Hamer, UK, 1947

Johnny One-Eye, Robert Florey, US, 1950

Kala Bazaar, Vijay Anand, India, 1960

Key Largo, John Huston, US, 1948

Kill Me Again, John Dahl, US, 1989

The Killers, Don Siegel, US, 1964

A Kiss before Dying, Gerd Oswald, US, 1955

Klute, Alan Pakula, US, 1971

The Last Seduction, John Dahl, US, 1993

Liebestraum, Mike Figgis, US, 1991

The Locket, John Brahm, US, 1946

The Long Good Friday, John Mackenzie, UK, 1980

Lost Highway, David Lynch, US, 1996

Miller's Crossing, Joel Coen, US, 1990

The Murderers Are amongst Us [*Die Mörder sind unter uns*], Wolfgang Staudte, Germany, 1946

The Naked City, Jules Dassin, US, 1948

Nightfall, Jacques Tourneur, US, 1957

Notorious, Alfred Hitchcock, US, 1946

One False Move, Carl Franklin, US, 1991

Ossessione, Luchino Visconti, Italy, 1943

Pépé le Moko, Julien Duvivier, France, 1936

The Prowler, Joseph Losey, US, 1951

Pulp Fiction, Quentin Tarantino, US, 1994

Le Quai des brumes, Marcel Carné, France, 1938

Quicksand, Irving Pichel, US, 1950

Raw Deal, Anthony Mann, US, 1948

Razzia sur le chnouf, Henri Decoin, France, 1955

Ride the Pink Horse, Robert Montgomery, US, 1947

Road House, Jean Negulesco, US, 1948

Sensualidad, Albert Gout, Mexico, 1951

Série noire, Alain Corneau, France, 1979

The Set-Up, Robert Wise, US, 1948

Se7en, David Fincher, US, 1995

Une si jolie petite plage, Yves Allégret, France, 1949

Somewhere in the Night, Joseph L. Mankiewicz, US, 1946

The Sound of Fury, Cy Endfield, US, 1951

The Spiral Staircase, Robert Siodmak, US, 1945

The Strange Love of Martha Ivers, Lewis Milestone, US, 1946

Stranger on the Third Floor, Boris Ingster, US, 1940

Stray Dog, Kurosawa Akira, Japan, 1949

The Street with No Name, William Keighley, US, 1948

Suture, Scott McGehee & David Siegel, US, 1993

Tenebrae, Dario Argento, Italy, 1982

La Tête d'un homme, Julien Duvivier, France, 1932

Index

Note: Credits have not been indexed. Page numbers for individual film entries are marked in **bold**.

List of Illustrations

While considerable effort has been made to correctly identify the copyright holders this has not been possible in all cases. We apologise for any apparent negligence and any omissions or corrections brought to our attention will be remedied in any future editions.